MOX

MOX

BY

JON MOXLEY

PERMUTED
PRESS

A PERMUTED PRESS BOOK
ISBN: 978-1-63758-038-7
ISBN (eBook): 978-1-63758-039-4

MOX
© 2021 by Jon Moxley
All Rights Reserved

Cover photos by Ryan Loco
Cover design by Tiffani Shea
Interior design by Donna McLeer / Tunnel Vizion Media LLC

This is a work of nonfiction. All people, locations, events, and situations
are portrayed to the best of the author's memory.

The author is represented by MacGregor & Luedeke.

PERMUTED
PRESS

Permuted Press, LLC
New York • Nashville
permutedpress.com

Published in the United States of America
1 2 3 4 5 6 7 8 9 10

CONTENTS

PROLOGUE BY MOX 8
WE'RE THE GOOD GUYS 10
BACKUP PLANS 14
THE G1 16
PERSONAL STORY 28
FOLEY 34
WHY I DON'T RIDE A MOTORCYCLE 40
TRAVEL AND FAVORITE CITIES 45
TONE IT DOWN 51
FAVORITE CITIES: HOMES AWAY FROM HOME 56
FCW 57
THE GREATEST THREE-MAN LUCHA SQUARE DANCE OF ALL TIME 65
TRUE VILLAINS 67
BRODIE LEE 73
SANDWICHES 77
DECEMBER 31, 2020 81
DECEMBER 31, 2018 82
CINCINNATI 87
BRIO 95
HWA CHUNK, LATE 2003 102
TRAINING 114
TAG MATCH 128
HOME AWAY FROM HOME: TORONTO 132
2008 CHUNK 142
JACKSONVILLE MARRIOTT, MARCH 7, 2021, 1:21 P.M. 150
LAS VEGAS, MARCH 13, 2021, 2:22 P.M. 152
HOME AWAY FROM HOME: PHILADELPHIA 155

CZW CHUNK 156

MORE CZW 160

ZANDIG 167

TOURNAMENT OF DEATH 172

NOVEMBER 2010 180

THE SHIELD 183

INTERLUDE NO. 1 202

JANUARY 2019 204

MAY 2019 207

MAY 25, 2019, LAS VEGAS 211

INTERLUDE NO. 2 217

OMAHA, NEBRASKA 220

PUERTO RICO, 2006 225

A WWE STORY 229

GRANT 233

JON MOXLEY'S GUIDE TO MARRIAGE 238

INTERLUDE NO. 3 248

MAY 14, 2021, CHICAGO ORD, ADMIRALS LOUNGE, 12:39 P.M. 251

MONEY IN THE BANK 2014, TD GARDEN, BOSTON 254

T-MOBILE ARENA, LAS VEGAS, JUNE 2016 256

CINCINNATI, PICCADILLY, 1996 259

... VEGAS, 2016 260

END OF THE BOOK 263

PHOTO CREDITS 268

ABOUT THE AUTHOR 269

PROLOGUE

BY MOX

I've never really considered my own identity.

Sure, I've occupied the vessels of characters in certain narratives over the years, and maybe some of these narratives, or the things that happened within these storylines, were informed or inspired by my real life. In those cases, I was tapping into elements of my own identity, as if this were all real. But it's also all fake. Point of clarification: As a wrestler, I'm allowed to say "fake," but you're not. Don't make me stab you. Did that make any sense to you? Have I lost you already?

Professional wrestlers are such a strangely specific type of athlete/performer/ artist/entertainer. We're impossible to categorize. I've heard people try ... even wrestlers themselves. Don't. Just don't. There's no specific word or term, it's just ... wrestling. And you'd only be shortchanging the thing we love if you tried to define it more than that. Wrestling can be ANYTHING. It's everything. It's world-class athletes. It's Broadway, Shakespeare, summer blockbusters, best-selling novels, soap operas, high art. It's nobodies from nowhere finding a way to say to the world: "Fuck you!" It's entertainment, it's movies, it's music. ... It's EVERYTHING.

If you don't like wrestling already, you're probably not reading this book, but just in case you're a civilian not initiated into our world ... WELCOME. You're gonna love it — there's something for everybody.

I never put much thought into my actual identity until I started writing this book. For many years, I simply didn't exist. Then I became a pro wrestler, and now I'm writing this and trying to figure out, like ... who the fuck do we say wrote it? What is my identity? OK, we can say it's a book by a pro wrestler ... at least that we know for certain. The rest? I've come to find as I go back and think about how I got here, about to have a little girl (who we're calling Nora, and who I'm gonna teach to be choking MFers out from an early age), that I'm a bunch of other things too: athlete, entertainer, storyteller, yes, but also ... socially challenged, borderline alcoholic, mildly sadomasochistic, headcase, poor kid, juvenile delinquent, brother, son, friend. I'm also a pretty damn good husband and a supernaturally potent sexual creature.

Above all, I hope to be a good father, which I know in my heart I will be. I have no fear of that. So who do we say wrote the book? Just say MOX, cuz that can mean everything. It's all that shit and everything else I've forgotten and even shit that hasn't happened yet. I make no apologies.

I don't profess to have any answers about anything. That being said, I've seen some shit and been some places and made some observations along the way. I want this book to be fun to read, and I sincerely hope that no one takes it too seriously, but maybe somebody can learn a little something. I know fuck-all about shit, but somehow I came out on the other side of the last 35 years having achieved everything I ever wanted, with the woman of my dreams. I'm blessed to do what I love for a living, and I like to think I'm pretty good at it. Maybe I just got lucky. Maybe this book just serves as a guide to what not to do. For instance: Don't smoke crack. I'll describe it for you now just so curiosity doesn't get the better of you: It's like doing a whip-it and eating wasabi at the same time. Still, if you really just love smoking crack and that's your thing, I won't stop you. In any case, just like any night I come back from the ring, in writing this book I hope I've created something people enjoy, just like any night I lay my soul bare, sweating and bleeding with all my effort and whatever physical ability I have left, just to tell a story or two. With this book, I share my experience with you.

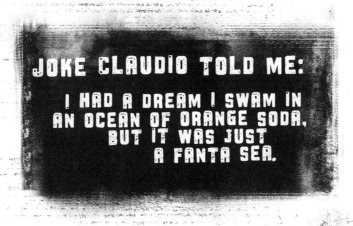

JOKE CLAUDIO TOLD ME:

I HAD A DREAM I SWAM IN AN OCEAN OF ORANGE SODA, BUT IT WAS JUST A FANTA SEA.

WE'RE THE GOOD GUYS

This is a crazy-ass ride I've been on for 16 years.

But recently now, finally, the whole world makes sense to me.

How did I get here?

How have I been AEW World Champion for so long?

The answer is ... my dad.

Six-foot-three, 250-pound brick shithouse, would box your ears if you got out of line.

Scary.

One day he's in town. He picks me up from the police station but doesn't hit me.

He looks at me and says something I'll never forget.

He says, "Son ... we're the good guys. No matter what happens, no matter what's going around you, just remember. We're the good guys."

They tried to lie, cheat, and steal this championship away from me.

I've been jumped, beat up, I've fought monsters, technicians, my own friends ... but I always know what to do. I always have.

"We're the good guys."

And now the whole world is bearing down on me, my body feels like hell, I can't even get out of bed in the morning. I have a pregnant wife at home. I'm holding two titles on two different continents. I have challengers coming from every which way.

What do I do?

I know what to do.

"We're the good guys."

So tonight, I'm going to walk to the ring. I'm going to sign that contract without any hesitation. I'm going to look into Kenny Omega's eye, I'm going to shake his hand and let him know in no uncertain terms, "I am the best wrestler in the world."

I am the AEW World Champion.

I am my dad's son.

And I am Jon Goddamn Moxley.

And that is never gonna change.

That story, taken from an interview I did on an episode of AEW Dynamite, is 99.9 percent true. I took the creative liberty to make my dad 6'3", 250 lbs. in order to enhance the idea of his physically intimidating presence when in reality he's 5'9", but he was still every bit the brick shithouse in his prime. My dad, Danny Burl Good, had meaty hands and a crushing grip that appeared superhuman to me as a child, fortified by baling hay in the humid summers of rural Clermont County in southern Ohio. Built like a human fire hydrant, my dad was an All-Conference football player for Clermont Northeastern high school, at center. Sturdy. Fortified. Dependable. In command. In control of the football. Nothing happens until I snap this ball. When

I do, I will gracefully and assuredly pass it between my legs to my teammate, the quarterback, who gets all the attention, praise and chicks, and then and only then … the play will commence. After that, some violent shit might go down. I'll do what I gotta do to make sure our prom king–quarterback gets to do his thing, and I'll get down and dirty to block who I need to and clear a path for the star running back, who gets his photos in the paper. Cool, calm, composed. Trustworthy. The bedrock. The center.

That's my dad. "We're the good guys" is my moral compass, the words that guide me to determine which path I take. When we sat in that car and my dad said the words that would be forever etched into my brain, he wasn't trying to philosophize, wax poetic or tell me some groundbreaking new idea I'd never heard before. It was simple. Common sense really. I was into some bad shit, hanging around other kids my age doing stupid things, but that wasn't who I was. He knew it. He knew I knew it. The message of "We're the good guys" is simple: If your life was a movie, are you doing things the bad guys in the movie are doing or things the good guys are doing? In film, it's usually easy to tell the difference: You know who the protagonist is, you know who the antagonist is. You don't have to be told. Now I'm not saying after this exact moment I never did anything stupid ever again. I went on to commit many stupid, regrettable and embarrassing offenses and probably will go on to commit more in the future. But as I get older, more experienced, collect more scars and become more grateful to God and the universe for my abundance of good fortune, I always come back to this simple philosophy: "We're the good guys."

There are exceptions to every rule. Robin Hood stole from the rich to give to the poor. Jack Reacher, one of my favorite literary characters and often an inspiration for my character in AEW, kills motherfuckers at a breakneck pace in pretty unforgiving fashion, but it's always because it's the right thing to do. Jack Reacher has no patience for bad guys doing bad-guy shit — he'll just shoot you — but his moral compass is always irrefutably on point. For long periods of time when I was young, my dad wasn't around. My mom, Caryn, and he divorced when I was little. Even when they were married it didn't feel to me like they were *together*, probably because it didn't seem like I saw them at the same time. Mostly I just remember my mom, soaked in sweat and tears, emerging from her room after a long shouting match with my dad over the phone. She told my sister, Lauren, and me that they were getting a divorce. All they did was fight. My reaction as a little tyke who could see the obvious was something like, "Yeah, no shit."

I have the two greatest parents anyone could ask for and they sacrificed to the utmost for us, but let's face it, they should never have been together. The thought of them as a couple today is comical to me, but they got married young and pregnant young. My dad was 19, his prefrontal lobe not even developed, and he had a wife and two babies. Dad did what he needed to do. He worked two jobs, moonlighting as a waiter at a Frisch's restaurant, and in the shop at Cadillac Plastic in Cincinnati by day. He would eventually work his way from the shop into a sales position in an office, where he would bring me on weekends when the place was empty and he was working overtime. I would vacuum the floors, throw out the trash and Windex all the glass for a *coool* two-dollar payday. He taught me how to melt a square sheet of plastic in two spots, bend them, clamp them into place and make a picture frame. Eventually, he did such a good job in his new position he was asked to move to Dallas and take a higher-paying position at another branch. My mom wouldn't go, refused to budge. My dad knew that to best provide for his family and our future he had to take this job. He knew he'd be lonely in a new city away from his young kids. He knew we wouldn't understand. And I wouldn't understand until I was in my twenties. He knew he wouldn't get the credit he deserved. He did what he had to. He walked up to the line, snapped the ball and did the dirty work. The center. Today my dad is the branch manager of Laird Plastic in Dayton, Ohio. Started from the bottom. He beat lymphoma. When he got the diagnosis, he reacted as if he'd had a hangnail. No sell.

During the pandemic he's been working 60-hour weeks as they're pumping out plastic protective equipment of all sorts to meet unimaginable demand. No problem. Walk to the line, snap the ball. Do what needs getting done. "We're the good guys."

BACKUP PLANS

I don't believe in backup plans. Wrestling is one of those pursuits where you'll hear you should have a backup plan. Go to school, get your degree. There is no guarantee of success, and even then it's often fleeting. Countless wrestlers who've had success have blown their money, spending it fast as if it will last forever, ending up with nothing when it's over. This business, like many, especially in the entertainment field, can be cruel. Jim Ross came down to FCW one time and gave the talent a good talk about setting yourself up for the future: "Pay your taxes, save your money, be a good citizen. ... Nothing good happens after midnight." It's all sound advice, of course. He stressed preparing for life after your career in the ring is over. Even if you are one of the lucky ones, your physical window as an athlete is finite. Having a degree, a fallback, a "backup plan," is a good idea. In theory, yes, I can't disagree with that logic. I took a lot of JR's advice to heart as it made a lot of sense, especially about keeping your financial house in order. There was no guarantee I would ever make it to the main roster in WWE, and if I did, who knows how long it would last? I saved my money. I always make sure my taxes are paid ... but the part about having a backup plan? I couldn't help but think as I listened that if I'd had a backup plan I probably wouldn't have made it even this far. A backup plan, to me, is planning to fail. An education is always a good thing, and I did later get my high school diploma online (which was so easy to do, it made me wonder what the point even was). Having more than one skill set, varied interests, passions and ways to earn income, diversifying yourself ... these are all great things, but I think if you really want something, whatever that is, you have to go after it with 100 percent of yourself. If you're gonna go for it, go for it. Great things aren't achieved with a safety net in place. Safety nets, backup plans — these are distractions, excuses to give up early. A backup plan may be put in place for your benefit, but what it really serves as is a way out. If you want something bad enough, if you believe in yourself, failure can't be an option. The very concept that you may not succeed simply can't exist. A backup plan may alleviate fear of failure, but you need that fear. When I set out on this journey, I was terrified to fail, thus it simply wasn't an option. So when it was time to learn an arm drag or some such thing in wrestling school, you'd better F'n believe I was paying attention. This was not a game, this was life. I'd now dedicated my existence to this pursuit. It was all or nothing: become a great professional wrestler, succeed (whatever that nebulous concept meant), or nothing. There was no other job, no other career, no money, no other anything. There was nothing on the other side but a meaningless existence in Piccadilly, sucking up oxygen, scraping out a living. That was about as acceptable as death. It terrified me to no end. It drove me to train the extra hours, drive the thousands of extra miles and work every rinky-dink independent show in the Western Hemisphere. That fear drove me to overcome obstacles, setbacks and failures. It drove me to soldier on in the face of adversity and overwhelming odds well past the point of reason, to a point others called "delusion" or "obsession." If people call you delusional for believing you can achieve your dreams, fuck them. If they call you obsessed, well yeah, you have to be obsessed. "Obsessed" is a word the lazy use to describe the dedicated. I couldn't stomach the thought of not succeeding. It caused me physical revulsion. During a dark period when I couldn't get booked anywhere, I found myself at 22 with no education, job skills or money and nothing to show for my years of hard work thus far. Not making it started to look like a real possibility. Failure had taken my back, it had its hooks in and was looking for the choke. I just refused to die. I moved forward because there was no choice but to move forward. I don't believe in backup plans. I call them "10th-hour plans." You can't win in the 11th hour if you quit in the 10th hour.

THE GI

I love wrestling in Japan. I love the fans, the culture. I love the style, the physicality. I love the 7-Eleven, which is what I was most excited to show my wife when I brought her to Tokyo with me for Wrestle Kingdom 13 at the Tokyo Dome. In Japanese pro wrestling, fighting spirit is revered above all else. Never say die. This idea, this attitude, is nowhere more present than in the Young Lions from the dojo of New Japan Pro Wrestling. I love to watch them work. Trainees at the NJPW dojo, the Young Lions, go through the most intense and disciplined training camp that exists today. The workouts are intense: endless hindu squats, pushups, intense wrestling drills, bending their spines backwards over a tire to develop the perfect bridge to deliver a beautiful suplex ... but the program is more than just the workouts, it's a way of life. It's designed to transform you, fully, completely, into something greater.

The Young Lions foster the fighting spirit. They demonstrate discipline daily, always at the bus early to carry and stow the bags of established veterans. They kneel by the ring during matches studying the moves of their elders intently. They dutifully dart into the ring after a three-count to place ice bags on the heads of those exhausted and possibly concussed elders. They take back bumps. Fuck, do they take back bumps. You will never see a more intense, crisp back bump than one performed by a Young Lion during a preshow training session.

When Young Lions get a chance to compete, usually against each other, it's always intense. They're fighting for their spot in the pecking order. Fighting to prove themselves to their teachers, to the veterans, to the fans and to each other.

I can relate. In February 2004, I was 18 and it was finally time for me to do more than sell sodas and sweep the floors at the HWA Main Event Pro Wrestling Camp. I was ready to F'n go. I never missed a two-hour, three-day-a-week training session for two years. I'd put in endless extra hours in the ring: running, lifting weights, watching tape ... ANYTHING extra I could do. This was my one shot at doing something in life, and I was dedicating my entire existence, fully and completely, to the pursuit of professional wrestling.

I threw every bit of myself into any opportunity to be in the ring, eager for the approval of my teachers. Reckless abandon. My favorite wrestling coach when I was a kid once told me: "Don't pace yourself. Just go until you fall over. We'll pick you up." That stuck with me, maybe too much. It was a pure time. I had little experience, skill or knowledge but I was full of piss, vinegar, MDog 20/20, and confidence. Fuck you and fuck anybody who doesn't think I'm gonna be a great professional wrestler. I'll show you. Watch me. Creating negativity just to feed off it. The only fuel I'd ever known.

Fifteen years later that same 18-year-old kid walked up the steps outside legendary Korakuen Hall in Tokyo, a Young Lion once again. As I get to the top floor following NJPW personnel and my second, Young Lion Shota Umino, down the hallway, I have the feeling I'm on a march to the bus stop to fight some Piccadilly bully, the feeling somebody mistreated my sister and I'm coming to beat the fuck out of them, the feeling somebody is trying to literally deny my right to exist as a professional wrestler. The fuel, the only fuel I'd ever known, burns intensely, heating up with every stride down these hallowed halls. I repeat to myself, "THIS is the night. Right F'n now is the moment, I will SHUT everybody the fuck up!" Anger building to a boiling point with every step until I reach the door and hear the raw guitar chords of my entrance music and explode into the arena to the gasps of the fans in Korakuen.

It's 100 degrees easy, the humidity thick. Kevin Kelly, veteran commentator, notes that he is scared. It's night three of B block competition in the 29th annual G1 Climax tournament, the most prestigious, the toughest, most grueling tournament in the sport. Tomohiro Ishii, my opponent, hasn't yet entered the ring as I make my way down the stairs, through the fans and palpable tension to the ring. Better get the fuck outta the way. Ishii, the Stone Pit Bull, is a hero, a legend, the definition of fighting spirit. What the fans here in this historic building know is that Ishii will give no quarter. He will go out on his shield. A samurai, he's happy to die in the ring tonight with honor. What they don't know is that I'm about to open my palm, rear back and bitch slap the entire wrestling world in the mouth. This is my first main event in NJPW and what I know — what I'm CERTAIN of — is that every person in this building and watching all over the world wants me to fail. I can hear their jokes and insults. You don't belong here, you can't cut it in the G1, you'll never make it as a pro wrestler. What a stupid dream! You'll never get a contract, you'll never make it in WWE, go ahead and leave WWE and we'll all watch you fall flat on your ass.

Fuck. You.

Tonight, I won't back down an inch. I will take what I want by any means necessary and the only way to deny me is to kill me ... Ishii will give no quarter ... Ishii enters the arena with his ever-present scowl, comes through the ropes with one step and is in my face before he completes a second. I push my forehead into Ishii's. I will not give an inch.

No quarter. This. Is. The. Moment. The bell rings ... how did we get here?

February 2019, it's a blustery, snowy day. I'm at the Courtyard Inn at the Winnipeg airport in Manitoba, Canada. I have a WWE house show at Bell MTS Place. Rumors have swirled for the last month that I'm not re-signing with Vince when my contract expires in April. I get a text from Rocky Romero, a liaison with New Japan Pro Wrestling. "Not sure what your plans are after April but would love to get you over to New Japan." I thanked him for reaching out and replied, "I'm extremely interested." We agreed to talk at a later date. At that point nobody knew anything about my post-WWE plans. I wasn't sure myself, but truth be told my confidence was low. I didn't feel like myself. A disastrous heel run in late 2018 had eroded any inkling in my mind that I would re-sign. I knew I was out when the clock struck midnight on April 29, but beyond that ... it was all a bit fuzzy. My first thought was that my next move would be to take myself off-Broadway, so to speak (a term I learned from Dusty Rhodes). Go wrestle off the grid. Maybe wrestle under a mask, just find a way to enjoy wrestling again, find a new style, a new concept, a new look ... maybe a new name? I wasn't sure. One thing I was knew was that I wanted to go to Japan. I loved wrestling in Japan. In WWE, we'd do a double shot at Sumo Hall in Tokyo every summer. I looked forward to those shows more than any show all year, more than the PPVs, more than WrestleMania. Those shows were FUN. I loved the atmosphere, the respect of the crowd, the engagement. In Japan you can just ... wrestle. At Sumo Hall on those shows I had a distinct feeling. I connected with the crowd in a particular way. I couldn't quite put my finger on it, but I knew in the back of my mind I could come back and work there one day. I quietly folded that up and put it in the back of my mind to save for a rainy day. It was pouring now. It became a goal of mine to have at least one solid run in a legit Japanese company. Which company? I didn't know. There are many different promotions in Japan, big and small. Many have distinct products and specialize in one style of wrestling. Where would I fit in? There are shoot-style promotions, deathmatch promotions (I wondered if I could do a big death match at Sumo Hall), promotions that specialize in comedy, some that specialize in featuring high-flying aerial artists ... but there is only one king today. New Japan Pro Wresting.

Of course, NJPW was the top choice for a run in Japan, but if I'm being perfectly honest, I was a little scared. I knew NJPW was home to the best wrestlers in the world. The highest standard of in-ring excellence. I remembered being enamored with Hiroshi Tanahashi vs. Minoru Suzuki while I was in FCW. I knew there were guys there I was familiar with and had worked with. I reasoned that if they could do it, I could do it, but my confidence was lacking. Still, New Japan, the top choice, had now called me. I wasn't gonna say no. I still couldn't picture myself in New Japan. I was inexperienced in the nuances of the style, and I didn't know if I could keep up with these guys, but I still figured: Hey, there's gotta be a place for me there somewhere, and this is the next move. One solid little run. No pressure.

Fast forward ... I'm standing in my garage/gym/fortress of solitude talking to Rocky. "Basically, it's whatever you want. If you wanna come over for a couple big shows? Cool. You wanna do a tour? Cool. ... We'd love to have you in the G1. That'd be sick."

Pause. Full stop. ... The G1? I hadn't even considered it, never expected they'd ask me. The G1 Climax tournament, aka the G1, is the most prestigious tournament in the sport, where the best wrestlers in the world go head-to-head in the most physically demanding high-level matches in the world. Best of the best, filet mignon, the crème de la crème. That much I knew ... but competing in a G1 was a foreign concept. I was intimidated.

After my casual conversation with Rocky, I came back in the house and sat down on the couch next to my wife. About 10 seconds later I said to her, "Shit! ... I HAVE to do the G1."

"What's the G1?" she asked.

It's this thing. ... Shit! You see, I was completely comfortable in my world where the G1 didn't exist until a few minutes ago, but now I feel like I have to go or I'm a coward. It intimidated me, but I can't live in a world where I backed down from a challenge, where I was scared, where I took the easy road, where I had the chance to do something extraordinary and I took the safe option. There was no choice now. Rocky couldn't have put less pressure on me the way he mentioned it, but the way my brain works, he may as well have said to me, "You won't do the G1, you pussy!"

I just ain't gonna back down on any shit. That's just my natural reaction. I didn't know I had this fear until three minutes ago, but now I had to conquer it. I figured there would be a lot of people out there that would scoff at the idea of me wrestling in the G1, who would say I was just some over-my-head, washed-out WWE superstar that was gonna get exposed as not the real deal. Fuck 'em, I figured. I wasn't doing this for them, I was doing this for me. I can't say for sure anyone wanted me to fail. Hell, in fact, most people all around the world were all super-supportive and happy for me. I have some great fans, and some great friends ... but supportive don't make the bacon, babe! I needed fuel, the only fuel I've ever known, so I turned all the little snarky fuckers out there with their little opinions into just that ... *mmmmyeeeeess!* Dean Ambrose in the G1! That's rich, councilman! Sit and type on your little computer while I'm out there in the world making history. Y'all about to get bitch slapped. (Y'all know who you were ... and thanks.)

So the G1 was going to happen ... first things first. At the end of my WWE run I wasn't quite in peak physical condition: Aches and pains, old injuries were piling up. I'd been on the road nonstop. I had been doing mostly six-man tags with The Shield and short TV matches toward the end, so I knew I wasn't ready to compete in the longer, faster-paced, more physically demanding matches that were waiting for me in the G1. It was time to get to work. On April 30, I called my friend Gil Guardado, whom I'd met at Xtreme Couture in 2015. Gil's a professional MMA fighter and a strength and conditioning specialist extraordinaire. He trains pro fighters to fight 25 minutes if necessary. I didn't know exactly what I was getting myself into. Grappling conditioning is different from striking, sprinters are different than marathon runners ... I didn't know what I needed, so I decided I needed it all. If I was trained to fight for 25 minutes, I figured I'd be trained for the G1. I wanted to make sure all of my energy systems were at full strength. Gil put me through a full MMA-style training camp for nine weeks. Strength and conditioning, wrestling, kickboxing, jiu-jitsu, two-a-days, the works. It. Was. A. Bitch. ... But I'll be damned if I wasn't in the best shape of my life. We also focused on rehab, lots of active stretching and mobility training to fix all the things that got all twisted up and bent out of shape over the years. I did cryotherapy in between workouts. Steam, sauna, massage, stretching, anything extra I could do ... an old Young Lion.

TOKYO, RYOGOKU, SUMO HALL

Next order of business was my debut in NJPW. I was delighted to hear from Rocky that the booker, Gedo, wanted to bring me in before the G1 to introduce me to the audience against my old friend from FCW, Juice Robinson ... you up. ... at Sumo Hall. I couldn't have asked for a better first opponent, someone I knew, someone who spoke English! Also, the NJPW United States title would be on the line, so I'd be sporting a fancy new championship belt! Not too bad. ... My AEW debut at Double or Nothing had already happened at this point, so some of the fears and anxieties I had about life outside WWE and the audience's willingness to accept me were gone, but this was my first time actually in the ring outside WWE since 2011 ... and this was Japan. Would the New Japan audience know or care who I am? I couldn't picture it. What would I do? How would I walk, talk and wrestle? I had no idea. I knew one thing, however, the most important thing, the only important thing, was getting over with the New Japan faithful live in the building.

It was weird being back in Sumo Hall but working for a different company. I was brought to the building early, the first one there. I stood atop the stands where I would enter that night and looked out at the ring. The New Japan ring. I'd seen it so many times on tape. Now I've been transported into a different universe, and I'm here. Not unlike the first time you're live on *WWE Raw.* You've seen it so many times

on TV and now you're here: Somehow you've been transported inside the TV screen. I had reservations about how I'd be accepted by the locker room. Some big-name dipshit WWE superstar coming into our house? How much they paying him? He don't belong here, he's a joke. As the various New Japan wrestlers filed in, I introduced myself to everyone. Everyone was so cool. Zack Sabre Jr., who I haven't seen in 10 years since we last partied at a discotheque in Germany arrived; we picked up right where we left off and shot the shit. I was calm. Relaxed. Remarkably calm considering the situation. There should have been a lot of pressure, but I felt none. I probably should have. If I stunk the joint out they might change their minds about putting me in the G1 ... how embarrassing would that be? There'd been a lot of hoopla around my debuting tonight. It was a big match. If I didn't win the fans over right now I'd be toast. I looked at the lineup, on second to last, following Hiroshi Tanahashi, the star equivalent to a John Cena in the US. This is a hell of a situation. ... I can't F'n picture it. ... Who the hell am I gonna be in the ring anymore?

I think maybe the Jon Moxley that escaped back into the world at Double or Nothing was in the final stage of battle with whatever the hell weak creature had been trying to maintain control of my consciousness. The real Jon Moxley would be set loose in the ring tonight again, in an actual wrestling match, and once that bell rang he would reclaim control of my body. For good.

Maybe it's cuz I'd already given up everything. There was nothing to lose anymore. I'd walked away from security, from being a WWE superstar, from I don't even know how many zeros on a check. I don't know what it was, but I was fine. It felt like the eye of the storm, eerily calm.

When it was time, I emerged from the top of the stands at Sumo Hall. Entering through the crowd was Rocky's idea. I was initially resistant to it because in the spirit of reinvention I didn't wanna rely on any old WWE tricks (entering through the crowd was the hallmark entrance of The Shield), but Rocky was right. I immediately set the tone as something ... different. *OOOOOHHH!* was the sound that came from the fans as I made my way to the ring. I was feeling the crowd, feeling the music, feeling the energy, feeling myself.

Juice and I immediately erupted into a furious exchange of blows. He met me at the ropes with an elbow that rang my bell. I clotheslined him over the top rope and the room was spinning. Great. Of all times. I hit the ropes to perform a suicide dive, praying I was running the right direction. As the match unfolded it became an out-of-body experience. Chains and locks were popping off my body. I was aggressive, I was mean, I was loose, I was having fun. ... Oh yeah! This is what I used to do all the time! Jon Moxley is back. He's out of jail ... and he's beating the fuck out of Juice Robinson. The extent of the instructions we received from Gedo was, "Fifteen, twenty minutes?"

Blood, sweat flying, tables breaking. ... God, I love this shit. ... I would debut an elevated version of the Dirty Deeds we called the Death Rider* and win the U.S. Title. I knew the match was pretty damn good. I felt many emotions but mostly ... I'm F'n BACK, baby ... and that was just a dry run. That was my baseline. That's what I just ... DO. It's only gonna get better from here. When I returned to the dressing room I received a standing ovation, common in New Japan, where the boys all watch the matches and support each other. We all love this shit. ... I was stunned. Elated. On Cloud Nine.

---

* The "Death Rider" became the name of my finish and sort of my moniker in Japan. It came by accident. In the mystery teaser videos that played before my arrival, produced by my boy Nick Mondo, the body double posing as me just happened to have a biker jacket from Goodwill that said "Death Riders" on the back. What it's actually in reference to is the guys who would ride motorcycles around the giant steel ball at carnivals. I think Ryan Gosling did that shit in a movie — you can Google it.

Osaka Jo Hall, three days later. I grabbed the microphone. "I bring a message from Cincinnati, Ohio. Jon Moxley, international purveyor of violence, gentleman and all-around sick son of a bitch wants in ... the G1!" ... *OOOOHH!* ... That's right, baby. You got somethin' to say, bitch? The guy who stood in his garage on the phone scared of the G1 doesn't exist anymore. I'm on the attack, the warpath. I returned to Las Vegas to train.

TOKYO, KORAKUEN HALL: G1, B BLOCK, NIGHT 3

Ishii and I have been beating the ever-loving hell out of each other for over 19 minutes at a breakneck pace. I've lost an incredible amount of body fluid in the summer humidity of the packed hall. My heart is beating hard. Korakuen is rocking. We've given them violence both spectacular and revolting, chairs and tables smashed, bodies flying through the air, skulls smashing into each other with sickening thuds. High drama, the audience can feel the contest in all its unapologetic, violent glory, and now we're building to a crescendo. I hear the timekeeper over the PA, "*Tuuweenty* minutes gone, *tuuuwenty* minutes past." ... Shit ... we're 20 minutes deep in this sumbitch. Self-assessment: I feel fine, I could go another 20, crowd's on fire. Finally, after a blistering exchange, I dump Ishii on the top of his head with the Death Rider. He grabs his neck in abject agony. The ref counts three.

In that moment, all the grueling hours and weeks of work I did to prepare for this tournament paid off. I felt like the king of the world, unstoppable. All those people who said I couldn't do it, whether I created them in my head or not, I've proved to them that there's no ceiling on what I can do in wrestling and in life.

I didn't realize I'd have to address the crowd after the match, as it turns out is customary for the winner of the main event in New Japan. *Booooooooooy* was I tired, hot and beat up, but when they motioned for me to take the mic, I grabbed it and delivered a dual message, from the heart, to the whole world. Whether you love me or hate me, for the fans in the building and all those who lifted me up, I expressed my sincere gratitude; for the doubters, for anyone who attempts to hold me down or stand in my way, well ... the message has always been the same: Fuck you.

ALBUMS - SPIN IT UP

Much has been said about the art of the album being lost: iTunes, singles, individual songs, TikTok (whatever the fuck that is), playlists, all that shit are the thing now. When I was a kid, when a band's new CD came out it was about the whole album, from the first track to the last. You were meant to study the cover art, pull out the booklet inside containing the lyrics and maybe a foldout poster, and read along for the duration of the recording. You were there to experience the journey, the whole album as one piece of work. Now, I love a good Spotify playlist, but there's something about the physical cassette or CD in your hands that just feels different, more personal. Renée is big into vinyl. She has a massive collection, which I appreciate. A lot of people are into collecting vinyl; they say it sounds better. Maybe ... but I think it's more about owning and experiencing a piece of an artist's work in its complete form, how it was meant to be experienced. I totally get that. On the other hand, I'm something of a minimalist by nature. I throw shit out all the time. I'm not sentimental. They used to send me boxes of my WWE action figures all the time. And sure, it's nice to be able to give some away to family and friends, but at a certain point it's like ... just STOP. Stop sending me F'n toys! I don't need them, and they're taking up space. I've taken several boxes to Goodwill. Some kid in Henderson may have wondered why there was such a surplus of Dean Ambrose figures at this particular location. One time I was so frustrated with these boxes in my garage I took them up the street and threw them in the dumpster. My mother, my biggest fan, reacted as if I'd drowned a litter of baby kittens.

I'm not what you would call tech-savvy. I had a flip phone until WWE basically forced me to get a smartphone (Android all day. I don't fuck with no cloud. That's right, bitch, I'm a green texter ... what?). I haven't played a video game since Sega Genesis and I wasn't good at them back then. Even writing this F'n book on my wife's MacBook is a challenge. This thing is constantly throwing curveballs at me. Writing on this MacBook, I feel like Will Smith in *Independence Day* piloting the alien craft.

All that being said, I love the fact that I can have thousands of my favorite albums all stored on my device in one place. It's crazy to think about. The technology we have today makes it so you don't have to have stacks of CDs and shelves of records taking up space. In this case I'm all for this F'n phone technology. It just makes sense. It's pragmatic. Still, I appreciate Renée's affinity for physical records, even though a part of me is like ..."You realize we can hook up your phone to Bluetooth and listen to all this shit without having to flip the record over, and there's no need for all these F'n things to be taking up space in our house? When does it end? We're gonna be on *Hoarders*!"

I've circled the runway here for a few paragraphs with a stream of consciousness that I'm sure is making you seriously question why you purchased this book, so let's prepare for landing: I love a good album and throughout this book, which you're now having serious second thoughts about, I will share some of my favorites with you. A playlist is great but sometimes it's fun to just commit ... for a workout, a drive, a hang on the couch with your woman, or a woman you *want* to be your woman, or by yourself in a Fairfield Inn in Bakersfield with a bottle of Schlitz.

Commit to the album, the journey. Rob MacIntyre was the former strength and conditioning coach at FCW. We'd pile into cars to save gas money and drive the 40 minutes out into the swamps of Florida to train at his customized warehouse gym, Hard Knocks South. Rob was something of a philosopher, one of the smartest guys I ever met. He would begin training sessions with stories and lessons, often quite educational, discussing strategies of war, or the incredible courage of our armed forces and the sacrifices they've made for our freedom. Other times we'd all watch some clips from cakefarts.com, not for enjoyment, not to make fun of it, but just to marvel at the ridiculousness and the beauty of the world we live in. Rob liked to have an album of the day. When we began a workout, he'd put on for example, Slayer, *Reign in Blood*, 1986. Rob would explain the history of the album, the state of music at the time it was recorded and its cultural impact. Now, when this training session began and the notes of the first track came through the speakers ... in this case, "Angel of Death," we were locked in, we were focused. No distractions, no external interruptions, we were listening to *Reign in Blood* and pumping some F'n iron.

Committing to the album is a surprisingly effective tool to achieve focus on a task, whether that task is to have a productive training session, score with that special chick, decorate your Christmas tree (which my wife is doing as I write this) or just have a good time alone in your hotel room with your malt liquor. I've somehow hit the tarmac, pulled up, got the plane back into the air and am circling the runway again so I'll finish this now ... Renée is right, I am long winded. We'll call these recommendations "Spin It Ups" ... and we'll start with the first CD I ever owned, Metallica, *Master of Puppets*, 1986.

I don't know how I acquired *Master of Puppets*. I was in the fifth grade and had a rudimentary CD player. Maybe I traded some baseball cards or a wrestling tape for it? I just remember another kid in school telling me about all these different metal bands and how cool they were. I didn't know shit about music at this point, but after hearing about all this heavy metal awesomeness that was going on that I wasn't a part of, I felt like I needed to be on the inside. I wanted to be cool too, to learn about new bands before I ever heard their music by reading copies of *Metal Edge* at the newsstand: Metallica, Pantera, Slayer ... they all certainly looked cool. *Master of Puppets* begins with 38 seconds of Spanish guitar: relaxing, mellow. You may picture Catherine Zeta-Jones sniffing *romneya* flowers in *The Mask of Zorro*, you're enjoying a nice breeze. ... Then BAM! ... The rest of the opening track, "Battery," announces its presence with grandiose electric guitar. Then it just gets F'n nasty. The album does not let up from there: The classic title track, the spooky "Welcome Home (Sanitarium)." "Disposable Heroes" rips right into "Leper Messiah." Those two songs have always felt like one long piece to me. Next it's the epic and inspiring "Orion," which highlights the legendary Cliff Burton's bass, then we finish with "Damage, Inc," which starts with what I used to think were whale sounds before just getting in your face with some mean, aggressive, unapologetic metal headbangery. This album F'n rules.

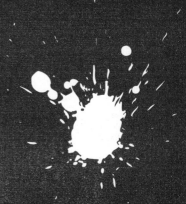

PERSONAL STORY

One day I get a call from my dad. He wants me to bring my truck to meet him at Cub Foods over by the Dayton Mall near his home in Springboro, Ohio. The vehicle in question is a beat up '97 Ford Ranger with the ignition box hanging out under the steering wheel cuz I lost my keys and had to have an associate of mine hotwire it. Dad told me to bring my buddy Mario, a strapping Italian fellow I met on the first day of first grade. He was the Iceman to my Goose as we navigated the route from adolescence to adulthood. Dad didn't say why he requested we come, but I knew why. I had a truck. If you have a truck, you know you are the one who everyone calls when they need something moved. Mario and I moved a lot of people. We moved my dad twice. We moved his wife, Julie. We moved brothers, sisters, family friends, acquaintances, girlfriends, cousins, godparents, wrestlers, wrestlers' friends, accountants, personal trainers, strippers. ... Sometimes we moved people by accident. Sometimes we moved people who didn't even wanna move just cuz we had the momentum.

Being the guy with a truck can be a curse. I'd get the call and then I'd call Mario, He was my guy. We had a system, being two strong college-aged guys (Mario was actually *in* college; I was a poor aspiring wrestler). We could effortlessly turn a corner carrying a dresser without scuffing the walls or knocking pictures off the wall. We could easily get a mattress down or up stairs without saying a word to one another ... simpatico. Got a 50-inch flat-screen? No problem. We were the best, babe. We talked about turning it into a business, couldn't think of a cool name though. ...

I'm not sure why we were meeting my dad in the parking lot of a grocery store. Usually it was a pretty straightforward job: boxes, couches, box springs, mattresses. We might be hauling an old fridge or washing machine to the dump, but whatever we hauled, I hoped to score a $20 payday at least.

Today's work, as it turned out, would be pro bono but I gained something much more valuable than some gas money. Dad arrived at the Cub Foods parking lot, and Mario and I followed him into the store. He instructed us to both grab a cart, and we followed him through the store as he instructed us to fill the carts with groceries.

"What kind?"

"What families eat for dinner. Fill 'em up."

We followed him up and down the aisles; we stocked up on eggs and milk. Then we were instructed to focus on non-perishables: rice, canned goods, pancake mix, cereal.

Dad asked, "What kind of cereal do kids like? Get some stuff kids like."

We loaded up on sugary cereals ... Golden Grahams, Fruity Pebbles, Cocoa Puffs, and my personal favorite, the MF'n Suga Bear. From there it was fruit snacks, Capri Suns. We grab giant-sized tubs of laundry detergent. Our carts are loaded. What the F is going on here? Is my dad preparing for nuclear winter? He was in the National Guard – does he have Cold War PTSD? You know the Wall came down, right?

And come to think of it, who are these kids we're buying for? Did my sister have quintuplets? Can we get her on a reality show? Also, who's paying for all this shit? After winding through the entire store and going full *Supermarket Sweep* in this bitch, we came to the checkout counter to start the long process of scanning and bagging this sizable haul. While the clerk was tackling this task item by item ... *beep ... beep* ... my dad took this time to give Mario and me further instructions. We were to load the groceries into the truck and follow him to an address. I have more questions. WTF is going on? But Dad is reluctant to give me details. He paid for the groceries with his debit card. As we were loading the truck, I pressed him further for information ... nothing. As he walked away to get in his truck, he said, "Just follow me."

We arrived in a residential neighborhood in Dayton, Ohio. Not a great neighborhood: houses in disrepair, lawns a foot tall, graffiti, broken windows, rusted-out vehicles. My dad stopped at a stop sign a couple turns away from our drop point. We stopped behind him. He got out, walked up to our driver-side window. I rolled the window down. Dad instructed us to knock on the door of a specific house, out of view from where we were, and deliver the groceries to the family inside. Most importantly, when asked about the source of this delivery we were to respond, "Anonymous friends," and nothing else. To say anything else besides "anonymous friends" would be a breach of our mission.

"Who are these people?" I asked.

"Doesn't matter."

We parked and walked up to the home: one story, cracked paint, rusty steel fence. We had bulky plastic bags stretched to their capacity at our sides. The man who answered the door, slightly concerned at the intrusion at first, was clearly a machine shop worker. He's wiry, ashen, clearly smokes two packs of Marlboros a day. He was wearing an open plaid shirt over a wifebeater, grease under his nails. I like him.

It takes all of three seconds for him to figure out what was going on and a warm smile came over his face, tears welled up in his eyes before Mario or I could even stammer out any awkward hello. He saw the groceries. His lip quivering, the kind of humble gratitude so evident in his body as he shook, made it clear instantly that this dude was in a real tough spot in life; something bad had happened. He needed help ... now.

Suddenly, EXCITEMENT! Kids, maybe three or four of various ages, rush out the door. Mario and I are swarmed like it's the F'n Puppy Bowl. We were trying to go back and forth from the house to the truck bringing in the supplies this family obviously needs desperately. The man is elated. You'd think he just won the lottery. He's praising Jesus, he's quoting scripture to ... I'm not sure to who, but he's damn sure excited. The kids are helping us unload the truck. They're F'n stoked. It was a wild scene. In all the action, this man asks me and Mario once or twice where all this came from.

"Who are you?"

"Anonymous friends."

We don't hang around and make conversation. We were in and out in maybe three minutes flat. It was a hailstorm of canned goods and Praise Jesuses. We were like the SEAL team from the militant wing of the Salvation Army. And then ... we vanished.

Meeting my dad back at the rendezvous point, I must admit we were on a bit of a high. That was a whole lot of excitement, a whole lot of people being happy.

"I gotta know, man, you gotta tell us what the hell that was all about!"

My Dad told us about the man to whom we'd just delivered those groceries: His wife was battling cancer, a long and grueling battle. Their medical bills were out of control. They couldn't afford to pay their bills or eat. I don't remember all the details but they were in a real bad spot. Desperate. The man worked in the shop at Laird Plastics, where my dad was the branch manager. Dad started in the shop for minimum wage, so he knew it was important to keep his ear to the ground and be aware of what was going on with everyone on his team. He'd heard of this family's troubles and he knew they needed groceries. Right now. He took it upon himself to fix the problem ... *We're the good guys.* ... The most important part of all this was that my dad not only didn't *need* anyone to give him credit for this ("Oh, that Dan is such a great guy!"), he actively *refused* credit for this. "Anonymous friends." Dad did not want that guy to feel any embarrassment over his boss buying every F'n box of cereal in Dayton to make sure his family ate. He explained to me that true, pure charity should be anonymous. ... You help your fellow man not because you want a tax break or a ticker tape parade for your generosity. You do it because it's the right thing to do. The man never found out.

FLICK PICK: POINT BREAK, 1991, KEANU REEVES, PATRICK SWAYZE

I have a hard time picking my all-time favorite anything, but over the years it's become clear and undeniable. *Point Break* is my favorite movie of all time. If you are of the opinion that any movie other than *Point Break* is the greatest movie of all time ... well, then ... I will not attempt to understand, let alone tolerate, your viewpoint. I am right and you are wrong. Nah, just kidding. That's what makes talking about movies so much fun — everybody's got their own favorites. For me, it's all about *Point Break.* What's not to love? This movie has everything: bank robbers, surfing, skydiving, memorable quotes and iconic scenes. Peak Gary Busey.

"UTAH! Get me two!"

And, of course, there's a smoking hot chick, Lori Petty with that short haircut. The scene where she changes clothes at the beach with the magical towel trick ... Bruh! This flick even has one of the Red Hot Chili Peppers! What really drives this movie is the two lead actors, Keanu Reeves and the great Patrick Swayze himself, one of the *coooolest* dudes of all time. And don't say shit about *Dirty Dancing* cuz you wouldn't have the balls to dance like that even if you could. Swayze plays Bodhi, the Zen guru surfer/leader of a pack of radical surfing bank robbers. ... Trust me, it's dope. Keanu plays Johnny Utah, former hot-shit QB from Ohio, fresh-out-of-the-academy stud FBI recruit. Things have been said about Keanu's acting. Well, it seems like he's done pretty well for himself to me, but what do I know? In any case, Keanu's trademark delivery and personality IS Johnny Utah. Swayze IS Bodhi. One of the most interesting things in this film to me ... besides all the obvious cool shit ... is the juxtaposition of the two main characters, which is first displayed during the opening credits, going back and forth between Utah, cornfed midwestern QB, shooting 100 percent target practice at Quantico*, and Bodhi, a free spirit, a searcher, just surfing the waves.

---

* Quantico is a town in Virginia where the FBI Academy is located. For some reason, it's raining in this scene. I don't know if they would really do target practice in the rain, but it does make the scene way cooler.

On my United flight from L.A. to Tokyo for my debut in New Japan, they had *Point Break* among the movie selections. I hadn't seen it in years. A couple of cocktails and the focus of being stuck in a pod for 10 hours where all I had to do was watch movies, get drunk and sleep, and nobody could get ahold of me if they wanted to. ... I've never enjoyed a movie more. It put me at peace and felt like a good omen. Renée and I watched *Point Break* with the balcony door open to the salty sea winds coming from Imperial Beach in San Diego. We had some excellent calamari. It was the perfect setting to enjoy my favorite movie of all time. We could see the surfers below, which really fit the motif. Let's be clear, however. No matter how much I love this movie or Swayze's performance. I don't fuck with the ocean. Maybe I'll wade out ankle/knee-deep, but I keep my ass on the land. I don't wanna get stung by no jellyfish. ... You ever read about a box jellyfish? ... And I do not fuck with sharks. I only occasionally go out far enough to where if I get attacked by a shark my feet are firmly on the bottom and I can punch down. They have their element, I have mine. Let's keep it that way. I can say with almost absolute certainty I will not be eaten by a shark. My ass won't even be in the water. ... "He's not coming back." ... "I am an FBI AGENT!" ... "This game, we both lose." ... What a radical movie.

Author's note: We did not discuss the 2015 remake of Point Break because it's never to be spoken of again. It does not exist. It's been taken care of by top men. ... TOP MEN!

By the fall of 2012, I had been on the road since the day after WrestleMania 28, doing dark matches and house-show loops, largely just sitting in catering or the stands, getting progressively more and more pissed off. The *Raw* after Mania in Miami, I wrestled JTG in a dark match and got a nice response from the crowd. A good portion of the more hardcore fans that attended Mania Week actually knew who I was. I was pumped. It was the time of the year for debuts, new characters and new angles, and I was about to come in and fuck everybody's world up.

I had THE PERFECT angle to do it. Coming back through Gorilla after the match, I had a conversation with Hunter: "This thing's picking up steam; it looks like a shoot," he said.

"Hell yeah," I replied, then I recounted to him how the previous day in the Axxess green room, I had been sitting at a table with Mark Henry, who had no idea who I was at the time. He asked some other folks at the table, "You hear about Foley last night, man? Some motherfucker came up to him in the lobby talking about how he ruined a generation and he needs to be held accountable or some damn thing. They got that motherfucker outta there. Lucky I wasn't there. I'da slapped the SHIT out that stupid motherfucker."

I sat quietly at the table and didn't say anything. The motherfucker who the world's strongest man was saying he would like to slap the shit out of was me. The previous night we had planted a seed for the potential angle of a lifetime between a yet-to-debut-on-WWE-TV Dean Ambrose and the hardcore legend Mick Foley. Foley had come back to the hotel after the Hall of Fame ceremony and was in the lobby meeting fans. I was up at the top of the escalator, awaiting his arrival. When he showed up, I let him mingle with the people for a couple minutes before coming up and introducing myself. Then I got in his face and explained that he was responsible for ruining a whole generation, my generation, a generation that went out and nearly killed themselves trying to emulate him. I told him he needed to be held accountable. "What does accountable mean to you?" he responded, clearly rattled.

It was all part of the plan. I was booted out of there by security while fans in the lobby vociferously told me to go fuck myself. I was shown to the elevator and returned to my room, mission accomplished. I had met Mick for the first time in the green room a few days before and we agreed to ad-lib the scene, meant to only be caught on camera phones and come off as very real.

The idea came from a day when I was bored in Dusty's promo class at FCW. Mick had just returned to the company, and in my mind, there was no way not to book us together if he still had some matches left in him. With our similar histories and our penchant for intense promos, it not only made perfect sense, it was a dream match for me and a hell of a way to debut. If they gave Foley to anyone but me, I'd be pissed. We were tailor-made for each other. ... This was MY match.

I hated Wednesdays in FCW, my least favorite day of the week. Fucking promo class, or excuse me, "The Art of Communication with Dusty Rhodes." Basically, everyone would go up and cut a promo, or people would do a skit or whatever. In theory, this practice could be beneficial to a talent with little experience with talking in front of people, but I just couldn't wrap my brain around it. Participating in this made me feel foolish. I hated it. Allegedly the office watched the promos we did every week, which I didn't really believe. In fact, I almost never put in any real effort in promo class. Dusty would try to get me to explore different ideas and try out new characters. ... We had a semi, mild, feud over the fact that I refused to try.

A lot of talent at FCW were coming up with new wacky gimmicks every week in hopes the office would bite on something. I chose not to do this for two reasons. For one, if I fucked around just for fun one week and came out with a full costume and a new character, "I'm ...THE BEEKEEPER!," I would run the risk that they actually saw it and liked it, and then I'd be on TV in an F'n beekeeping outfit and my career would be over six months later. They knew exactly who I was; they knew I could talk. For another, if I had a really good idea for a promo or a concept and the office actually did watch this stuff, I sure as hell wasn't gonna give away good material to the fuckstick creative team and have my ideas stolen and given to some other dipshit. No sir, I'll keep my good ideas to myself, thank you.

When Foley came back into the WWE fold, however, I wanted to scream from the rooftops that they better not even fucking think about having him work with anybody else but me, and I chose to express this in a promo. What would be my motivation for wanting to take down Mick? To prove who's more hardcore? No, that's lame. To try to take the torch from my hero? Yawn. No, I gotta hate this motherfucker. Why would I hate him? I devised a concept where I looked around at my contemporaries on the indie scene, especially the deathmatch scene, and realized we were all poor, our bodies were torn up, we had no future, we'd suffer long-term health issues. In actuality some of these guys were now dead. I decided I would blame Mick Foley for inspiring all of us to jump off our roofs and balconies as kids and then eventually mutilate ourselves in the name of being hardcore, like Mick, our messiah. It was all bullshit he sold us. ... Where were our Beefaroni commercials? Where were our beautiful wives, families and fat contracts? Fuck Mick Foley. I would be the lucky one. I made it out. I would go to WWE and I would rid the world of the hardcore legend, but not before I put him on trial for his crimes. It was intense stuff. It was good, maybe too good. The office saw the promo, Hunter ended up seeing it. He bit and he bit hard. It was a green light.

Twitter was just starting to become a big deal. I had no idea what it was when they told me the plan. First, I'd have a public confrontation with Mick. The hope was that video of the incident would gain traction on the internet. Secondly, I was to start insulting him on Twitter, a proto-social media feud. They made an official Twitter account for me and anyone at FCW who didn't have one to avoid suspicion this might be a work. I was instructed to just start talking shit, basically. They told me to become a presence on social media and tweet all kinds of different stuff as well as the angle-related bits, to gain followers and make it all seem real. It seems hilarious now that I, of all people, was made to be in a social media feud, but at the time I was into it, seemed like some cutting-edge shit. So, I played with this Twitter. It was amusing, and I used it effectively for my purposes. I started posting links to videos of backyard wrestlers nearly killing themselves in cringeworthy clips, attaching the hashtag #thanksmick (See, I know how hashtags work. ... I figured that shit out a decade ago).

The plan was for me to debut at Extreme Rules, the PPV after Mania, and slam Mick's head through a car windshield after building heat in a work/shoot feud online. Shit started getting a little weird. At a *SmackDown!* taping in Hampton, Virginia, the plan was for Mick to confront me in front of a good number of wrestlers about my online activities. I guess it was supposed to be some working-the-boys type shit, which is always a poor idea, but again at the time, I was into it. It was different. So Mick says something to me in front of a bunch of the boys and specifically says, "Don't talk about my family," in reference to something I must have tweeted. I'm then brought into the talent relations office and told in order to blow the incident out of proportion and get the rumor mill started I am to fly out immediately as if the incident had resulted in me being sent home for insubordination of some sort. I am told to tweet about this. I go to the airport and get on the flight, and I take to Twitter to voice my displeasure. I even take a picture of my boarding pass so it's clear I'm actually flying out just as *SmackDown!* has started, hopefully adding some realism and making it all murky for the hardcore fans following this story.

Then it gets weirder. We go to London for TVs. I have a shitty cheap phone that doesn't work in Europe so I'm basically out of communication for a few days. In my mind, since we were "working the boys" when Mick said, "Don't talk about my family," in front of those who I thought we were working, that was a signal to me that talking about his family was exactly what he wanted me to do. At the TV hotel in London, I go to the business center, get on the computer and tweet more shit about his family because that's what I think I'm supposed to do.

Mick had been texting me that while this angle was going great, he actually did not want me to make mention of his family. In Europe with my cheap phone, I was not receiving these texts and happily went on to do exactly what Mick had asked me not to. Mick did not appreciate this. We didn't know each other well, and he just figured I was an asshole. He was pretty upset with me and almost pulled the plug on the whole thing.

When I returned to U.S. soil my phone lit up with messages, among them several long texts from Mick asking me what the fuck my problem was. I was mortified. I would never have said anything intentionally disrespectful or out of line with our story if not for the fact that that's exactly what I thought he wanted me to do. I cursed my shitty phone for blowing the biggest opportunity of my life. I profusely apologized, explained it was a misunderstanding, and we smoothed it over quickly, but there must be a lesson to be learned here about trying so hard to work other people that you end up not knowing what's real and what's not.

Crisis averted, we were back on, Dean Ambrose versus Mick Foley, on a collision course for some kind of gimmick match, like a cage or something, at SummerSlam. Sure it would be a star-making performance, I figured I'd be cutting promos and talking mad shit to the top guys on *Raw* in main event segments in no time. All I had to do was do what I do and get over. Give me a mic and get out of the way, I'd be the top heel by the end of the year, I figured. Then I got a call from Hunter, and it all went up in flames.

They couldn't get Mick medically cleared. That was it. He was done. It was over. I was crushed. I don't know the details of Mick's evaluation, but I believe it was due to his history with concussions. Mick had tried. He suggested to the doctor we could work an entire match around his leg and play it safe as possible. 'Twas not to be. I believed that feud could go down as an all-time "what could have been" thing, but looking at it now I see it differently than I did then. At the time, I assumed it would be Mick and I coming up with our own angle and cutting our own interviews, crafting our own story.

In FCW I was largely left to my own devices. I'd never read a script in my life. I had heard the phrase "scripted promos," but I just thought it was a turn of phrase. Like, it's a television show with a format that's timed out. When I heard about scripted promos or heard the term "verbiage," a word that now makes me physically ill when I hear it, I just thought it was TV industry jargon: "cold open," "pyro," "ballyhoo" and all that. I didn't take it literally. It hadn't hit me that there would be actual scripts to memorize. I thought the writers just came up with ideas, booked matches and angles. The concept of somebody else writing words for me was completely alien.

Had the feud between Dean Ambrose and Mick Foley actually came to pass, the reality is I would have shown up to that first TV with a truckload of promo in my head, then I would have been handed a script. I would have reacted poorly to this to say the least. I would have immediately been deemed difficult to work with. I would have been confused and frustrated that they wanted me to read from a script. Red light of the camera on, live mic in hand, I would have trusted my own instincts over some writer's and been summarily punished for it. I would have quickly developed a bad reputation, and they would have soured on my attitude. Vince would feel he couldn't trust me, and the push would have fizzled within a couple of months.

A feud between the Moxley of today or even 2009 vs. 1995/96 Cactus Jack, I'm confident would be a classic — an emotional, cerebral and violent campaign. But the likely scenario in 2012 WWE is we would have been handcuffed. It's possible that Mick, being a Hall of Famer and all-time promo master could have afforded us a little more freedom, but I doubt they would have let us take it where we wanted. I would have come in so excited and confident, and the whole thing would be clear in my head. It would have been real to me at that point. To be handed a script would have been unmercifully galling and resulted in a clash. For all my passion and creativity, I would have been future-endeavored or sent straight back to developmental.

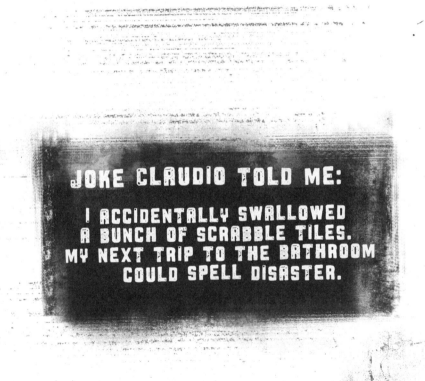

JOKE CLAUDIO TOLD ME:

I ACCIDENTALLY SWALLOWED A BUNCH OF SCRABBLE TILES. MY NEXT TRIP TO THE BATHROOM COULD SPELL DISASTER.

WHY I DON'T RIDE A MOTORCYCLE

I'd love to be a motorcycle guy. Often people think I am, probably cuz I have such a sick jacket game. I like the thought of flying down the 15 on a Harley, burning through the desert, but I am, in fact, not a motorcycle guy. I've often had to clarify for people when telling a story about crashing my bike, that I am referring to ... my mountain bike, a specialized 29er. The look on the listener's face is always disappointment. Yes, reader, despite the plethora of leather jackets I've sported over the years and my innate ability to look cool AF in them, I do not ride motorcycles. The reason I don't is simple. It's the same reason I don't like being on the top rope: I'm clumsy. I know what you're thinking: In the ring you move like a *panther*, well maybe not a panther, but you don't seem *thaaat* clumsy. When I'm in the ring and my brain is switched on and focused, performing moves I've practiced thousands of times, and then, yes, I can create the illusion that I'm a reasonable facsimile of a world-class athlete, but outside of the ring I can be shockingly ungainly. It might be cuz I can be absentminded, a daydreamer, my head in the clouds and not paying attention to what my feet are doing. I've fallen down our stairs at least four times, partly because my wife hates carpet, and running in socks on hardwood can be hazardous. I always wear shoes around the house now, but the threat always looms. Just the other day I ate shit face-first on the sidewalk while out for a run. Why? I couldn't tell you. But I did make sure to signal the concerned onlookers that I was OK with a double bicep pose and a thumbs-up.

One time I ran to answer the front door. I bounded down the two-step landing and somehow managed to launch myself in the air with such velocity that it defied the laws of thermodynamics. Did I step on one of those things from *Super Mario*? I thought I was walking DOWN the steps, so how am I in a fully horizontal Superman-like position hovering three feet above the ground? ... This can't end well. My life is often like a scene from *Home Alone*. We're expecting a child as I write this, and I fear my ultimate demise will result from a Tonka truck or maybe some Hot Wheels left on the floor.

Which brings me back to the motorcycle. If I rode a motorcycle it would be an inevitability that one day I'd be cruising down the highway feeling myself when I notice the gorgeous sunset on the horizon. The sight would fill me with joy and inspiration. I'd consider all the splendor and beauty of this world and my place in it and then ... *BAM!!!!!* Roadkill! Or I'd get distracted by a Pizza Hut sign. Either way, same result. Every time I've considered getting a motorcycle I come back to the same conclusion. I would be a danger to myself and others. I'm keeping myself on four wheels.

I'll tell you a story that illustrates this point further: September 19, 2015, Henderson, Nevada, Renée's birthday. In recent weeks, she had casually mentioned her desire for a motor scooter. She had just moved into an apartment with me in Las Vegas and didn't have a car yet. She used my truck when I was on the road, but if we wanted to be in two places at once it presented a problem. For whatever reason she liked the idea of a scooter. Her friend, the incomparable Amy Dumas, has had a Vespa for years and loves it. Seems like fun, bopping around town, going to yoga, getting your nails done. ... Now remember, brothers, **YOU GOTTA CRUSH YOUR WOMAN'S BIRTHDAY**, and with that in mind you know what I did. ... *Aaaaahhh* man, y'all making this too easy. I decided: I'll buy Renée a scooter.

I went to a dealer in Vegas, described my needs and was soon loading my truck up with a badass little piece of scootery. They rigged the engine so it could reach speeds up to 50mph. We were still in the apartment, so I had no place to store this hog until September 19. I rented a storage unit on St. Rose Parkway and inside I parked the gift that was sure to make me a hero.

September 19 arrives, and even better, my sister is in town! Now I have double the audience for my best-boyfriend-in-the-world moment, now there are two women to discuss how great this gift is, how great I am, how they are all so lucky to have me in their lives. ... How to debut the scooter? It can't just come down the aisle with a generic ring jacket and raise one arm to the crowd. This ain't earrings, this ain't a basket of decorative soaps ... this is a scooter, dammit! I need pomp and circumstance. ... I need to create a moment they'll never forget. Let's take a ride, babe! This is cool-guy shit.

My plan was to park the truck about 30 feet away from the storage unit so my audience could see me enter the unit 30 feet in front and to their left. They won't know what's inside and will have no idea what to expect. I will get on the bike, start it up inside the unit, anticipation building. At the precise right moment ... I'll know it when I feel it ... I'll come flying out of the storage unit like Ghost Rider leaving a trail of flames behind me!!

In my mind, it's going to be better than any pageantry Evel Knievel ever came up with. There will be confetti, trumpets, maybe a speedboat pulling one of those towers of water skiers. ... It's gonna be F'n *coooooool*! I'll be a hero, Renée will be the envy of women worldwide, and my sister will know she has THE coolest brother in the world. ... I know how to GIFT. Bitches won't know what hit 'em.

The moment arrived. My audience got in the truck expecting they were going to Target or some shit, little do they know they're going on a rollercoaster ride, about to experience true cool, the perfect birthday gift. I get on St. Rose Parkway and start going in the opposite direction of our supposed destination. ... I say nothing.

"Where are we going?" Renée asked.

I say nothing.

We drove a few more miles, and I remained silent as Lauren and Renée chatted. We eventually reached the storage facility. Renée asked more questions, but sunglasses on, hand steady on the wheel, I betray nothing. I have the surgical precision of a hitman as we pull up to the gate and I punch in a code that swings the door open, provoking suspicion.

"Why do you have a storage locker?" Renée asked. (She would later admit that she thought this was finally where the other shoe was gonna drop and she found out I had a meth lab or some shit.)

I betrayed nothing, not saying a word, completely stoic. ... In time, my dear. ...

I parked the truck and got out. Calmly. All business. Renée's questions faded in the distance behind me as I walked the 30 feet and put the key into the padlock. I intentionally looked around to make sure no one was watching, the suspense building with every passing moment. I opened the door and disappeared inside.

Ha ha ... I got 'em right where I want 'em ... a captive audience.

I prepared the bike, took off the e-brake, started her up. I waited for the exact right moment. Two minutes passed. I heard the truck doors slam, my audience has gotten out of the truck, now curious and impatient ... right where I want 'em.

It was time to fly! VROOOOOM! I came blasting out of the storage unit on my metal steed!!! I made a hard left away from the audience, and I could hear the cheers behind me. ... Got 'em. I circled the storage complex and now I was coming at the audience from behind! More cheers as I came back into view. Renée was jumping up and down as I zipped by at 30 mph. Big smiles. WooooHooo! This couldn't have gone better, exactly how I pictured it.

Now it was time to just sit back and bask in the glory of adulation. The best boyfriend in the world. I circled the complex again and made another pass, this time at 35 mph. I pulled my shades down and gave a wink. The coolest guy in the world. ... I decided to make one more pass, show off one more time for the audience before slowing to a stop amidst my fawning, adoring public. ... The coolest gu—

Shit!!!! I hit the front brake. My ass is definitely not on the seat anymore. ... In fact, it seems to be about three feet below me. At this point it became one of those slo-mo scenes from *Deadpool*. ... I definitely have two fingers left on one handlebar, but I can feel them coming off. ... I'm going airborne. It's time to tuck and roll, babe.

When I hit the front brake — which you are NOT supposed to do on a scooter — I was catapulted over the handlebars, ass over teakettle 10 feet into the air. I must have flown 20 feet. Thank God I fall down for a living. That's the only explanation I have for how I was able to stay relaxed and somehow F'n ninja roll back to my feet, where I immediately did a quick five-point diagnostic on myself: No broken bones, no bleeding, no concussion, my brains aren't splattered anywhere. Just a little road rash. ... I'm alive!

I know I'm not like a Patrick Swayze in *Ghost* because I see my wife and sister running toward me in shock and horror!

"OH MY GOD! ARE YOU OK?!" they shout in unison.

I tried to play it cool. As my audience ran up to me in panic, I explained, "You see, what I was demonstrating there was the most important safety rule of this scooter — never hit the front brake."

But there was so no saving this one. I. Was. A. Geek.

Renée did *looove* the gift, which miraculously emerged unharmed, and despite my near-death experience I did, in fact, crush her birthday. On the drive home, I was hoping for, "You're the best boyfriend," and instead what I got, over and over, was, "I thought you were a goner!" Dammit. There's always next year.

TRAVEL AND FAVORITE CITIES

I've been able to travel the world on another man's dime. It's one of the perks of the job. For a chunk of that time, I've had my wife by my side, which is even cooler. Renée and I have listened to music in a piano bar on Beale Street in Memphis and done shots on Bourbon Street in New Orleans. We've hung out at the Viper Room in Hollywood and cracked fresh crab legs at Pike Place Market in Seattle. We've meditated at a Buddhist temple and did a weird sound bath in a yurt in Sedona (that was some *Total Divas* bullshit but still cool). We've made love on a balcony in Times Square (hours after I successfully defended the WWE Championship at MSG. ... *What, bitch?*). We've done karaoke in Tokyo and filled up on gas and stocked up on snacks at Buc-ees truck stop in Texas (THE BEST truck stops).

Wrestling 250-plus days a year does two things: It makes you never want to travel again, and it makes you want to do nothing but travel. I was in and out of New Zealand in 24 hours, but it seemed pretty cool. I did a signing at a mall, wrestled that night and was back on a plane immediately thereafter. But looking out at the mountains from the window and checking out some travel brochures from the airport, I decided I needed to get back and really explore the place one day. When I got TIME. I still hope to. I hope to return to many places where I was in and out too fast to truly experience the place, but still there long enough just to get a taste. ... Got another shot in another town tomorrow night — gotta roll.

But also ... how good is HOOOME?! I've realized I never truly had a specific home until I met my wife. Renée is my home, and with her I've lived all over the world, from a fun night at a motel in Coldwater, Michigan (the home of Dan Severn), where I opened her wine bottle with a pen, to staying at Mr. C's in L.A. and getting free Bellinis at check-in.

But my official home is in Las Vegas. My stuff, my couch, my bed, my garage, my wife's little decorative touches everywhere. My dogs! If the dogs aren't there, just a lil' something's missing. We bring them everywhere we can. Blue's fat ass can't fly commercial. I've driven that fat bitch across the country, even flew the bougie little fucker private to Jacksonville twice, just so we could all be together and make away from home into ... home. Cincinnati's my original home, will always be my No. 1 home away from home, but I have others. Places that have taken me in, welcomed me. Places I've had great experiences, where I've enjoyed and explored. Places where I've grown, loved, lost, laughed, cried. Many places where, when I land at the airport and hop in a rental car, I know where I'm going without having to use my GPS. I'm in a home away from home. Throughout this book I'll tell you about a few of my homes away from home and why I love them. I encourage you to find some of your own, whether it's a quick day drive or a Southwest flight (*transparency*, bitch!) to wherever's cheap, it's a big world out there ... and, trust me: It's not as scary as you think.

I'll start with where I currently reside: Sin City.

Welcome to Fabulous! Las Vegas! Nevada!

I love that recording that plays over the P.A. in the airport. One thing about having a job that takes place on the road is you can make your residence any place you want. In early 2013, I had been living in Tampa since May of 2011. The Shield had been on the main roster for a few months. I was starting to make a little money and was officially free from Developmental. Change was in the air, and I felt like it was time to move on. I loved Tampa, but it seemed like everybody lived there, and it was where I had been stationed. It was a place I was in for a specific reason, and that objective had been accomplished. Now I wanted a little slice of the world for myself. Now that I could live anywhere, where should I go? I first looked at the tax-free states: Florida, Texas, Nevada ... wait, Nevada? As in Las Vegas, Nevada? The entertainment capital of the world? The fight capital of the world? I researched life in Las Vegas. I quizzed Ryback (born and raised in L.V.), and I had an enlightening conversation with

Bryan Danielson, who'd spent time living in Vegas. He loved it, told me all about the great vegan bakeries, which I have still not as of yet visited.

Obviously, the first thing you think of when you think of Las Vegas is the bright lights, the gambling, partying until dawn ... but Bryan was the farthest thing from a partier of any sort. Bryan is a man you're more likely to see picking berries in his garden than being within 100 yards of anything debaucherous. If HE liked living in Vegas, it must be nice. I had narrowed it down to either Vegas or Austin, Texas. I flipped a coin, and it was Vegas. I was single back then and didn't see that changing any time soon, so I figured I'd try it for one year, and if I didn't like it, I'd try the other for a year. If I didn't like either one, I'd try somewhere else. I'm a rambling man.

I never left Las Vegas, at least not as of this writing. I fell in love immediately. I left my apartment in Tampa with nothing more than I could carry with me on the imminent European tour. We landed back in the States two weeks later, did TV tapings, and then instead of flying to Tampa, I flew to Fabulous! Las Vegas! Nevada! I'd never been here before. I hopped in a cab and gave the driver the address to where I had procured a modest one-bedroom apartment.

"Do you gamble?" the driver asked.

Nah. ... I still don't really aside from throwing a little action on a fight occasionally or killing time on a slot machine at the airport.

"Good. Don't start," he replied.

He explained to me how many people he's seen over the years come to this town and leave with nothing. Sage advice. The cab driver gave me his card and dropped me off at the office. I went in and explained that I thought I lived there now. They had been expecting me. A woman walked me to my new second-floor digs. You could see the Stratosphere from the balcony, mountains in the distance. She gave me the numbers to call to set up my various utilities and left me alone in the empty apartment with my two bags. I called to set up my electricity. ... It would take 24 hours to turn on. Well, shit, I'm not gonna build a campfire in my living room. I called the cab driver, and he came back to pick me up and drop me off at the Mandalay Bay, where I'd Pricelined a suite for something like 36 bucks.

Time to explore Sin City! I checked in at the Mandalay and was prepared to explore my new hometown. I couldn't believe the dope-ass room I got for so cheap. The good vibrations were flowing already when I realized I was out of chewing tobacco (terrible habit). I figured I would have to find a gas station to buy some, but I was right in the middle of resort land, so I'd probably have to walk across the highway or some such pain in the ass.

I came out of the elevator on the main casino floor, took a few steps and immediately in front of me was one of those little bodega/gift shop-type stores that are all over the strip. Behind the counter I see stacks of cans of tobacco, all flavors and brands ... sweet, that's convenient! But wait, there's more: They got Red Man, cigarettes, any kind of liquor, beer, wine, champagne, cigars, literally any kind of Sin City supplies you could want. I loved this place! I went on a solo exploration of as much as the strip as I could over the next 36 hours. The details of the events that occurred on my first night in town will remain classified, unless that chick with the face tattoo ever writes a book — or her friend, who I'm pretty sure was a witch, does.

I couldn't wait to tell all my friends back on the road how cool Vegas was, and now I get to live there! Even though I don't really gamble, I still like casinos. There's something fun about them. I like just walking around, or posting up at a bar with Renée and people watching. I like the atmosphere.

I would soon grow to love living here for reasons that have nothing to do with casinos or the strip or even staying up past 9:00 p.m. First came falling in love with the desert. Yes, it does, in fact, get hot as an MFer here. We can't walk the dogs from 11:00 a.m. to 9:00 p.m. in the summer, but there is something about the feel of the desert heat wrapping around you like a blanket when the sun's already down and you're taking a piss off your back porch.

I'd never really hiked before. You know where I'm from? I don't know shit about no trails ... but my first trip to Red Rock Canyon solidified my relationship with this place. It's beautiful, quiet, calm, eerie, humbling. I hiked the Calico Tanks trail in Red Rock, my favorite local hike and the one I usually bring visitors on. I'd never breathed air like this, never seen scenery like this in real life. I'm walking across giant red stones like I'm on Mars. I didn't realize I've been searching for quiet like this my whole life: no sirens, no cars, no yelling. Just my thoughts, clarity, a healthy sweat, a raised heart rate, breathing a little heavy but not blown up ... endorphins, nature. I don't feel like some cog in a big media machine or a number on some government paperwork. I feel ... like a human. I feel alive. I feel like I felt when I was seven years old playing in a creek, exploring the woods behind our apartment. I feel like myself. I love hiking.

And if you thought that was cheesy, you can go get fucked.

I come to what looks like the end of the trail and there's a pond, surrounded by cliffs on all sides. I forge on up the cliffs behind the pond cuz they look climbable, so let's keep going. It's, in fact, not the end of the trail. The payoff of Calico Tanks trail is a stunning mountaintop view of Red Rock Canyon and the Las Vegas valley. I can see for miles, and it's dead silent. I sit and chill on a big-ass rock. I hear wings in the distance ... *whoosh, whoosh, whoosh* ... and a hawk emerges from the mountainside, flying toward me, getting closer, startling me. *Whoosh, WHOOSH!*

I feel like a 747 is passing overhead, the sound of this bird cutting through the air in the dead silence of the desert. It flies by. *WHOOOSH! ... Whoosh ... whoosh.* ... Silence again. That was F'n dope. We would pop champagne and celebrate my sister's engagement on that rock.

I decided to bike the 15-mile loop around Red Rock, the scenic drive. I got to the first mile marker after pedaling uphill for what seemed like forever and quickly realized I had made a mistake. This sucks! I pedaled on, the first half of the trip miserably trudging uphill, wondering how those MFers in the stupid neon outfits on the side of the road make this look so easy. At the halfway point, there's a lookout; cars stop to take pictures of the Las Vegas Valley and Red Rock canyon. It was like I popped a few Oxys looking out over the valley, checking out the mountains, seeing how much ground I'd covered. My truck was a tiny speck in the distance in the visitor center parking lot that I couldn't make out.

I hydrated. I ate a green Nature Valley granola bar, my favorite. Endorphins rushed through my system, and I hopped back on the bike. The second half of the ride is like a roller coaster, mostly downhill ... barreling down, cacti rushing past my peripheral vision and then being catapulted up the other side. The mountain peaks were humbling to take in as I came up over the horizon on the last few miles of the loop. I rolled back to the truck on a high.

Skin baked, mouth parched, muscles punished. My soul was full ... GET FUCKED. Our house sits on a golf course, and when they take the flag down at sunset every night, we take the dogs out behind the house to throw the ball and run. The skies are incredible: blues, purples, oranges. I'm filled with gratitude nightly. I love the weather most of the year. I love seeing mountains, clear in the distance in the morning. I love the Valley of Fire. I love kitschy little casinos, the Double Down, karaoke at Dino's. Rock concerts at The Joint or Brooklyn Bowl.

I love the people, the locals. I learned early on there is a clear delineation. A girl born and raised here once explained to me that her dad used to say the tourists are how we make a living, so we gotta put up with them. When your waiter or bartender finds out that you're a local, it's almost like a facade comes off. They can relax, you're cool, they don't need to put on a show. I've met great friends here. I bought my first house here. I got married for 250 bucks in my backyard at 3:00 a.m. here: ninety minutes door to door, proposal to consummation. ... Pistol Pastor Pete — I added the pistol.

I flipped a coin to get here, a gamble brought me to Sin City. Fabulous Las Vegas has indeed been good to me.

TONE IT DOWN

I was always getting told to tone it down, whatever that means. Tone it down. Once, I did a dark match against Ted DiBiase Jr. in Philly. Our match went great and I cut a kickass little promo beforehand. The response from the crowd to all of it was great. I had been hitting on all cylinders that evening. The note I got from Vince: "Tone it down." The next night I went out and had basically the same match in Richmond, except this time I felt strangely self-conscious. It was not as good. I didn't really do anything different, but I felt like I was wrestling in fucking bowling shoes with "tone it down" ever present in my mind. Afterwards, Hunter came up to me excited and said Vince was impressed. "He did everything he was supposed to," Vince had told him.

"Great job," Hunter said. WTF? I didn't do anything. I might have sucked a little more is all. In the early days of The Shield, as soon as we started wrestling matches, that's all I heard all the time. Tone it down. Strangely, this would always come right after some really awesome shit just happened or we tore the house down. I'm in the zone, dialed in like a motherfucker and then here comes some pusscake coming at me with a "tone it down." I remember Hunter telling me, "You just don't wanna become Terry Funk spinning around in a circle like Homer Simpson. ... *Whooop ... wooooop woooop woop woop.*"

OK. I guess. My thoughts were, Did you see me spinning around in a circle? Also, Terry Funk rules, bitch. But at the time I was open to exploring the merit of this input. After all, you never stop learning in this business. Sometimes you get great advice from the most unexpected places. It's important to always keep your ears and your mind open. That being said, if I received that advice today, I would tell whoever told me to tone it down to go fuck themselves with a Brillo pad on a stick. If you're a young wrestler reading this and you take away one thing, let it be the following: If someone comes up to you and tells you to tone it down, don't worry about it. The reason they're telling you that is probably just because they have no charisma.

FLICK PICK: HIGHLANDER, 1986, CHRISTOPHER LAMBERT, SEAN CONNERY

"There can be only one," although they tried. Multiple *Highlander* sequels have been attempted over the years, and they've all bombed. The original, however, remains a cult classic science fiction film. Christopher Lambert (the dude who played Raiden in the '90s *Mortal Kombat* movie) plays Connor MacLeod, the "Highlander" (he's from the Scottish Highlands). He gets killed in the 16th century, but he comes back to life and is understandably befuddled. He's found by Sean Connery who explains that they are both immortals. The only way they can die is to be beheaded. For centuries, all the immortals of the world have been sword fighting and trying to chop each other's heads off. When one immortal decapitates another, they experience "the Quickening." A big-ass lightning storm ensues, and the loser's power is absorbed by the guy with his head still attached. The last immortal left standing will receive "the prize," hence, "There can be only one."

The heel in this movie is awesome, a coked-up Frankenstein-looking immortal played by the guy who played the drill sergeant in *Starship Troopers* and voices Mr. Krabs in *Spongebob*. What puts this film over the top, and cements it as a classic, is the soundtrack by Queen. Yep, THE MF'n Queen. It includes the badass track, "Princes of the Universe," also the theme for the '90s *Highlander* TV series, which was actually pretty good.

Highlander's opening scene actually takes place at, of all places, a pro-wrestling event. MacLeod and another immortal sword fight to death in the parking lot while the Fabulous Freebirds are in the ring. No matter what kind of egregious, brightly colored pimp suit I ever saw Michael P.S. Hayes wear at TV, I always had to give him a pass. Not so much because he's a WWE hall of famer, but because he was in *Highlander*. You can never take that away from him. Michael Hayes. There can be only one.

LAS VEGAS, APRIL 4, 2021 6:23 P.M.

Renée is preparing a beef Wellington for dinner. Who. The Fuck. Eats. Beef Wellington? Is this an episode of *The Crown*? What the fuck is even going on? Last night we ordered Subway on Postmates. What are you trying to prove? You're probably gonna eat one bite of it and decide you wanna make a peanut butter sandwich anyway because you're pregnant and insane. Renée is seven months knocked up, and we're restocking peanut butter at such a rate you'd think we were provisioning rations for WWI battalions in Europe.

Anyway, Renée, our little miss cookbook, is using liquid measuring cups for dry goods. I ask her, Why? She says there is no difference. I maintain that there are both dry and liquid measuring cups. She says, No, they are all the same. Bitch! I was in Impact for two years! I know they're different! Not Impact Wrestling — IMPACT was the program they put you in during seventh and eighth grade after you got suspended or arrested enough times. Upon being placed in Impact, you'd spend half your day in the home ec room with Mrs. Davis, who I actually really liked, learning life skills such as sewing and cooking. We made something called Fast and Flawless Candy, a gooey baked good whose chief ingredient was corn flakes. Sometimes, we'd visit nursing homes. When the weather was warm, we would garden, landscaping around the premises of the entire school in plain sight of our classmates, who would mock us while they watched through the windows. No, being one of those kids in Impact was not cool. I guess we were placed there because we were the kids so beyond help that they felt they might as well teach us something, anything, we might be able to actually use to feed or clothe ourselves one day. For instance, how to measure dry goods. For 20 years I thought all Impact brought me was embarrassment ... that is until today. I Googled whether there is a difference between dry and liquid measuring cups and won the day. Whoever stuck me in Impact would probably be pleased to know it finally paid off, if they didn't first die of shock after learning I was eating like a king, being served beef Wellington by a beautiful woman while I'm writing a book.

ST. LOUIS, MISSOURI, MAY 19, 2013

"Did you say 'fuck' out there?" Road Dogg asks me. It's the Extreme Rules PPV. I am in the tunnel by Gorilla as he passes by. I think he's making a joke at first. It's Road Dogg, he's always kidding around. I notice he's not smiling, he's just looking at me.

"I didn't do a promo," I respond.

"In the ring, did you drop an F-word or something?" he asks again, leaning in, loud music and pyro going off around us.

"Huh? I don't think so, maybe. ... what?"

I am confused. I had just won the United States championship from Kofi Kingston. I hit him with the headlock driver I stole from Sami Callihan and scored my first WWE belt to a big reaction. When I first started doing that move, it looked devastating because I was doing it to guys like Kofi and RVD who could take a spike bump on the top of their heads, making it look like they were dead. But it was hard to make it look good with bigger, taller guys, so I would eventually scrap it for the double-arm DDT. I wouldn't bust it out again until years later in the G1 against Tetsuya Naito. To explain the move, I just showed Naito a clip of Kofi taking it.

Right now, I am about to go out and celebrate with Seth and Roman. They were in the ring with Kane and Bryan and about to score the tag belts. Road Dogg just walked on, but the look on his face gave me an indication that I was in trouble. But for what? *Huh?* I went out to celebrate with my teammates. We were commanding championships now. A logical next step. It's pretty cool to win a belt in WWE. It was another first for us. We were in a pretty good mood as we rode on to Kansas City. The celebration would be over by the time we got to our hotel. We'd grab a few hours' sleep and be in the gym the next morning. Always a CrossFit gym in those days. Seth loves CrossFit. I don't need all the acronyms, but I like a sweaty garage gym and weights, so it was cool with me. We were working our asses off, the siege of WWE continued. The next night we would cut our first in-ring promo on live TV, but that's a whole other fucking story. We'll see if I have time for it. I'm getting close to my deadline.

I didn't think much about my interaction with Road Dogg.

Might as well, here's all the story is:

They gave us a three-page script. Paragraph after paragraph of words. Roman: paragraph. Seth: paragraph. Dean: paragraph. None of it made a goddamn bit of sense. We spent all fucking day memorizing these lines, going over it over and over again. We went out there in the ring and delivered that sumbitch verbatim, exactly as we'd been instructed to. Afterward was all high-fives and congratulations. Yet another new challenge. We stepped up to the plate and knocked it out of the park. About an hour later, I had a strange empty feeling. Something felt a little off. After the adrenaline of live TV wore off and with the stress of having to memorize every single note of Beethoven's Piano Sonata No. 14 in C sharp minor lifted, we sat in the car getting ready to drive to the next town, and I asked my partners, "What the fuck did we even say?"

FAVORITE CITIES: HOMES AWAY FROM HOME

Tampa, Florida. Tampa's a great place to live and I had a couple of great years there. Thinking of Tampa puts me in the mind of sitting at a bar on dock, eating coconut shrimp, looking out over the water at the sunset. There will usually be a guy playing guitar, without fail he'll be playing "Wagon Wheel." (*Heeeey, mama, rock me. ... I swear it's like the official song of Tampa.*) Sometimes you can spot a dolphin. You will learn more about my time in Tampa with this next story.

Florida Championship Wrestling was a WWE developmental territory. I signed there in May 2011 for the minimum, 600 bucks a week. I'd had some buzz on the indies in the past year, but I showed up there with little fanfare. I later learned that Joey Mercury, one of their trainers, basically told the talent relations, "We need him." They decided to give me a shot. Joey would become something of a mentor to me during my time in Florida.

This opportunity was coming out of the blue and I decided I was going for broke. I'd watch WWE programming from time to time and I reasoned I could talk as well as anyone there, and with nothing to worry about but training full-time, I could forge myself into the best version of me I'd ever been. I was not gonna blow this.

I was nervous to go to Pittsburgh for the standard medical evaluation. I'd been taking bigger and bigger risks with my body, sliding farther down the slippery slope of death matches. I was afraid I'd get to Pittsburgh and find out I had injuries I didn't know about that would disqualify me. I thought of HWA alum Nigel McGuinness, who signed with WWE only to have his contract rescinded after his trip to Pittsburgh. ... And what about this drug test? I drank gallons and gallons of water to flush out any traces of any substance that could be lingering in my system. The results came in the mail, and I stared at that envelope for a good while. I said a final prayer. ... Hallelujah, clean bill of health!

I also committed to a conscious decision to not change for anybody: They hired Jon F'n Moxley, and that was what they were gonna get. I knew I'd have to adjust my style to a degree: Obviously there would be no bleeding, swearing or skill saws to the face, but I was NOT going there to be anyone other than ME. I'd heard whispers about how I'd be down there for a few months and end up back in CZW, how I'd never adjust to family-friendly sports entertainment. Not only did I succeed at molding myself into a successful WWE product, but in later years I would actually become a little too kid-friendly! All that was left was to get to Tampa from Philly, where I was staying with my boy Devon Moore and sleeping on a floor.

WWE sent me a moving bonus, 1,200 bucks. I signed the check over to Dev's girlfriend Mag so she could cash it using her bank account. I didn't even have one. I loaded my wresting bag into the "Love Machine," my beater car I bought from my buddy Buffalo for 200 bucks. I threw in a few books and the rest of my meager possessions, stuffed that giant wad of cash into my pocket, and headed south. I drove nonstop.

When I arrived in Tampa, I'd been up all night and the Florida sun burned my eyes. Because of a prior eviction on my record, I was unsuccessful in securing an apartment. They offered to set me up with a roommate, but I was too proud, and antisocial, to take them up on it. I searched Craigslist for a room and found one that looked nice for 100 bucks a week in cash (it would turn out to not be nice, like not at all, in the slightest). I finally arrived at the property manager's address and followed him over to check out my accommodations. My house, where six other rooms were occupied by some unsavory-looking individuals, looked decent enough from the outside. I followed the guy around back to discover an unkempt backyard with weeds sprouting everywhere, garbage, paint cans, old car parts and a washing machine from the Great Depression. This was not a good sign.

He opened the door to a small rectangular room that was tiny, maybe three or four feet wide and 10-ish feet long, with a rickety dresser and a creepy-looking bed. There was no mistaking this was basically a crack den, but I was exhausted and didn't have any other options. At least the FCW building was only a mile away. When he asked me what I thought, I said, "I'll take it."

The next morning, I had to report for my first day on the journey to taking over WWE. (My only original goal was to make enough to pay off my mom's house; if I did that, I would consider myself a success.) I walked across the street to a strange-looking building that sold used appliances and bought a small TV for 25 bucks from a man who was also selling oranges. I walked it back across the street, put it on a milk crate, and plugged it in. I had cable at least. I was proud of that TV.

I woke up early, went across to McDonald's and got a coffee, then stood in my open door sipping it and smoking a cigarette. I looked out over my new *Mad Max* backyard as the sun rose, excitement and nerves welling up inside me. The road ahead was not clear.

I showed up to the FCW building and was led into an office where I met Dr. Tom Prichard and Norman Smiley. They would become two of my favorite people I've ever met. There were a lot of big dudes here, bodybuilder types, football player types. Seth Rollins arrived looking sleepy. Seth and Xavier Woods were the only two guys I'd ever met before. I'd met Seth at an Ian Rotten show in Peoria, Illinois, where I was drinking a beer in the ring truck. I'd once shared an Egg McMuffin with Woods (who I still call Creed) at the Orlando airport after an unsuccessful TNA tryout. I knew they were both good workers, so I gravitated toward them that first morning. I asked them questions and they filled me in on the day-to-day of life in Developmental.

We began with our daily stretching routine, which was always painful, mostly cuz it was so boring. We stretched cold muscles at 9:00 a.m. while we counted off numbers for what seemed like an eternity, then, still stiff and cold, we would begin our morning meeting.

We'd discuss new business, the upcoming schedule, whatever. Sometimes our *Raw* reports would be read aloud after we turned them in. These meetings were where Dr. Tom shined: His goal was to make this meeting last as long as possible — "filibustering" as he would call it, easily filling an hour if he so chose. He'd sometimes tell stories, or he'd lead discussions or he'd just yell and scream about anything that was on his mind, a master promo.

On one's first day it was customary for Doc to bring the new person up to the front of the class to introduce themselves. Doc would ask you to tell a joke. ... I had been warned of this tradition, so when I got up in front of everyone I was prepared.

"So, you got a joke" Doc asked.

I hit the audience with the following gem: "How'd the computer get so fat? ... He downloaded too many cookies."

Crickets.

A complete swing and a miss. Maybe not complete. One person laughed: Derrick Bateman, who would go on to become one of my first Tampa friends. *Raw and SmackDown* were filmed in Tampa and Orlando that week, so it just so happened that on my third day, a bunch of the office were there: the creative team, writers, Michael P.S. Hayes and Hunter. So was his lordship, William Regal. We gathered in the

"FCW arena" that morning, in the part of the building that was a little studio where we filmed TV. All the wrestlers sat where the crowd would sit. They put a big table at the front of the room where all the WWE main-roster luminaries sat like an episode of *America's Got Talent.* There was a wrestling card with all of the top prospects at FCW who were trying to impress the bigwigs. The rest of us played along as a mock crowd. I found the whole thing very bizarre. The wrestlers came out to their music, in their gear, oiled up, hair greased. Full elaborate entrances. They proceeded to have mock matches, hitting all their best shit. It was pretty weird, but it did give me something of a look at the competition. After all, there were only so many spots. I saw a lot of great talents perform that morning in an attempt to impress their bosses and hopefully earn a main-roster spot, but FCW didn't have anything, *ehhh,* quite ... like me.

After the matches, it was time to talk. There was a litany of promos, some good, some heinous. Some guys volunteered, got in the ring and gave it their best shots, some debuted new wacky characters they'd devised, some were called up unprepared and floundered. I was sitting in the back row keeping to myself, head low. I wasn't looking for any action that day. I didn't think anyone really knew who I was, so I wasn't too worried about getting called up. I was a wolf, hiding in the brush, just surveying the scene. ... Maybe a mountain lion is a better analogy (mountain lions terrify me). Then suddenly, I was the one being stalked. I felt William Regal's eyes on me, heating up my insides like laser beams, adrenaline starting to pump. I fidgeted in my chair. I knew what was coming: Regal was gonna call me up. I'd be foolish to not be prepared, so throughout this laborious and awkward Developmental showcase, I'd been toying with something in the back of my head, an introductory promo – a Jon F'n Moxley promo. Now I knew it was coming any minute, and I was ready, maybe even a little cocky. I was very confident in my verbal abilities at this time. (By the end of my run in FCW I believed I was as good on the mic as anyone in the world. Whether that was true or not didn't matter. I FELT IT!)

When Regal had a moment to get the table's attention, I could see him motioning in my general direction. He nodded his head, looked my way and called my name in a way that suggested he was excited to show something off to his colleagues. I coolly got up and walked into the ring, grabbed the mic and laced into a tirade introducing myself to the WWE at large. It might have been a story, an anecdote, a haiku, a limerick. ... I have no idea.

I don't remember a single word I said, but the response I got after this whole F'n strange event was over couldn't have been more positive. I had knocked it out of the park, and thanks to Regal I was given an important chance to make a good impression to the higher-ups and stand out. For some reason, after it was over, Michael Hayes cut a very aggressive promo yelling at everyone. I think he was trying to inspire passion in us, but I was just like, Dude, why are you screaming? ... We just took it all in.

The next day after practice, Dr. Tom got a call from the office and told me I was to start training with Rob MacIntyre, the strength and conditioning coach, that afternoon. This was a good sign because normally you have to earn that privilege over a few months. I was being fast-tracked. I never talked with Hunter (Triple H, Paul, HHH. ... I would just call him H) that first day, but the next time he came down a month later, he brought me in for a meeting in the office. I could tell he was trying to read me. I was grateful for this opportunity and ready to work my ass off, but I wasn't about to be a suckass. I told him it was going great, asked some questions, gave some of my opinions about how I saw wrestling, where I thought it was going, what I hoped to accomplish. He seemed to listen intently. We were feeling each other out. He told me I was doing great and that I should just keep doing what I was doing, and that they saw big potential in me. Off to a good start. I was pretty pumped.

The next step was to debut on FCW television. Dusty Rhodes was the creative vision, and I loved Dusty, as did everyone. I loved just chillin' in his office listening to stories and waxing creative. He said he wanted Seth Rollins vs. the newly minted Dean Ambrose ("Dean, James Dean ... AMBROSE! Dean Ambrose is *strong*, baby"). Dusty said, "Good enough for me." Dean Ambrose was born, although it was a little awkward using a new name at first. Dusty said he wanted Ambrose/Rollins to be his Pacquiao/Mayweather. We would begin working the house shows immediately, "off-Broadway," to build our chemistry. My first match with Seth, who'd come to be synonymous with me as a partner and one of my greatest opponents, was in Largo, Florida, in front of fewer than 50 people, and that's being generous. We'd never worked together before, and it was something of an indie dream match. He was ROH Champion while I was CZW champ, two diametrically opposed promotions, and we would now meet on neutral ground.

At this time Seth was getting a little frustrated in FCW. He wasn't having quite the matches he wanted with the type of opponents he'd been given. I understood completely. We put together a 15-minute match (the FCW Jack Brisco 15 Championship medal was on the line, a medal defended solely in 15-minute Iron Man matches). We clicked instantly. Everything was tight, smooth, right in the pocket. We complemented each other perfectly in style and character. It was a perfect marriage, and we'd be married for a long time.

I debuted on television with a promo announcing my arrival and intent to go after Seth Rollins. We built an angle culminating in a 15-minute Iron Man match for the gold. By the time we got there, we'd perfected our routines, our timing and our highspots. There was anticipation in the air around FCW as our matches in the house shows were routinely tearing up the (very small) houses. A few main-roster talents from Tampa came down to watch the match, giving us an extra boost of motivation (Watch this, you superstar MFers!).

Adding more gravity to the moment was that we were taping multiple episodes in one night. We'd wrestle to a 15-minute draw in the Tampa humidity, then come back out shortly thereafter with five extra minutes and go to a 20-minute draw. The matches couldn't have gone better – we tore it up for 15 minutes with the crowd on the edge of their seats, and by the time we crashed and burned off the stage to end the 20-minute draw, we knew we'd done something special.

The real money was still to come. Well, not *really* money but it was magical: the biggest match in FCW history, Dusty's Pacquiao/Mayweather, a 30-minute Iron Man match. There was definitely a buzz that day, and the small building was about as full as it could be. I got myself DQ'd intentionally to give away a fall but then scored two in a row on the prone Seth. Seth made a comeback as we pulled out all the stops. With eight seconds to go, Seth's foot struck my face with his patented finishing kick in the mouth. I kicked out.

The crowd was stunned – 65 minutes of wrestling with no winner. The GM, Maxine, declared that there must be a winner and announced sudden death overtime. We sped into overdrive for the next few minutes. ... My adrenaline was so high I could have gone another 30. I felt no fatigue, just pure joy at what we were experiencing. It was pandemonium in the building. Finally, Seth debuted his Small Package Driver to score the pin.

We both knew we had done something special. We were made men, at least in our little Developmental bubble. I would next move on to a feud with Regal himself, but more on that later, cuz this chapter's already getting long.

I remember the FCW Summer Slamarama Tour. I can still hear the voice of Ryan Nemeth, who emceed those shows. We drove all over Florida piled into cars, hit every little town there was, wrestling in sweltering armories. Sometimes there were 25 people, sometimes there were several hundred. I made a lot of great memories that summer, driving up and down the Sunshine State's highways, getting caught in summer Florida rainstorms with Seth, Juice and Corey Graves. Eventually Big Cass needed a roommate. He'd been staying with someone who got fired. I'd been in my crack den for a full year at that point, embarrassed to let any of the boys see where I lived. The high point of my stay in the house came late one night when I heard a commotion in the common living room. I walked out to see one of my roomies wielding a kitchen knife at two other residents. I took two inquisitive steps toward the scene when a cop burst in and tackled the offender. I returned to my room and put my headphones on.

I jumped at the chance to live in an actual apartment.

SPIN IT UP:
LANA DEL REY, *ULTRAVIOLENCE*, 2014

What a F'n voice!

I'm a big Lana Del Rey fan. She's a pure talent, a beautiful woman as well. ... I suspect she'd be a challenging woman to date, the kind of chick who might set all your clothes ablaze in a dumpster fire at the drop of a hat. Renée lived in Queens, an apartment in Astoria, when we first started dating, and we'd often spend our off days there. She introduced me to Del Rey's 2012 record *Born to Die*, which we used to listen to amidst the backdrop of beautiful New York City. *Born to Die* is kind of set in NYC, and anytime I hear a track from it I'm transported back to that time and place. My favorite Lana album, however, is *Ultraviolence*, not just because of my affinity for barbwire. This album is different from *Born to Die* in that its "setting" is the West Coast, as embodied by the track "West Coast" ... obviously. "Brooklyn Baby," a great song, might be the exception here, but this album feels distinctly West Coast to me, whatever that means. There's also a song called "Florida Kilos," so maybe my whole theory is off base. (Seriously, why did you buy this book? I clearly don't know what the hell I'm talking about.)

I first listened to this album while shooting a movie in Vancouver and when I hear it now it always takes me back to that time and place, walking along the water with Renée, hiking the Grouse Grind and having a beer on the mountaintop, getting some Japadog (amazing Asian-fusion hot dog carts; if you ever see one, stop!).

Sit on your porch with some sangria, light some candles, and take a bath with a glass of wine, or take a nice walk through the park while you listen to the first five tracks of *Ultraviolence*. Let me know how you feel afterward. For me, this album is relaxing and inspiring. I don't light candles or drink wine, but I'm all about an Epsom salts bath (GET FUCKED! It's a legitimate therapy tool! It's not like I use bubble bath and shit).

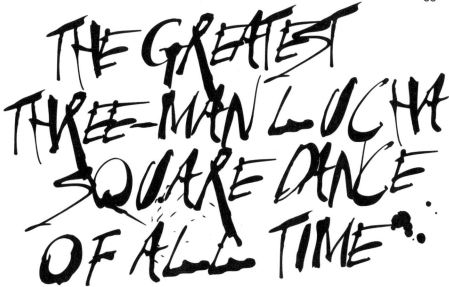

THE GREATEST THREE-MAN LUCHA SQUARE DANCE OF ALL TIME

I quickly made friends with Cass. We'd drink beers and talk wrestling. He was pretty new to the business, and he'd ask me for advice. Cass has had some well-publicized problems in later years but he's doing well and staying healthy now. I just talked to him the other day. He's still a sweet kid at heart. Our apartment became kind of the official hangout spot/staging area for pregaming before group outings to the infamous South Howard. We pretty much went out every night back then, and by "we," I mean at least half the locker room.

I would be determined to stay in: "Nah, I'm just gonna chill tonight." But inevitably, someone would show up at our place around 10, then two more people, and so on. "Fine, I'll just come out for a little bit, then I'm bailing." ... Next thing I know I'm running to the gas station from MacDinton's to buy more beer before the cutoff time so we can keep the party alive back at our place. One time, Trent Beretta pulled the fire alarm in that bar, because it was a very Trent thing to do. We liked this place called The Dubliner that had a nice patio and this delicious blueberry draft beer, with actual blueberries floating in it. One time at a country bar over by where those good-for-nothing Windham boys lived, Trent, Bo and I did the greatest three-man lucha square dance of all time.

FCW could be a frustrating time, having to be at practice every day, the small crowds, feeling like you were on an island, and you just wanna hurry up and get to the big show. I spent a great deal of time feeling that way ... the fear of not getting called up, that this might all be for nothing. Now I look back on FCW as one of the most fun times of my life. I made a ton of friends, forged some real bonds, and I learned a lot, specifically how to work for television, taking into account replays, facials, camera switches, slowing down the beats ... all invaluable things to know. Now I mostly only remember the good times, the laughs and the great stories (many of which I can't include here so as not to incriminate anyone). I will always be grateful for my time at FCW. It set me up for success.

FLICK PICK: MAJOR LEAGUE, 1989, TOM BERENGER, CHARLIE SHEEN, CORBIN BERNSEN

This was my favorite movie as a kid, a hilarious, feel-good classic. I watched this VHS so many times I have the whole thing pretty much memorized. I could perform this movie as a one-man show on Broadway. "Wild Thing"* Ricky Vaughn ... what a great name. Charlie Sheen walking to the mound in the ninth inning to the strains of "Wild Thing" was probably what inspired to me to try Little League. ... Boy, was that a poor idea! I was terrible at baseball; it's just not my sport. I have the hand-eye coordination of Hans Moleman. I would swing wildly at the ball like I was trying to whack a bee out of the air. I spent a lot of time riding the pine, definitely not as cool as Jake Taylor or Willie Mays Hayes. I wouldn't call myself a baseball fan nowadays. You couldn't pay me to sit and watch a game, but I will always watch *Major League*.

* Coincidentally, months after I wrote this, Tony has me coming out to "Wild Thing." Maybe Eddie

TRUE VILLAINS

One of my favorite pieces of work, which also took place at FCW, was a slow-burning feud that lasted almost a year with Lord Regal himself. The chance to work with Regal, one of my biggest supporters and a true legend, was a huge opportunity for me. I appreciate him endlessly for wanting to do it. Best of all, this was not just a one-off, but a full-blown, long-term story we could both sink our teeth into.

Regal was born in Blackpool, England, and had wrestled all over Europe and Japan, developing a hard-nosed, technical style before becoming a star in WCW and WWE. Some of his most memorable stuff was when he was WWE Commissioner in the early 2000s. His comedic timing and delivery were classic. But there were to be no laughs or sight gags here. The first act would be a story about pain and punishment. The second about one man hunting the other one down to the ends of the earth for a revenge that both men knew would inevitably come. The final act would be tragic.

Regal was an announcer on FCW TV, and he went out of his way to compliment me on my attitude in the ring: "That's exactly what we need more of here!"

Not only did we have no issue, he was a fan. We began in earnest one night when there was something of a locker-room-clearing melee in the ring, I ambled out to see what all the commotion was about. Maxine, the GM, was knocked down and possibly hurt in the ring. Regal had left the announce table to tend to her as the ring cleared. I lingered, went to step through the ropes and looked back, went to leave again, paused and looked back again. ... Then I rushed Regal and knocked him over with a body check and started pummeling him, seemingly for no reason, just cuz I spotted the opportunity, like it wasn't planned. When the fight was stopped, the camera panned to a shot of Maxine with a devilish grin, all but signaling the match was made: Regal vs. Ambrose.

He worked mostly backstage with talent at this point, so having Regal actually wrestle on FCW was a big deal. I explained myself in a promo, painting the picture: I just wanted to poke the hornets' nest, fly close to the flame, fuck it ... just cuz. It was too much to resist. Next, Regal would cut a stylized backstage promo, the one quoted below. He was really into it, he knew what he wanted to do, a chance to do something serious and violent and thought-provoking.

> *It's very strange when it comes to oneself – look at this, a drop, a tear. Believe me, it's not through sorrow; it's actually a tear of joy. I've got so complacent with myself for the last few years. ... I'm everybody's Mr. Entertainment, Mr. Go-To-Guy. There's a reason that I like Dean Ambrose so much, and that is because I see a kindred spirit. I see a man that I would drag somebody I didn't like outside into a carpark and set fire to them. Everybody else here in FCW would run away. I know Dean Ambrose. He'd come and stand next to me and warm his hands on the bloody flames. That's why I like Dean Ambrose. Now I'm indebted to him. I've got a mind that just works ... as a villain. True villains can't pretend to be anything else. They are what they are.*

We were all set to go. Regal was confident, a veteran ready to teach an impetuous young lion a lesson. I was confident in the sense that I didn't give a fuck. Let's just see what happens. It might get wild, but I bet I take this old-timer out. The match was simple. Regal beat the hell out of me. He mercilessly pummeled me, beat me pillar to post, as they say. I took a cool, nasty-looking bump on the apron, injuring my arm. He did creative stuff like trapping my hand in the bottom turnbuckle, sticking my arm in between the steel steps, and kicking me. He destroyed my arm and beat the hell out of me for most of the match. I got humbled.

Regal let me know that I got too ambitious too soon, and he punished me for it. He would go back to the announcing booth, and I would pick myself up and dust myself off. I popped my shoulder back into place and got back to the drawing board ... but it wasn't over. I did learn a lesson: Next time it would be different. Wherever, whenever this match happened again, and I'd make sure it did, I would redeem myself. Regal would go back to the announce desk and commentate on my matches. During this time, I was improving in my FCW training in every way. Every time I'd wrestle, I'd give Regal a death stare, signifying that this wasn't over. He never sold it. Eventually, I'd start cutting promos calling Regal out. This lasted for months. No matter whatever else I had going on, I'd make sure to keep throwing gas on the fire of a potential rematch. I was getting better every day, and I let him know it. He knew I was coming for him, on commentary he made it clear in the most casual of ways that he knew one day I'd be the man to take him out, but he betrayed no emotion — all class.

He continued to ignore me, which made me grow more incensed and made my verbal attacks more pointed. I did not like being ignored. As far as I was concerned, months and months of improving and climbing the ranks of FCW *earned* me this rematch. In my mind, it was the only match I wanted. I almost won the FCW title, but my shoulder failed me ... the shoulder Regal had chewed up like a hyena months earlier. He'd taken something else from me, and now, no matter what, I wouldn't let him deny me a rematch.

I'm here to take what's mine and I want my F'n rematch and my revenge, I've F'n *earned* it. Despite attacking him for no reason, we had bonded over our love of violence and chaos. I'd started to look at him as a father figure, and he was F'n ignoring me, and now he would not give me any credit for working my way back to a rematch. This grew animosity, not hatred. Deep down I wanted Regal's approval, and there was clearly only one way to get it now: to destroy him. He finally told me, "Good things come to those who wait." Eventually, he began to stare right back at me when I stared down at the table. I cornered my prey in ever-tightening concentric circles. The time had come. The rematch.

FCW were moving operations to Orlando, so this would be the final episode of FCW television. We were the main event. Dusty and the GOAT, Jim Ross, were on commentary, which was very cool for me. JR was the voice of so much of my childhood, so it was surreal having him call a match I was actually in.

I came to the ring with focused intensity, different from last time. I had a dope leather jacket. During my entrance, Dusty compared me to James Dean, and I felt as cool as the legend (although I nearly wrecked it by almost tripping as I entered the ring, but I covered it rather nicely). I had worked myself up all afternoon to achieve the right mindset. By the time I got to the ring, I actually hated and was going to kill Regal. This was real to me at this point. I had my headphones on all afternoon, pacing (this memory always makes me think of The Game's "Red Nation," which I was into at the time). I was an animal to be unchained when the bell rang. Regal, "the veteran outlaw," as JR described him brilliantly, entered stoically. This match would unfold as the inverse of the last. At the outset, Regal went after my arm, outwrestling me with his technical-but-vicious English style. This time, I would survive the early onslaught and send Regal's head flying into the ring post. It fucked him up. His eyes were glassy, his equilibrium off kilter ... a busted eardrum maybe? He expertly sold that he couldn't walk or stand straight. I proceeded to beat the fuck out of him. I had his head trapped in the same turnbuckle where he'd once trapped my hand, but the turnbuckle pad was exposed. I slammed my knee into his face multiple times, his questionable ear cheese-gratered on the steel. It began to bleed.

Now, I was always supposed to go over, destroying my mentor. Problem was, if I destroyed him, I would never get the approval I was seeking from my mentor. I would be victorious but unsatisfied. ... What happened instead was even more beautiful.

Blood was a no-no. That stupid WWE bullshit when they would stop a match and the ref puts on rubber gloves for a F'n paper cut in the middle of a match on live TV. Bill DeMott had just taken over as head coach, replacing Doc ... which was a wildly unpopular decision with the boys. He was on headset. When Regal's ear started bleeding, the trainer jumped in to check on him. I'm pacing like a tiger, seething. ... DO NOT STOP THIS FUCKING MATCH. But DeMott made the call.

"He jumped right out of the trainer's arms!" Dusty exclaimed as Regal leapt from a kneeling position, blasting through trainers and refs to drill me with a HARD forearm. Now we were both down.

The ref told us to get to a finish, something ... *anything*. In all the chaos and confusion, we ended up in the penultimate moment, where Regal was bloody, beaten, helpless, with just enough strength to clap his hands, point at me and signal for me to put the nail in his coffin as he always knew I would.

He lowered his defenses and I hit him with his own Knee Trembler to the face (I had stolen it from him out of disrespect in recent months). I leveled him into a motionless heap. Instead of going for the pin, I paced around in frustration and anger, continuing to assault his carcass. The whole locker room emptied to pull me off of him. The match was stopped. There was never an official winner, but it was an even more beautiful and tragic finish because of it. I'd set out to destroy him and I did, but I never got my victory, nor my validation.

I was so in the "this is F'n real" zone at the time. I was furious that a little blood put an abrupt end to the match we'd been building for so long. I wanted to punch DeMott badly for taking such liberties on the headset. I stormed to the back, made a quick right turn, and blew through the doors to the parking lot to cool down. Joey came out to console me, all smiles.

"It couldn't have worked out any better," he said.

I calmed down quickly. Regal, who I just now call "Lordship," has often told me this was one of his favorite things he's ever done. That means a lot to me. We were kindred spirits. This was a local little rasslin' TV show, but the final episode of FCW Television went off the air with some Shakespearean shit.

This movie still holds up. I assume everyone my age loved Ninja Turtles when they were a kid. I loved the cartoon. I still have the theme song memorized . . . but I'm not gonna type all the lyrics here cuz I got nothing to prove to you. . . and you might just assume my editor looked them up anyway. You probably know the lyrics too, and now you know that makes two of us.

TMNT in the '90s was a marketing powerhouse. They made a bunch of stupid toys. I remember seeing some at the store where Donatello was a basketball player. . . . He's like five feet tall. I guess he could have been a John Stockton type, but the pick-and-roll wouldn't have worked cuz none of the other turtles were tall either; they would have needed that giant robot body with Krang in his stomach to play power forward, and by that point I think there would have been just too much animosity for them to gel as a team. This book sucks. The kids' cartoon and toys aside, this movie had some edge to it. . . . Seedy, crime-ridden NYC, Raphael with the "*DAAAAMN!!*" This movie was popular with kids but stayed true to the original comic, which was the darkest version of TMNT. The music is good. Shredder is terrifying. I could feel the sexual tension between Casey Jones and April O'Neil before I even knew what that was. All the fight scenes are classic, and, of course, my favorite line: "Ninja-kick the damn rabbit!" Many times when The Shield was getting our asses kicked by the bad guys, I'd crawl over to one of my partners and say, "At what point . . . did we lose control here?" just to pop myself. There have been many other versions of TMNT over the years, but I can't get behind any of them. Fuck Michael Bay. Still, I will completely flip-flop my stance on that if there's another remake. If the director has any sense, they'll cast me as Casey Jones. . . . "Pizza dude's got thirty seconds."

BRODIE LEE

Brodie died today. Details are still sketchy. All we've known for the last six or seven weeks is that he was in the hospital on life support and might need a lung transplant. Today is December 26. I can't imagine what kind of Christmas it was for Amanda and the rest of his family. I'm numb at this point; it doesn't feel real. I've yet to shed a tear, but I know they're coming. This whole time my brain hasn't been able to wrap itself around the situation. I'm at a loss and I've just been praying constantly. Renée has kept in touch with Amanda through this. Every time we talk about it, all I can say is, Let's just keep praying and waiting for good news. ... What else can you do? Amanda told Renée that when Brodie found out she was pregnant he smiled, which was a good sign, as much emotion as he'd been able to show in a long time.

By the time this book comes out every nice thing to be said about Jonathan Huber will have been. Brodie (a fellow Jonathan, but he'll always be Brodie to me) was one of the best people in the business, one of the best people I knew. Cliché as it sounds, you'll never find anyone who had a bad word to say about him. He'd been my friend for over a decade and one of my favorite and most frequent opponents. On the indies, in the Shield/Wyatt Family wars, and ultimately in AEW where we wrestled our final match, on PPV, for the World Championship.

He was brought into FCW for a tryout several months after I got there. Since we were friends and had wrestled each other many times before, Joey Mercury asked me if I would work a match with him to be filmed and sent to the office. I obliged without hesitation, of course, but this was a lot of pressure. All of this man's hopes and dreams, his family's future, were riding on this. I had to make him look like a million dollars. I took his Boss Man slam so good it looked like a tornado tore through the gym. I bumped my ass off and took a hell of a beating. Brodie got hired, and I never let him forget he'd be substitute teaching in Rochester if not for me selling it like I was Jamie Lee Curtis to make him look like Michael Myers in his tryout.

We joked about that often but, of course, Brodie was hired because of his exceptional talent. He was an athletic big man who could work circles around almost anybody. Brodie's upside was can't-miss. He ended up opposite me in the Wyatt Family. As I was part of The Shield, we were on opposite sides of the demarcation line that divided the SWAT dudes and the swamp dudes. I can't begin to count how many matches we had on TV, PPV and at live events in every town you can think of all across the U.S. Sometimes on long, grueling European tours we'd do lucha spots just to pop the boys at the monitor. We shared the closest thing I'd have to a "WrestleMania

Moment" in a multi-man ladder match. I figured the best way to make the highlight reel was to nearly kill myself with a death-defying bump. We devised a spot where he would power bomb me from the ring through a steel ladder to the floor: Falling backward at such an angle was an extremely high-risk bump. I said at the time and have always maintained that I wouldn't have trusted anybody else on the planet with that spot but Brodie. I literally put my life into his hands: Jesus and Brodie, take the wheel. A couple of staples in my head, but I walked away unscathed thanks to my friend's guiding hands.

Vince freaked the fuck out in Gorilla. He thought I was dead. It was a gnarly bump and we made the highlight reel. When Brodie got his release from WWE, I was texting with him from Sapporo. I gave him the lay of the land from my experience so far outside the WWE bubble. I was excited that he was coming to AEW, if for no other reason than to just have him around again, to laugh, to joke, to tell stories. I was always on the same wavelength as Brodie. Like me, he was a big MMA fan, and I'd always hunt him down to discuss the latest fights. An opportunity opened up for him to jump in and wrestle me at Double or Nothing on PPV on a few weeks' notice. When Tony suggested Brodie, I said, "Hell, yeah, I can wrestle him in my sleep!"

I was so happy he'd get to show the world what he could do in a main-event spot. Tony, Brodie and I had a three-way phone call and mapped out a three-week angle that had Brodie and the Dark Order stealing the championship belt. He took it home, and Amanda sent Renée a video of his son, little Brodie, proudly holding it while cutting a hellacious promo on me. We were on the same wavelength. Our vision for the match was a 12- to 15-minute hailstorm of violence. Brodie had the idea of crashing through the stage. I won with a choke. That match was the embodiment of what I wanted my style to be: a mixture of wild violence and pure wrestling, an in-your-face, thrash-metal sprint.

I am eternally grateful to Brodie for creating and sharing that night with me. I think it was our best match. The year 2020 has hit everyone hard, but this is particularly tough to swallow. I feel sick. I'll miss him every time I'm in a locker room. I had an idea tucked away in the back of my mind to make a run at the tag belts with Brodie as a Shield-Wyatt superteam. We'll have to save that one for the next life.

Yesterday was Christmas Day, and as for many people, it was a little different for us due to the pandemic. Just me and Renée at home this year, so we decided to go on a Christmas morning hike in Red Rock Canyon. At the end of the Calico Tanks trail,

I looked up on the ridge and spotted a bighorn sheep. I'm always on the lookout for 'em. I've seen them in Utah and Valley of Fire but never in Red Rock. It came down the side of the cliff, passed by us, and went back up the other side of the canyon in less than a minute. It felt like a Christmas gift, maybe a sign. Maybe a sign to keep your eyes open and enjoy the beauty around you while it's here. Enjoy people and love people while they're here. Maybe a sign that 2021 will be better for everyone. I don't know what it meant, if anything, but I'll remember that sheep. Brodie, it was a pleasure to share the ring with you and an honor to be your friend. I love you. PS: If you see Grant up there, tell him I said what's up. He'll be at the bar.

JOKE CLAUDIO TOLD ME:

LANCE IS NOT THAT POPULAR OF A NAME ANYMORE, BUT IN THE MIDDLE AGES PEOPLE WERE NAMED LANCE A LOT.

SANDWICHES

I consider myself a connoisseur of sandwiches, one of life's great simple pleasures. Sandwiches are a delicious, pragmatic and beautiful thing when the artist truly understands the complexities of the sandwiching medium. I can't cook. Like, at all. I have no desire or need to be around a stove, oven or broiler. After all, I have the Postmates app and I married a chick who wrote a cookbook. I do, however, have a passion for the art of the perfect sandwich. If you're gonna do something, do it right.

Les Thatcher always said, "Train hard and master your craft." Well, I've spent many years on mine, and chomped through countless BLTs, turkey clubs, pastrami on ryes, and bologna sandwiches to perfect my system. When I see an outlaw mud-show sandwich haphazardly thrown together, I feel the way Les would while watching backyard wrestling. I take this shit seriously, maybe too seriously.

Case in point. We sat down at the restaurant of a pretty nice hotel a few weeks ago, and I ordered what they called a Pretzel Club. The ingredients individually were all great: toasted pretzel bun, grilled turkey, spectacular perfectly cooked bacon, avocado and Bibb lettuce.*

I picked the thing up to take a bite, and I could feel that the integrity of the sandwich was lacking, a house of cards. I opened my mouth wide to take the first bite, and as I bit down, I immediately felt avocado bursting out the back, dragging precious bacon and turkey with it. My thumbs and forefingers were now pinching down on each other. I let go of one hand and palmed the sandwich like an overfilled water balloon. I had to put the whole thing down and eat all the ingredients individually like a savage. Delicious as the individual components were, this sandwich was worth much less than the sum of its parts: poorly conceived, planned and executed.

---

* I generally don't give a shit about lettuce. What am I, a rabbit? The exception that proves the rule, however, is in a BLT.

There are four key points to consider when executing a perfect sandwich, four pillars if you will. They are as follows:

1.   Bread
2.   Ingredients
3.   Balance
4.   Entry point

Bread is the first pillar because it literally holds the sandwich together. What type of bread is this? Rye, sourdough, a bagel? Is this bread sliced, grilled? You gotta know what you're working with. For example, say I'm working with one of my favorites: Wonder Bread. It's a classic, but very light with a small surface area. If you start thinking about saucy meatballs or Sloppy Joes, you're gonna be in trouble, but slap on a piece of crunchy lettuce, two strips of bacon, one slice of tomato, Miracle Whip,** salt and pepper and you're in business. If you do wanna push the boundaries of a basic slice of white bread's integrity you can toast it. This will stiffen it up and it'll hold stronger. See? You gotta be thinking ahead.

Your ingredients largely provide the sandwich's identity. They are the items that are being "sandwiched," after all. "What didja have?" A turkey sandwich, a cold-cut trio, you name it.

This is the fun part, here is where your creativity can shine. Starting with pastrami? OK, you putting mustard on that? Pickles? Going with bologna? You gonna fry that shit or no? PB and J? What else can you put on that? Honey? Banana? Reese's Pieces? There's no rules. Let your imagination run wild.

One of my favorites is a Chipwich: Wonder Bread, a handful of potato or tortilla chips, Miracle Whip. Done. You can use any chips you want. Cool Ranch Doritos are one of my favorites, but when I can get them from Canada, Sour Cream and Bacon Ruffles are the best. I don't toast the bread because it should be soft and sticky to counterbalance the crunch of the chips and keep them in place. See ... thinking ahead. (Another life hack involving Canadian snacks is topping an original Chick-fil-A sandwich with ketchup chips.)

** That's right, I said Miracle Whip. I understand most people prefer mayo and that's fine, but don't you dare call Miracle Whip (and its tangy zip) gross. I don't like raw onions, garlic or (shudder) truffle oil, but I respect your right to enjoy these things. You do you, and I'll do me. Live and let live. Sandwich and let sandwich.

You might have noticed I don't classify the main ingredients like turkey or pastrami separately from sauces or toppings. To me it's all one living organism. The elements work together like a symphony, which bring us to … balance. The first mistake the aforementioned Pretzel Club made was an imbalance of ingredients. It was overloaded on avocado. Avocados are fine and all, healthy fats or whatever, but on its own it's gooey and tasteless. They went to the trouble of cooking this incredible bacon and then smothered it in wet slop. Had they spread a much lighter layer of avocado on the bread with a knife, they could have kept the sandwich together, but what they did caused flood damage: Turkey and bacon swept away, left covered in muck, all consistency destroyed.

The first bite of a sandwich should strike a perfect harmonious balance of all the ingredients, and the sandwich should maintain its structure, leading me to their second mistake and this crucial pillar that's all too often overlooked: entry point. The Pretzel Club that you're now very familiar with was large, packed to the gills, and in one round piece: no corners, no edges, no point of attack. The eater had no choice but to create a bite vacuum, the phenomenon that sucks the pieces of bread toward each other, creating a black hole where matter collapses upon itself and pushes ingredients outward in an explosion. What they should have done was cut the Pretzel Club in half, creating four entry points on which to seize in a balanced bite attack (see figure A).

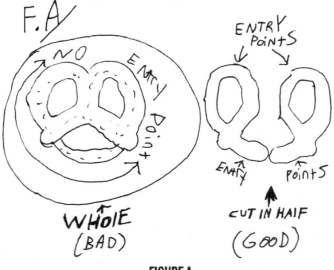

FIGURE A

To be fair, this is often a problem with breakfast sandwiches on bagels. When Great American Bagel in the Vegas airport doesn't cut my ham, egg and cheese with tomato in half, I blow a F'n gasket in my head, although I never say anything cuz I don't wanna be one of those people. But, dude, I'm not a Burmese python. How the fuck am I supposed to get my mouth around this?

This is less of a problem with square breads, but I still find it more efficient to cut them in half diagonally (see figure B).

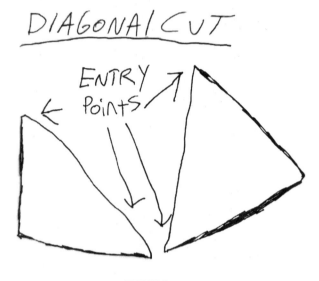

FIGURE B

Now take this guide and go forward, letting your only limit be your imagination as you prepare a snack or decide to raid the fridge at 2:00 a.m. When you're at the touchscreen ordering a custom sandwich at Wawa and they ask you all those questions, take them seriously. My dad always told me, "Measure twice, cut once." Make any kind of sandwich you want ... *your sandwich* ... but if you're gonna do it, do it right.

DECEMBER 31, 2020

It's New Year's Eve. I'm typing at the kitchen counter. Renée is making a "mocktail," something called a sparkling pomegranate punch, and stealing potato chips from my bowl. She's pregnant and can't drink. Also, this pesky pandemic is still going on, so it's likely to be my most tame New Year's Eve in recent memory. We were both born on East Coast time, so that's our excuse to do our countdown to midnight at 9:00 p.m. We'll be in bed by 11. Lame, I know. I'm drinking a Heineken 0.0, for Christ's sake, a far cry from one year ago when we were at the AEW New Year's Eve party in Jacksonville, taking full advantage of the open bar, but life has changed even more dramatically from where we sat exactly two years ago.

DECEMBER 31, 2018

Renée and I sit at the bar of our favorite local spot. The bartender is pouring my second double-Jack, splash-a-coke, on the rocks about 10 seconds after he puts the first in front of me. Renée sips her wine as the conversation inevitably steers itself toward my misery. I begin bitching about the same stuff I've been bitching about over and over for years now: Vince, WWE creative, WWE and everything about them, and everything about the way they do everything. I'd grown to hate WWE. I'd tried not to for a long time. I tried to stay humble, grateful to God and the universe; after all, I was living my dream ... right? It's only with the clarity of looking back on it that I realize how truly depressed and miserable I was, and how long it'd been that way.

Things had finally reached a tipping point. Actually, tipping point is an understatement. That pitcher had tipped over, fell off the F'n counter and shattered on the floor. The last couple months since I'd turned heel ... a change I once hoped would be my salvation ... had been the lowest, most disappointing, infuriating, frustrating, agonizing period of my career. Vince was very hands-on with my new heel persona, whatever the fuck that was supposed to be, writing scripts I was to follow verbatim. They all sucked. He even went so far as to script my matches. They all sucked. He had begun to infiltrate the house shows now too, sending detailed formats to the stressed-out producers 30 minutes before bell time, and demanding I cut cheesy heel promos to the audience as I walked to the ring.

House shows are typically free of Vince and the TV writers. They are more laid-back, and they had been my sanctuary for years. Vince started interfering and putting his fingerprints on these shows after he came to the traditional post-Christmas Madison Square Garden event, sat by the curtain, watched the whole show and shit on the whole thing. Seth and I tore the house down in a steel cage match that night at MSG, but for some reason Vince made us change the entire match on the rest of the loop to fit his vision, which was a less exciting, far shittier version of a steel cage match.

I had nothing even close to heat. I was once one of the most popular performers in all of WWE, and now I was lost in the ring in front of confused or apathetic audiences. I was F'n dead in the water, irreconcilable, a dog to be taken out back and shot ... and I knew it. I was fully aware of it through every slow and excruciating second, yet my objections went ignored or refuted, like that movie where the guy is still awake but paralyzed during open-heart surgery. If you sat through any of my segments on TV during this timeframe, you know what I'm talking about ... unless you blocked it from your memory. If you thought *you* were confused, imagine what it was like being me? Shit, at least you had a remote control. I couldn't just turn the channel on my own life. I was in a living hell. Gee, it's fun reminiscing.

I wasn't just depressed, I was angry. It's not like I don't like money. I don't WANT things to be this way. Why do they have to make it impossible? Why does everything have to be so F'n stupid? They're really gonna make me walk away from all this money, aren't they? They can't just write one good angle, let me cut one good F'n promo? Fuck! I can't believe it's come to this. There was a time I thought I'd be a lifer with WWE, but this whole place has gone F'n MAD, and I feel like I'm the only one who can see it ... buncha MFers just playing violins while the ship sinks and Vince continues to lose his mind.

"Fuck 'em, I'm just gonna go to Japan or something," I tell Renée, while sipping on my third stiff drink. "I'm telling you, April thirtieth, I'm F'n done."

I had been talking about leaving for months and my mind was long made up, but when I was in a bad mood or three drinks in, I would feel the need to reaffirm it for some reason, as if I suspected she didn't believe me.

"Six months, I'm gone!"

"Five months, I'm outta here, I'm telling ya!"

On it went.

Renée had always been supportive and patient with my ramblings, but in this case she finally had enough of me bringing down the mood on New Year's Eve

"Good! Go then! Go to Japan! You should! Do whatever you wanna do!"

"Well, I'm gonna."

"Good, Go!"

"I'm gonna."

"Great!"

"Well, good then."

The next morning, we decided to ring in the New Year with a hike. 2018 had largely sucked for me, even before the recent dumpster fire segments I was starring in on television. I had spent the majority of the year recovering from a December triceps surgery. In fact, I woke up New Year's Day 2018 covered in blood and gooey pus. It was the first sign of what I'd find out was a staph infection in my elbow that would require a second surgery.

We were gonna start off 2019 right! With fresh air and a beautiful hike: the toughest hike in Red Rock Canyon, Turtlehead Peak. ... I'd done Turtlehead a couple times solo, but this would be Renée's first trek up there. It takes a few hours round trip and it's a bit of a bitch, but totally worth it at the top. We began trudging out into the desert brush, slowly gaining elevation. The sun was bright, the weather was great, peace and quiet. As your heart rate increases and a little sweat forms on your brow, endorphins begin to flow. The repetitive sound of your steps amidst the silence of the canyon brings focus, stress melts away, the cloudiness in your mind clears up like the sky above you. It began to hit me as we started climbing uphill at a steeper grade. ... Oh, this is real, I'm leaving, and it's only five months away. ... I'll be free, free as a F'n bird. I began to say things to Renée like, "You know, it'll be cool cuz I'll just, like, make my own schedule. If we wanna take a vacation, I just won't book myself on a show that week."

What an attractive idea. Simple things like "I can design my own T-shirts!" The notion that I'll be in control, able to call my own shots, do what I wanna do and be who I wanna be filled my heart with hope and my veins with adrenaline. We got to the top and spent 10 or 15 minutes enjoying the view, satisfied with our New Year's Day accomplishment. Renée took her obligatory Instagram photo and we headed down. By the time we were halfway back to the truck, I was bursting with optimism. It had become real for me. I wasn't mad that I was leaving WWE anymore, I was just excited for the future. I felt the way a kid feels on the morning of the last day of school, freedom and adventure in my sights. I'm almost there. It was a subtle yet dramatic change in perspective for me. That day put me in the right frame of mind to survive the coming months in WWE and leave with my head held high.

In a strange coincidence, unbeknownst to me, at this exact moment an announcement was being made to the wrestling world. A new promotion had been formed and, it was called All Elite Wrestling.

I don't know why we needed more than two Terminators. What are we on now? Six? Seven? When Nirvana did *MTV Unplugged*, they finished the set with Lead Belly's "Where Did You Sleep Last Night?" The producers wanted them to go out for an encore. Kurt Cobain refused because that performance was so good there was no way they could top what they had just done. You gotta know when to walk off stage. The Terminator with the thumbs up as he's being lowered into the molten lava steel pit! That's it! That's the end of the story! Any time you add time travel into the mix, things get confusing, and the first two Terminators are no exception, but you had it! The story was perfectly wrapped up in a little bow. Humanity saved, all the computer chips destroyed, and you had to go and rip the wound open and basically shit on everything we went through to stop Judgment Day by saying it was inevitable! The only inevitability is that Hollywood studios will squeeze every bit of juice they can out of a bankable franchise, even if it's at the expense of a perfect story. *T2*, in my opinion, is a rare case where the sequel is better than the original. *T2* had cutting-edge special effects for the time, specifically for the T-1000 liquid metal Terminator that scared the bejesus out of me as a kid, but this film doesn't rely on CGI like you see today. Back in the '90s they really blew shit up — they drove a real bus over the gap in the freeway in *Speed*. My mom loved *T2*. She always did push-ups and crunches at night before she went to work. I think she wanted to be like Linda Hamilton, doing pull-ups in the psych ward.

The crazy thing about this being one of my favorite movies of all time is that I actually got to reenact the iconic scene where Arnold walks into a bar naked and demands, "Your clothes, your boots and your motorcycle," from a rugged-looking patron while Dwight Yoakam plays on the jukebox. The guy replies, "You forgot to say please," before putting out his cigar on Arnold's giant pec. The WWE 2K16 video game had some kind of Terminator tie-in, and they got ACTUAL Arnold Schwarzenegger to be in the commercial. The 2K people asked me if I was familiar with *Terminator 2*. "Hell, yeah," I said, "It's one of my favorite movies!" and I told them I was quite familiar with the biker bar scene. I flew to L.A. on an off day on very little sleep, so when I found out exactly what we were doing and Arnold himself showed up with a bevy of security (including a couple of badass-looking Dobermans) I thought I had accidentally eaten a pot cookie. I stood in an exact replica of a scene from *T2* with the real-life Terminator standing in front of me. It. Was. A. Trip. ... It's one of those unexpected cool experiences that are the bonuses of the job, just one of those things that pops up sometimes. "Remember that one time you recreated a scene from *Terminator 2* with Arnold?"

"Oh, yeah . ... Weird. ... I thought he'd be taller."

CINCINNATI

As you may have learned from many ring announcers over the years, I'm from Cincinnati, Ohio, and it will always be home. Like Superman gets his powers from the sun, I'm always energized by coming back to where I was born and raised. I had been trying hard to get an *AEW Dynamite* at the arena in Cincinnati, where I worked event staff as a teenager. At the time it was called Firstar Center, then it changed to US Bank Arena. As I write this, it's called Heritage Bank Arena.

I spent many nights standing in the voms, watching the Cincinnati Cyclones play in front of 800 people, manning the smoking doors for six bucks an hour. We also got to do security at Riverbed Music Center, tackling people with lawn seats who tried to sneak into the pavilion. We worked concerts at Bogart's, breaking up fights. Even though I was underage, I got to do some security gigs at that nightclub on Pete Rose Way that had a million different names over the years, where I did ecstasy for the first time. At the arena I'd look around and imagine it full of screaming wrestling fans as I entered the ring. When I showed up for work and clocked in at the loading dock entrance, I'd imagine I was walking into the arena to wrestle in the main event that night. I walked down the halls with swagger. I could picture it. Some years later I'd walk through the same door to wrestle in the main event that night ... as planned. That arena did not want to host AEW as it turned out — they said they only do business with WWE. Well, Heritage Bank center, you fucked up.

We had a different venue in Cincinnati locked up for the fall, but then like so many other things ... sigh ... the pandemic hit. I look forward to performing at home again. Cincinnati is kind of a little big city: We have two major sports teams, arts, theater, museums (the natural history museum has a giant, dope T. rex skeleton). But if I had to sell you on visiting the 'Nati, it would be for the chili.

Cincinnati-style chili, that is, known to the locals as simply Skyline or Gold Star, the two rival chains in the CSC game. Most of us could tell the difference between Skyline and Gold Star in a blind taste test 10 out of 10 times, but they aren't very dissimilar, served over spaghetti or on a hot dog with cheese. There's either a Gold Star or a Skyline on just about every corner in the greater Cincinnati area, and growing up, it becomes a large part of your diet.

One time I was in the main event of *SmackDown!* in Cincinnati and I asked a favor of Bruno, WWE backstage legend and a guy who you can count on for anything — I would call him if I woke up next to a dead hooker. I asked if he would pick me up two cheese coneys from the Skyline on the concourse level, no onion. He brought me the steamy, hot, gooey, cheesy goods as I was making my way to Gorilla. They'd be there when I got back, but they were hot now, the cheese was fluffy, the smell was tantalizing. I dropped them off back in the locker room, intent to head to the ring and enjoy the glory of Skyline afterward, but the steam transformed into long cartoon fingers, followed me down the hall, enveloped my body and traveled up my nose. My feet floated off the ground as I was pulled back toward the source, arms dangling at my sides, my eyes glazed over, drool dripping from my mouth. Who knew when I'd be back in town? This was my chance. I scarfed those suckers a few minutes before I went to the ring, burping all the way, fighting through heartburn on the way to victory. Totally worth it.

What's a typical Cincinnatian like? Hard to say. Like any city, there are some nice parts, some not-so-nice parts and hip urban neighborhoods that aren't far from the Ohio River. Just several miles south of that and you're in Kentucky … and you're really in Kentucky. You might live in a mansion overlooking the river, you might live in a trailer park, you might have gone to a rich Catholic high school on the West Side, or you might have gone to a public shithole. You might be country, you might be city, you might be something in between … an urban redneck. Cincinnati is a beautiful midwestern menagerie of people, places and things. Blue-collar, small town, big city. Chili that makes no sense to anyone else but us. Hard to pin down. I couldn't have come from anywhere else.

Where do I fit in, exactly? A place where it seemed all the economy-class passengers in life were gathered, where all the have-nots and ne'er-do-wells washed up together on the east side of town in a gutter where they would be given low-income housing but be largely ignored. A place you chose to live but didn't really have a choice. At this time, on this side of town, for a certain socio-economic class, Piccadilly was an inevitability. Piccadilly was several dozen six-unit apartment buildings owned and operated by dozens of different landlords, a sprawling ghetto paradise tucked away off of State Route 125. Just out of sight from the main drag, Beechmont Avenue, lined with shopping, restaurants and the Beechmont Racquet Club. Beyond the tree line in the distance you might be able to make out a rooftop, a sign of the ugly secret hiding in plain sight. Most would never know this kingdom was here, unless you were an explorer searching for lost Section 8 cities.

Turn down Hamblen Drive past some quaint houses and a right turn onto Piccadilly Circle. The splendor will soon come into full view as you look out across a valley of endless apartment buildings, most tan-brown, some blue or grey – one particular eyesore is red. Many windows are broken. You'll see parking lots of gravel, cracked pavement, or dirt. Avoiding the potholes as you drive down the hill, you'll twist and turn through Piccadilly. Budweiser cans and cigarette butts litter the roadside, and stray animals scavenge the dumpsters.

You'll drive across the creek that winds through our little paradise, over a giant storm drain dammed up by shopping carts (residents often walk across 125 to Kroger and bring the whole shopping cart back with them, discarding it in the creek or simply leaving it strewn about). Many vehicles look like they haven't been driven in years, rusted out, spray-painted. You'll likely see a police car or two outside a building and a shirtless guy with bad tattoos, beer in hand pleading his case to the officers regarding some routine disturbance. There's a barefoot woman with frosty blue eyeshadow screaming expletives at him, waving a cigarette in her unflattering cutoff jean shorts.

All kinds of folks ended up in Piccadilly for one reason or another, but the common denominator was that it was cheap, and there were always apartments available. For many, Piccadilly was temporary, a place for transients, a place you came when your home was foreclosed on, when you lost your job, got out of jail, or left your shitty husband and took the kids. A place to be until you found something better.

For others, it was simply the only place you could afford to live. We moved to Piccadilly when I was six, to a second-floor apartment, Apartment C in building 102. Directly underneath us in apartment A lived a couple of kids about my age named Donnie and Kevin. We spent most of our free time together, throwing rocks, riding bikes with our shirts tucked in the back of our shorts like real renegades, and skulking around the creek.

We played baseball with tennis balls because we had access to a surplus of tennis balls. ... That is to say, the Beechmont Racquet Club had tennis balls. We'd sneak onto the courts, behind the tarp, and steal them right out of the machines, filling up our backpacks. I'll always remember this dude in bright white shoes, a polo shirt, and khaki shorts, chasing us through the parking lot while we sped away on our bikes laughing.

Piccadilly had a lot of kids. Every day there would be a knock on your door. One to three kids with scabbed elbows and knees on the other side when you answered:

"You wanna play baseball?"

"Wanna ride bikes?"

"You wanna play football?"

We were the dumb kind of kids that played tackle football on concrete.

"You wanna wrestle?"

Oh yeah, we played wrestling. ... Many of my contemporaries in the business have great memories of backyard wrestling as kids. In fact, that's where a lot of them first practiced the athletic maneuvers they perform today. They have home video footage of themselves in homemade costumes, playing flashy characters created in their imaginations, performing leg drops and flying elbows on their friends, all in great fun. ... Heartwarming stuff.

I can't say I was ever a backyard wrestler, mostly cuz I didn't have a backyard, but we played wrestling. Even though we may have suspected wrestling was a work, a show, it didn't occur to us that we could work together, like the wrestlers on TV were really doing. We could have had fun mimicking the moves and engaging in morality plays for our entertainment. ... Instead we just beat the shit out of each other.

"You wanna wrestle?" would go like this: We'd all meet out front of an apartment building on the dirt, amidst sparse patches of grass, and we'd choose a wrestler to be.

"I'm Bret."

"I'm Razor."

"I'm Undertaker."

We would assign a referee to count someone's shoulders to the ground for a pinfall. One kid would hide behind a bush and enter the imaginary gladiatorial arena, another would enter from behind the dumpster, not bothering with an attempt to portray any of his designated wrestler's trademark mannerisms or put on any sort of performance. The ref would "ring the bell," knocking three times on "the green thing," a square metal box we'd often sit on that I assume had something to do with the building's electricity. I really don't know what it did.

We would then proceed to just ... fight: throwing punches, pulling hair, biting, kicking shins, whatever juvenile offense we could muster up in an attempt to maneuver our opponent into a pinning position. Often, a head would be cradled, a leg hooked, and a three-count slapped on the cracked dirt to great protest.

"That wasn't three!!!" a kid might scream, tears in his eyes. Wrestling was my favorite activity of ours. Not just cuz wrestling was my favorite thing to watch. I was good at it, far better at it than any other sport we played. I mostly always won. I had a secret weapon too, a move I'd taught myself watching John "Earthquake" Tenta in the first wrestling tape I ever owned: SummerSlam 1990. Twenty-five years before I'd face Chris Jericho and his vaunted Walls of Jericho, I was Piccadilly's master of the Boston crab. I wouldn't turn it over in the traditional way. I devised something more practical for my situation. I would get a kid face-down, slam my knee into his lower back, several times if need be, and maneuver into the Boston crab position, pulling his legs up toward the back of his head until he screamed for mercy, signaling defeat by verbalizing, "I give!" Tapping out wasn't a thing yet.

Donnie and Kevin introduced me to wrestling. I knew Ninja Turtles, but when we compared action figures, they had all these guys I didn't know. Some of them, it would turn out, were the likes of Demolition, Bret Hart, Ultimate Warrior, Jake the Snake. They had wrestling tapes, Survivor Series and Royal Rumble both recorded on a six-hour VHS. All of these action figures came to life on screen, but this wasn't a cartoon. It was a real-life sport, like the Reds, but this was better than baseball. They would explain to me who was who in wrestling. We'd play with the figures and watch the tapes. They had some different figures too. Guys I was told were Ric Flair and Sting, who had the Warrior paint but also a flattop with a badass rat tail, a hairstyle which Donnie and Kevin both adopted.

Brian Pillman, I was told, and as evidenced by his tiger-striped trunks, also played for the Bengals (which he had years earlier). This was WCW.

"You don't know WCW?" Kevin asked.

I wasn't in the know, not cool enough yet. I needed to see these guys come to life on screen too.

"This is real wrestling, though," said Donnie.

He was showing me a copy of *I Like to Hurt People*, which was a cult-classic tape from the '80s, featuring Dusty sans polka dots and Terry Funk. It claimed to be "disgustingly real." There was so much to learn. These are my first memories of wrestling ... my first memories of much of anything, for that matter.

Some kids in Piccadilly were darker than others. Sure, there might be some nice kids with nice parents who wanted to play sports and run around, but there seemed to be an inordinate number of kids who were for sure ... troubled. This one kid who moved in across from Donnie and Kevin is a prime example. We were all hanging out on his back porch when he pulled out a lizard of some sort, a small gecko or newt or something that he must've pulled from the creek. He took out a syringe filled with water (don't ask me where a nine-year-old got a syringe) and stuck it into the poor little reptile. He pushed the plunger and pumped it full of water like a balloon. Its arms got all stubby, and its eyes bugged out of its head until it burst. I don't know where that kid is, but it wouldn't surprise me if he's got dead bodies in his basement.

Early childhood in Piccadilly was fun. You'd be out all day running around, then play hide-and-seek at night, darting in and out from behind cars until everyone's parents made them go inside. Then you'd start again the next morning. These were innocent times, but as we got a little older, the overarching depression of Piccadilly and its residents' place in the world wouldn't be lost on us, nor would the weight of the crushing realities of life that kept people from getting out. Food stamps, welfare checks, robberies, evictions, alcoholism, drug arrests and domestic violence painted the picture of what life had in store for us, even if we didn't fully understand those things.

For a kid who's never known anything different, you might not know to think of yourself or where you live as anything less than, but our reputation amongst teachers, administrators and classmates made it clear that to them, to everyone, we were "Piccadilly kids." We were a burden, a drain on time and resources. Irredeemable miscreants, we were an obligation placed on the school until we were old enough to go to jail. The beginnings of alienation.

To other kids we were a curiosity of which to make fun. "Na Na. ... You live in Piccadilly!!!!" ... Yeah, so what?

I never understood when kids would ridicule your clothes. I wore sweatpants to school. Those were the pants I had.

"You look like a hobo," said some little shit with a bowl cut.

"Shut up, Dylan, he's poor!" a little girl says, making me feel worse.

It's like, OK, your parents bought you that Starter jacket, dude. You don't have a job. You're nine. Fuck both y'all.

I felt a neon sign flashing over my head at all times, an asterisk next to my name every time a teacher spoke to me like a charity case. ... Y'all don't know me. You've never even been to my house. Who cares where I live anyway? I'm just living. I didn't do anything to anybody. I didn't get it. I turned inward.

"Piccadilly kids" became a badge we wore with pride. They don't need us, we don't need them. Our home base became our sanctuary. We would raise ourselves on our own territory. While parents were at work, at the bar or self-medicating while watching daytime TV, Piccadilly became a wild ecosystem, a *Lord of the Flies* experiment. A motley assortment of latchkey kids, feral products of broken condoms that roamed the streets marking their territory.

The fights. ... Jesus Christ, the fights. Everybody in Piccadilly fought everybody. All the time. It was exhausting. I was never the type to start fights or look for trouble. It's not my nature. I didn't like that negativity, but it was inescapable. My first taste of this harsh new world came one day while riding my bike. Three kids a couple years older than me, maybe 11 or 12, flagged me down on the side of the street. Naively, I pulled over to chat with them. They complimented my bike. They were being nice. As I talked with them I sensed they were being a little too nice. I noticed the glances between them, and my instincts knew ... they were toying with me.

"Hey, didn't you say he wanted to fight us?" one says.

"Yeah, he does!"

"Nah, I didn't say nothing. I don't know you," I said as I tried to get my wheels out of the grass and back on the pavement. The third kid blocked my way. I tried to keep my cool, but I knew this was a bad deal. I could feel it.

"You have to fight us" the kid said, smirking. Before I knew it my ass was flying up in the air. They had grabbed underneath the seat of my bike and flipped it over, I could feel the wheels spinning underneath. I was out of control and I hit the ground hard. Then it came, a hard soccer kick in the ribs that knocked the wind outta me completely. I couldn't take a breath, it felt like I'd been stabbed. The three of them proceeded to beat the fuck out of me for no reason at all. They kicked me repeatedly as I squirmed around gasping for air. It was something of an out-of-body experience. I just kept trying to pull air into my lungs.

They celebrated, quite proud of themselves. Slapping hands and laughing as they jogged away. Why did they do this? Were these kids mentally damaged sadists? Most likely, but at best they were garden-variety bullies. I hate bullies.

As I pulled myself up, I realized I couldn't breathe through my nose, so I started sucking in air through my mouth in bursts as I fought back tears. I gathered myself quickly and rode home as fast I could in such a state. I went straight to the room I shared with my sister and broke down, punching the walls in frustration, crying. What just happened? Why? It made no sense. I didn't do anything to anybody. Nothing was gained.

Later I would look in the mirror and see a grotesque scrape on the side of my face, as well as what would be the first of somewhere in the ballpark of a million black eyes over the next couple of decades. It was kinda cool. I looked like one of the wrestlers from the black-and-white pages in the back of the magazines, the guys with the blood. I grabbed my cardboard championship belt and put it over my shoulder, unknowingly gazing into the mirror at my future.

SPIN IT UP:
GREEN DAY, *INSOMNIAC*, 1995

This is one of the first CDs I ever had and still my favorite Green Day album. Hard-charging riffs from beginning to end, every song bleeds seamlessly into the next. The standout here is the classic track "Brain Stew," which I appreciated on another level in later years. Any former (or current, I guess) methamphetamine user will appreciate how this song so eloquently and accurately depicts what it's like to have insomnia and be "fucked up and spun out" in one's room.

If I had any illusions that the random beatdown was an isolated incident, they didn't last long. I'd soon learn the final lesson that would shape my view of people, of Piccadilly, of the world around me. My bike was my most prized possession. My Huffy Dirt Dog, with the badass green-and-black color scheme, bought for me by my mom. My WHEELS! One night I left it unattended, proudly on its kickstand, out in front of the apartment, before going in for the evening. I came out the next morning and it was gone. Just. Gone. Stolen. How could somebody do that? I wondered. Just take something that's not yours? What kind of shitty person would do such a thing? I was angry, furious ... mad at whoever stole from me, and mad at myself for being so stupid. I just left my bike out there, unlocked. What did I expect to happen? Why did I assume people were nice?

It was obvious now. Everybody sucked. The world was full of nothing but shitty people who steal your bike, jump you and mock you. Fuck everyone. I'd never be taken advantage of again. I'm no fool. I won't make the same mistakes. I'd be on the lookout, hoodie up, head down. I'd power walk the neighborhood with a sneer, deftly avoiding the traps and obstacles set by those who sought to take from me. If they got too close, I'd snap at them like a copperhead snake. I'll get you before you get me. I became intensely antisocial at times ... and mean. I didn't like to be fucked with.

At school I put forth every signal that I was to be left the hell alone. I did my work — sometimes I even listened, if the subject was interesting. I liked history, still do. I like watching documentaries on the Battle of Midway or Lewis and Clark, stuff like that. But I rarely spoke, interacted or participated. Everyone was an enemy. At home in Piccadilly we ran in packs, strength in numbers. You wouldn't want to be a straggler. You may come across a rival pack that would surely mess with you.

"Hey, kid, come here. We wanna talk to you!"

We knew what that meant. When two packs crossed paths, we'd bristle and bark like hyenas. It might devolve into the two sides throwing rocks at each other, a kid getting pelted badly in the face and everyone scattering, or representatives of similar age or size might be chosen from each group to fight each other.

I was often a target when I was younger. They'd try to pick me off. At first I was scared to fight, wishing these other kids would just go away ... but there was no other choice. People would never just leave me alone. I'd learned that by now. I remember me and another kid, circling, surrounded by kids cheering us on, throwing ridiculous Jean-Claude Van Damme strikes and ninja kicks at the air cuz we didn't know how to fight. I wrangled him down to all fours by the shirt collar and kicked him flush in the mouth, hard. He got up and ran away, turned back to scream some threats, blood running down his chin, then turned to run again. Holy shit, I won!

My friends celebrated with me as we walked down the street reliving the play-by-play. All of this fighting, all of this negativity, as exhausting as it was ... was inescapable. I figured I might as well lean into it. After all, this was a much better feeling than being on the opposite end of a Payless sneaker to the face. There was a kid who we'll call Scott Baio (cuz he kinda looked like him). A couple of years older than me, a real cocky eighth grader, pretty jacked for a middle schooler, even had abs and shit. He'd sit there on his BMX shirtless, while the girls hung all over him. One of those kids who people talked about like he was to be feared.

I didn't care for him. He was loud, made fun of people. Scott played football with us one evening, pretty good-size game, maybe six-on-six on a good grassy area by the first of Piccadilly's two bus stops. It was a central hangout spot, good to play football or for groups to stand around in a circle, get high, and play hacky sack. Girls would hang out, sitting on the air conditioners, smoking cigarettes and drawing in their notebooks.

Scott was bigger and stronger than most any other player. He'd run back kickoffs every time, hugging the ball and charging in a straight line, running as hard as possible. Nobody could tackle him. Kids bounced right off him, physically outmatched. He took great amusement in this. Being an eighth grader playing with younger kids, it was like he had a cheat code. Real hot shit.

As fate would have it, we were on opposite teams. Scott intercepted a pass and looked to run it back for a touchdown. I cut across the field at an angle in hot pursuit, now directly behind Baio. I lunged and grabbed a hold of the very nice basketball jersey he was wearing, yanking and pulling hard, dragging him to the ground in a dusty tornado of limbs, audibly ripping polyester as we crossed into the end zone.

There it was again. ... A now-familiar feeling, the new F'n standard, I guess. Piccadilly soccer kick in the ribs. Oxygen sucked out of my lungs in an instant. Prone on all fours after the tackle. A loud *crack* as Baio's foot slammed into my gut. Still couldn't breathe. ... Lemme check and make sure there isn't a knife in my sternum.

Scott Baio was incensed now, his precious fancy NBA jersey ripped to shreds, hanging off his neck like a cape. "Stupid! You ripped my F'n jersey, you little F'n punk!! You owe me fifty bucks, MFer!!"

Now, I obviously felt that all I did was tackle him and it's his own fault for wearing his precious F'n jersey, and I did my best to communicate this while struggling to breathe. Baio was apoplectic, screaming for all to hear, "He ripped my jersey!" as I struggled to my feet.

"You better have my money or I'm gonna beat your ass!!" he proclaimed as he rode away in a hurry on his BMX. The shock of his sudden crisis enough to cause him to flee the scene immediately, as if he needed to rush his NBA Jersey to the emergency room. Later that night, my mom answered a knock at our door. I soon realized who she was talking to in the hall when I heard her blankly stating, "You're not getting any money."

I moved closer to the door and saw F'n Baio standing in the hallway! He found out where I lived and was trying to F'n gouge my mother for the cash!

"Ma'am, I just need you to realize somebody owes me fifty dollars."

THE GALL! My blood boiled. My mom had zero patience for this fucker. He's lucky she didn't brain him with the baseball bat we kept by the door. The next morning on the school bus, I pass dickhead as I walk down the aisle.

"You better have my fifty bucks, or we're gonna have to fight. You don't wanna fight me."

I remained cold. As he got off the bus, he reminded me, "You better have my money or you're gonna get your ass beat."

Now, under normal circumstances, I wouldn't particularly wanna fight this dude. He was two years older than me. Bigger, stronger. ... But I had a strong sense of justification on my side. The fight had already begun, and he threw the first shot by kicking me while I was down, unprovoked (I'm not counting his jersey ripping as provocation. He was just being a little bitch about it). He'd been talking shit for everyone to hear, and on top of that he came to my door and talked to my mom! WTF? Was that a PTA meeting? I'd been completely and totally disrespected. I had no choice but to fight him.

The buzz on the school bus home was electric.

"Jon's gonna fight Scott!"

"Dude, you're gonna get your ass beat."

All the chatter from the pundits around me put butterflies in my stomach. I stood up in the aisle as we turned onto Piccadilly Circle, too much nervous energy to sit still. Soon we'd be at the first bus stop, where Scott got off. I assumed this is where it would go down. I normally got off on the second stop, but if I didn't get off here it gave him the opportunity to stay on the bus. Then it would be like I didn't want to fight and he was following me to my stop, chasing me down, like I was trying to get away. I thought that would give him a psychological edge and more opportunity to talk shit for his friends' entertainment like, "Where do you think you're going?" or "You trying to run home, pussy?" or something to that effect. Nah, I'll get off here.

Donnie held onto my backpack for me as I got up and walked the aisle, my heart pounding. Kids filed out seat by seat. Scott sat near the front and was off the bus already. As I neared the front, I looked through the door to see he was standing maybe 15 yards away with his friends and some girls, in a circle, by the air conditioners, his back to the bus and to me. There was laughing, smiling, the joy of the first moments of freedom after a day in school. When I came off the stairs and my feet hit the pavement, I casually walked a few feet, observing them. ... I realized he had no idea I planned to fight him. Even though he's the one who told me I better pay him 50 bucks or get my ass beat, he was oblivious. I guess he just thought he could run his mouth all day, trying to look tough in front of his friends and impress girls, but he wouldn't actually have to follow through on anything, or he just planned to beat my ass on his own schedule. Either way, fuck this guy. You asked for it, you got me all worked up for it. You might be two years older than me, but I got the jump on you. I'll get you before you get me.

I charged straight at him and bodychecked that bitch hard into the air conditioners. The girls standing nearby jumped and screamed. His friends were caught completely off guard.

"What the fuck, dude!?"

The rusted metal of the air conditioners cut him up badly. His arm was covered in bright red blood from the forearm down. His backpack was still on and I tried to sling him by it, which actually almost brought him to his feet but then he fell straight on his back then rolled to his side. I took the one loose strap with my left hand and tried to choke him with it, pelting him in the eye over and over with my right hand.

Baio was in shock. it all happened too fast for him. His friends yelled encouragement. Eventually, his surprise turned to anger, and he tried to fight back, powering me off of him briefly. But I jumped back on top of him. At this point, one of his friends shoved me off of Baio, which prompted Donnie and Kevin to start throwing wild haymakers, and for a brief moment complete chaos erupted around me as I kept wrestling the asshole who started all this in the first place to the ground. Then, not unlike a cattle rancher in the movies who stops a stampeding herd in its tracks by firing a pistol into the air, the bus driver arrived. She had stopped the bus 50 yards up the street and came running back to break up the fracas. This bus driver took no shit. She was screaming, hollering and slapping kids on the head, threatening to call the cops, the principal, the National Guard and everyone else. She said she'd have us all suspended – the bus stop was school grounds. One kid comically tried to argue we weren't on school property, but by then it was over. Fuck yous were already being exchanged between the retreating parties as the bus driver explained with great animation to the onlookers who had gathered, steam coming out of her ears, what all the commotion was and how she was "sick of this Goddamn shit!"

Cops would be here next if the situation didn't dissipate immediately, and that meant angry parents – both sides knew that. Time to get the hell outta here.

We ran like the wind to Donnie and Kev's apartment, on a high, like we won the World Series. Their dad was drinking a Budweiser, grilling burgers on the porch. We told him the story and he gave me a cheers. I took a long swig of my Citrus Drop soda. I'd never been so thirsty.

"That's what I'm talkin' 'bout!" he said, a little buzzed, smiling broadly.

"That kid's a fuckin' punk!"

FLICK PICK: CRIMSON TIDE, 1995,
DENZEL WASHINGTON, GENE HACKMAN

"I am the commander of this fucking ship!"

This movie rules. All due respect to *The Hunt for Red October*, but I think *Crimson Tide* is better. Hackman plays an old embattled naval commander aboard the USS Alabama, a nuclear submarine, during a fictional overseas conflict with Russian rebels. I squirm in my seat to this day watching this movie as Cold War-like tension runs high and nuclear trigger fingers are getting itchy, particularly Hackman's, as a partial message comes in from the U.S. seemingly ordering a missile launch. Denzel, the SO, second in command, wants to wait until the radio gets back online and they can retrieve the full message before taking action and starting a war. Hackman believes they have to strike *now*. The crew is split. It's an unthinkable position to be in, and mutiny erupts on board. Hackman and Denzel are so good and believable as diametrically opposed naval commanders. I wish Denzel's character in this movie was a real person who was running for president, cuz I'd vote for him.

This film also has an epic and iconic soundtrack by Hans Zimmer. The track "Roll Tide" is a great pump-up tune to throw into your workout mix as a change of pace. As part of WWE's Tribute to the Troops one year, I actually got to go aboard a nuclear sub, the biggest one in the U.S. Navy, actually. ... Those Tribute to the Troops events were always a privilege, a chance to get to give back a little something to our brave men and women in the service and experience some amazing things. One year Renée and I got to fly in a military helicopter over some of the most restricted airspace in the world, right over the White House and the Pentagon. This particular year, I and a few others got a tour of the submarine, which, if it were its own sovereign nation, would be the third most powerful nation on earth in terms of firepower, behind only Russia and the U.S. That's power-of-God type shit. ... I have incredible respect for the sailors on these submarines. They go down for MONTHS at a time, no sunlight, no fresh air, and lemme tell you, it's cramped. As someone who gets claustrophobic in hotel rooms, I can't imagine what it's like to serve on a submarine, and this was the biggest in the

Navy! We were told other attack submarines are much smaller. *Daaamn.* ... I'm on the biggest sub in the Navy, and I already feel like Buddy the Elf. They bunked six to a room in quarters as big as my wife's closet. Our tour guide explained their job was basically to be the world's bouncer. They go out to sea and just hang out. If there's no trouble, they just chill. They know what their job is, but they hope and pray, as we all do, that they will never have to do it and that their presence alone will be enough to deter conflict. It was a humbling experience I'll never forget. Watch *Crimson Tide* and say a thank you to all our brave sailors out there ducking their heads as they move through the halls of their ships, sleeping on their little bunks, away from their family for months at a time, proudly serving their country and keeping us all safe. I salute you all.

JOKE CLAUDIO TOLD ME:

WE DIDN'T LIKE OUR TRIP TO PENNSYLVANIA DUTCH COUNTRY. IT JUST FELT LIKE SOMETHING WAS AMISH.

HWA CHUNK, LATE 2003

Bang! Bang! Bang!

It sounded like gunshots, I thought. I parked my truck, got out and looked around. As I was striding across the parking lot, unsure of where I was going, I thought there must be an indoor shooting range here in this industrial complex, maybe behind one of these bay doors? I'd been to enough gun ranges with my dad, in places just like this ... a bleak, grey area in Woodlawn, north of downtown Cincinnati. I recognized that sound, swallowed up by steel and concrete, but still loud enough to hear from the parking lot. It was unmistakable. Four truck bays on either side of the lot, small staircases leading to numbered doors. There were no signs. There were some cars in the parking lot, but no indication as to which door I was looking for. Was I in the right place? I had written down the directions and taped them to my dashboard: 275N to 75S, Glendale/Woodlawn exit. I looked around for clues, inspecting every door. All eight units were identical. Perplexed, I continued to aimlessly snoop around. I was already fairly anxious, and being lost wasn't helping. The lost city of gold was supposed to be right here. I've come this far already – It's gotta be here. I was even wearing a collared shirt, a statement that I was to be taken seriously.

Bang! Bang!

The gunshots returned, only closer now. They drew me in.

Bang!

Nah, that's not gunshots, but it's loud. I hear voices.

Bang!

As I get closer and closer to the final unit in the back of the parking lot, that sound – the sound of metal crashing and bouncing to the bay door – reveals itself, becoming clear in my mind as it echoes through the early evening air. Somehow, I now know exactly what that sound is. I found it. The lost city of gold. The hidden door to the magical world I've dreamed about through countless long, sleepless nights. I would make my escape. The possibilities on the other side of the door were endless, but one must leave everything behind. Trade in your old life for what's on the other side. My mind was long made up, and now my search is over. I've found it: the Heartland Wrestling Association.

The actual door was just like the others in the complex, numbered but unremarkable, no doorknob, opening only from the inside. I walked up a few steps and just, well ... knocked. I was close enough now to hear more clearly the sound of what I knew was happening on the other side, though I had no idea what that actually looked like or meant.

The *bang* sounds I had briefly mistaken for gunshots were, in fact, the sound a wrestling ring makes when a wrestler takes a bump. I would soon find out that the more continuous, rhythmic crashing sounds I could hear from inside the bay door were the sounds of one or more wrestlers running the ropes. I didn't expect it to be this loud. The only time I'd ever been up close to an actual ring was some time earlier when I'd attended an HWA show at the Red Barn Flea Market in Batavia, Ohio. Wandering the streets one afternoon I had seen a flyer on a telephone pole ... one of those standard old-school, multi-colored posters used for wrestling, boxing or tough-man contests, one of those pink, purple and green ones that all looked the same. Live pro wrestling?! I knew the Red Barn. It was 10 to 15 minutes up the road. I had scavenged that place for wrestling tapes. I know the Red Barn. ... They're having wrestling?! I was there!

I stood in line with great anticipation, outside in the gravel parking lot of the Red Barn, amongst something of a county fair–type crowd. This event would feel comparable with a tractor pull to most, but not me. I felt like I was at a Rolling Stones concert ... despite the fact that I had absolutely no idea what to expect. Is this HWA thing legit? Wrestling just like on TV? As we made our way inside, AC/DC playing on the house speakers, the smell of popcorn in the air ... the ring came into view, real as can be, bathed in a couple of overhead ring lights.

Electricity hung in the air like the moments before a thunderstorm. I took my seat on the bleachers, about eye level with the top rope. I inspected the ring, the ropes, the mat, wondered what they felt like. It was close enough I felt like I could reach out and touch it, jump right in. A bell rang and a ring announcer named Hoss with frosted tips and a Hawaiian shirt made his way down the aisle, signaling the start of the show.

The first wrestler through the curtain was named Johnny the Bull. He was *jaaaacked.* The most jacked dude I'd ever seen in real life ... an impossible tan, giant bodybuilder muscles, tattoos, and shiny pleather trunks. He looked superhuman. Why hadn't I heard of him before? I didn't know anything about the business other than what I saw on TV or read in the magazines, but this guy is definitely a real pro wrestler, "Yes, he is, dude, he's standing ten F'n feet from me. Look, he's right there!"

I ask myself, What the hell is going on here? ... Oh, shit! So this is like the minor leagues, like the Cincinnati Cyclones? Where do these HWA guys come from? How much money do they make? Are they rich? Do they have belts? How the hell does any of this work!? My head is spinning. I have a lot of goddamn questions, and somebody better start answering them!

By this point in my life, I knew somewhere deep in my subconscious that I was gonna be a pro wrestler. My soul was already leading me toward that path, but I couldn't quite articulate or even understand what that meant. How does one become a pro wrestler? I had no idea, but still there was this ... *feeling. This is what I could be good at.* It sure wasn't an option on any of the aptitude tests we took in school, but I felt particularly suited for it. After all, I'd been studying wrestling as long as I could remember for reasons I couldn't explain, reading any magazine or piece of literature I could find, learning whatever history was available to learn, booking fantasy cards, and compiling decades of championship records in my notebooks during class, collecting boxes of tapes and studying them endlessly. When you're younger this type of thing is normal. Kids go through phases where they get really into different stuff ... be it wrestling, cartoons, sports teams, or comics. Just kids playing, exercising their imaginations ... but as I got older, I had taken my obsession to another level. By now my interest in wrestling had become academic. I was seeking to understand wrestling in a deeper way without even realizing what I was doing or why. Now as a young man in the spring of 2003, it was as if something inside me was saying, Well if anyone was gonna become a pro wrestler, who's more qualified than me? and, If I'm qualified for anything, it's wrestling. But at this point, there was no tangible goal, no clear path, it was still just ... a *feeling.* That would all change on this night at the Red Barn Flea Market.

Les Thatcher's Main Event Pro Wrestling Camp, it was called. I had been thumbing through the event program, hand-stapled together, which ran down the night's card and promoted sponsors such as Grammas Pizza, when I saw the ad in the back, beneath the HWA logo. This was it. X marks the spot. I was Indiana Jones, and I had just discovered the artifact that would point me to the Ark of the Covenant. A light shone from the heavens. Angels sang. I didn't know what I was looking for until I found it. There was no mistaking it. ... This is where I was supposed to go. The adventure was just beginning. I'd been studying this mythical world from a distance, in a classroom I created with boxes of tapes and dual VCR setups, the PWI Almanac, black-and-white wrestling magazines with color pinups. The answers lay ahead — I was sure of it.

The ad simply listed the address and phone number and noted that only those 18 and up need apply. ... I didn't care for that part; I chose to ignore it. After all, they just didn't know me YET ... but they soon would. I am supposed to be here. I was ahead of the game, I figured. I was ready. I had some good size and was still growing. I'd been amateur wrestling for years, I even got trophies and shit. I play football. ... They love that, right? I'm a good athlete, and more importantly... I get this. I know this. Once I learned what to do, how this actually worked, I'd be off to the races.

It was all still just a mystery. How are these guys doing this? I know they're not really fighting, but how does this all ... come together, I wondered as I watched a litany of talent come through the curtain and dazzle me by performing this mysterious art, this thing I was obsessed with and longed to learn, to be a part of ... pro wrestling.

What I didn't know was that HWA at the time was a WWE developmental territory. This meant it was home to several talents under WWE contract, awaiting their shot to be called up to the big leagues (as I would be years later). HWA was also a destination for both indie wrestlers hoping to get noticed and score a contract and prospective students seeking to train at one of the most reputable and well-respected camps in the country.

HWA was a hot spot, and unbeknownst to me, this whole time, it had been right underneath my feet. I sat on those bleachers transfixed, amazed at what I was seeing, studying everything intently. One after another, they came down the aisle, not just real-life pro wrestlers, but as I'd soon realize, some of the top talent in the country.

Johnny the Bull's giant traps disappeared behind the curtain. Out next was Matt Stryker.* The Unibrow, he was affectionately called, for obvious reasons. He was an explosive spark plug of a wrestler who busted his ass in the ring. Known as HWA's "Charlie Hustle," he was the gold standard of homegrown talent and would be my first real-world example of excellence to which I could aspire.

There was Chad Collyer, a superb, polished technician who reminded me of Dean Malenko. To this day he is still among the smoothest technical wrestlers I've ever seen. The chicks screamed for a Billy Idol-looking Englishman who slid backward into the ring, sticking his ass up in the air. His name was Nigel McGuinness. The Ice Cream Man, Tony B, came to the ring and passed out frosty treats to the fans in the front row. I watched "Surfer" Cody Hawk literally "surf" his opponent, hanging 10 on his back after planting him face-first with a drop toehold. Little did I know that drop toehold was one of a million maneuvers I would learn from Cody himself, as he would become my teacher and mentor. He would be the guy who would help me figure all this out one day, but right now I was just sitting on those steel bleachers with my eyes and ears open. "Tackle." ... Whoa! Wait! Did I hear that right? I know my mind is racing right now and my imagination is running wild, but I'm almost positive I heard that right: "tackle."

Chet "The Jet" Jablonski was in the ring. He was a cocky, gum chewing, blond heel who was built like a tank. My eyes are locked on the action now. I'm practically squinting, as if the secrets of the business will come into focus if I look hard enough. I swear he just said "tackle" ... between the heavy breaths of hard work in the ring, I heard it, ever so subtly, "tackle." Soft enough that it must have been only for his opponent to hear, because all the other grunts, exertions and vocalizations thus far have been at a higher volume, meant for the audience to hear. ... And I think I even saw his mouth move. ... Am I imagining that? No! Because less than even a full second after that, Chet's opponent was careening to the ropes, running into a flying shoulder tackle! I know what I just witnessed. A wrestler called for a move and another one took that move. So these guys talk to each other? In the ring? Nobody notices? I did barely hear it, I guess, and after all, I'm really close to the ring. This is unbelievable. ... But OK, cool. Well, then how do they know what moves to call for? And when? I have a million questions.

---

* Not to be confused with veteran commentator Matt Striker.

The gears continued to whirr in my head, my adrenaline buzzed as I watched the rest of the show, taking mental notes. I'd be in that ring with all you guys soon enough, you just don't know it yet.

A young, fresh-faced Brian Kendrick, then known as Spanky, hit the ring and impressed with his athleticism. There was a mean little fucker named Jamie Noble, who would become one of my favorite wrestlers. B.J. Whitmer, a beloved veteran, now a producer at AEW, was a standout, in the early stages of a memorable career. Then there were Kimo and Ekmo, The Island Boys. The Island Boys, two 400-pound Samoans who would soon be known as 3-Minute Warning in WWE, were a part of the Anoa'i family, professional wrestling's legendary bloodline and the two largest humans I'd ever seen in real life. When Kimo, the size of a Honda Civic, did a split-legged moonsault my jaw dropped. That poor soul laying on the mat must be crushed like an aluminum can. Little did I know that Kimo, called Rosey in WWE and who I'd come to know as Matty, was the brother of my future Shield partner, Roman Reigns. Ekmo would go on to be best remembered as Umaga, a top-tier WWE monster.

In retrospect, this card was stacked. ... I left the Red Barn that night on a high, gliding on air over the gravel parking lot, buzzing with excitement. I sped away in my '97 Ranger with the windows down, crisp night air rushing over me, WEBN blasting on the little boombox with the tape deck I kept in the passenger seat.

Wrestling had become a tangible thing, right in front of my face. Only a guardrail now separated me from being in the ring myself. ... I still had to navigate those several feet of mysterious waters that separated the bleachers from the squared circle, but now there was an arrow pointing me in the right direction. ... Now I knew exactly where to start.

Knock, knock, knock ... I waited on the steps about 60 seconds. No response. Now I felt stupid, self-conscious. I'm awkward in situations like this under normal social circumstances, but this is even more nerve-racking, like trying to join some kind of secret society. Is there a secret knock? Am I not supposed to knock on the door? Now I feel like an intruder, unwanted. I know they're in there. This must be a breach of etiquette; that's why they're not answering. Unless they didn't hear me. Maybe they're ignoring me. Shit. What if I've done something wrong and if I knock again I'll make it worse? I became nervous, my feet shuffled, a bead of sweat formed on my brow. I should just bail. I messed up somehow. ... Nah, fuck that. I've come this far, I will not be denied! ... Jesus! Would you just F'n relax, dude! Just knock again.

I clench my fist and try again, harder this time: *knock, knock, knock!*

I hear voices. Shit, they heard me! I could feel my skin getting red. Just chill, dude you're bein– the door swung open and a head burst out. The wild eyes hit me like a searchlight. I felt like a raccoon caught in a trash can, the way this guy looked at me. He didn't say anything – he didn't have to. I was obviously an intruder, and this was highly irregular. I'd stepped in some sort of shit. What's worse, this wasn't some sort of secretary. This wasn't a concierge. ... The square, chiseled jaw, hulking shoulders and the trademark black unibrow. He stood still, but his image jumped out of the doorway at me and nearly knocked me back down the steps. He was a cartoon character, a superhero. This was a scene from F'n *Who Framed Roger Rabbit*. This was Matt Stryker. Holy shit. I collected myself and stammered, "Uh, I called on the phone before. I'm here to check out the school."

It was as awkward as you can imagine, me at 17, about to have a stroke and all, but a smile appeared on Stryker's face. His guard came down, his annoyance with this interruption abated.

"Oh, cool, Come on in!"

Relief. Then: *Holy shit, I'm in!!*

"You came in the back door. The front door's on the other side," he said and laughed.

Dammit. *Idiot.* ... I followed Stryker through the gym, soaking everything up as he spoke. I was in a whirlwind. *Things are gonna move fast now. Pay attention.*

I took it all in: two rings, one large rectangular warehouse space, eight to ten wrestlers in workout gear, cutoff shirts, knee and elbow pads, tall patent leather wrestling boots, standing circularly in the ring, action happening in the center, suitcases strewn about the floor. Not gym bags, but roller bags. Quotes painted on the walls. I'll read those later.

"I'll take you back to meet Les," ... Les Thatcher. The name on the marquee. Les Thatcher wrestled professionally in top territories all over the country, debuting in 1960. A deep wealth of knowledge, he was and is as old-school as old-school gets. After retiring from the ring, he had success as an announcer, and in 1996 he started the Heartland Wrestling Association, finding yet another life in the only business he'd ever known as a trainer, one of the most respected and sought-after trainers in the game.

I'd communicated with Les once before. I'd written a letter to him, an actual physical letter, in which I described my desire to begin training for professional wrestling. I included my background in sports, stats such as my height and weight, and for unknown reasons, how much I could bench press, which I'm sure I lied about. Les wrote me back, in a letter typed on an actual typewriter, surely the last in existence by 2003.

I was pretty pumped when I received my reply, my first contact! This letter was a real piece of correspondence with the world of pro wrestling! Les thanked me for my interest and explained that I should continue on a good weight training program and the fact that I was in school would be no problem, as they'd had several student-athletes train while earning their degrees.

I think something I wrote in the gibberish of my letter referred to my being in school, leading him to believe I was in college. Sure as fuck not in college, dude. I was in high school obviously ... for the time being at least. It wasn't too long before I'd drop out.

There would be no college athletics for me. Reading Les's letter F'n napalmed any notion that I might graduate in good standing, graduate at all or even attend classes with any regularity. High school? We still talking about that? Dude, I told you: I'm gonna be a Professional Wrestler!

Stryker led me back towards Les's office. I peered around the corner and saw his stark white hair. He looked up from his desk, putting his glasses on. I couldn't help but notice the Greek statue on the shelf of two naked dudes wrestling, in a tight grappling entanglement, leaves covering their junk. How would you get those leaves to stay on? Les came out and shook my hand happily, looking at me through his thick spectacles. I explained who I was. ... I had written him and called on the phone and was told I could come down and check out a practice. I didn't mention my age. I had just turned 17. ... Close enough, I figured. We went back out into the gym to watch some training as Les chatted with me. I tried to play it cool, trying hard not to get too excited and start asking too many of the million questions I had.

I'd dressed carefully. My polo shirt tucked in, sleeves rolled up to highlight my burgeoning guns, a polished and professional presentation, I thought. A real goddamn blue chipper, if I don't say so myself. Just don't say anything stupid. Les asked me a question about who some of my favorite wrestlers were. This must be some kind of test.

"Take it to the mat, take it to the air, but take it seriously, or take it home."

"Train hard and master your craft."

Those were the quotes painted on the wall.

This was not the time to mention I once dressed up as the The Sandman for Halloween, wielding a broken pool cue as my Singapore cane. Although my Budweiser can and the gnarly, pus-dripping black eye I was sporting from a recent fight did make it quite an authentic costume. I didn't expect that was the sort of thing Les was looking for. No, surely HWA was a place for serious wrestlers. I discerningly answered with examples such as Benoit, Jericho, Bret and Malenko as the wrestlers I liked to watch: the technicians, wrestler's wrestlers. Les's eyes lit up, looking even bigger behind his Coke-bottle lenses. That was a right answer. Les's enthusiasm for the conversation grew now. Have I won him over? I wondered as he told me how sometimes when he asked that question of potential recruits they respond with answers like the Ultimate Warrior, which, as I had suspected, was not what he wanted to hear.

"Guys sit at home watching TV and think, 'Well I can do that,'" Les explained, "but there's a lot more to this than painting your face and running around the ring, shaking the ropes. You have to learn how to work."

I sure as hell didn't know how to work yet. In fact, I didn't even know what that meant. It's probably the first time I heard the phrase. Thinking back on it now, I wonder if Les's personal disdain for the Ultimate Warrior had been going back for years by that point. Lord knows the horrible things he must have thought about The Sandman. ... Sandman rules.

My answer was correct for a few reasons. Les took wrestling, his craft, very seriously and did not have time for anyone who didn't. If you thought pro wrestling was some get-rich-quick scheme, if you thought "Oh, well, I can do that," as Les put it, if you thought wrestling was just cheap theatrics and play-fighting, if you thought your frat-house wrestling character where you dropped an elbow on the porch through the beer pong table while you and your friends were watching *Nitro* made you ready for an HWA event, Les had no time for you.

Chris Benoit and Kurt Angle had just recently put on a ferocious technical wrestling masterpiece at Royal Rumble '03 that garnered a long, standing ovation from those in attendance. Mentioning Benoit as a guy whose work I appreciated sent Les into a soliloquy about that match and the beauty of the art of professional wrestling. Two people in the ring, going hold-for-hold taking the audience on a ride.

I was mesmerized. I couldn't believe the things I was hearing. These were the answers I was searching for, but they were coming at me so fast I couldn't process them. I must've done something right, I thought, because now, Les wasn't just giving me the spiel about *X* amount down, *Y* per month, here, sign these release papers. ... No. He brought me in; he was giving me the real scoop. This polo shirt paid off.

Les launched into another story, one I'd hear approximately another 2.8 million times over the years. If you are a wrestler who comes from where I do, you are told a legend about the greatest match that ever took place in the history of time. It's just a fact that one does not question lest they be shunned. Like a Catholic is taught that Jesus is God incarnate, a wrestler from this time and place is taught to believe that Chris Benoit vs. William Regal from the third annual Brian Pillman Memorial Show is the best match in the history of the sport. Bar none. Water is wet, the sky is blue and Regal-Benoit from the Pillman is the best match ever.

Many have heard the story. ... "Chris is sitting in the dressing room, and Regal walks in, drops his bag, and sits down. Chris says, 'What do you wanna do tonight?' Regal says, 'How about that finish we did that one time?' Chris says. 'Great.' Regal says, 'OK,' and gets up and walks away. They didn't talk to each other again until they locked up."

Mind. F'n. blown. I didn't understand why what I just heard was awesome, but it was awesome. I'm goddamn Charlie in the Chocolate Factory. ... This match of mythical proportions took place in Cincinnati.

The Pillman Memorial Shows were four charity events Les promoted from '98 to '01 and they included stars from WWF, WCW and ECW all on the same card at the height of the boom period, which is pretty crazy. Dr. Tom Prichard, another renowned trainer (and a future coach of mine at FCW) would frequently use this match as a blueprint to teach aspiring wrestlers. Regal-Benoit begins with sharp and aggressive technical wrestling, building intensity as the combatants start unleashing hard strikes. Regal gets busted open, a nasty hardway that sends the crowd abuzz. The tension builds to a fever pitch as Regal stretches his foe with a nasty surfboard, grimacing behind eyes burning with the sting of the rivulets of sweat and blood dripping down his face. "Regal, Regal, Regal!" the audience chants as the contest builds to its conclusion.

Legend has it that Les kept creeping closer and closer to the ring as the match unfolded, transfixed with the beautiful work being displayed, literally being pulled in by the story. And sure enough, as soon as the final bell rings, Les can be seen popping up on the apron behind those Coke bottle lenses with a huge smile on his face, unbridled passion for the craft bursting out of him.

"When the match starts, it's lukewarm, some bonehead in the crowd starts chanting 'boring,'" Les explained to me. "By the end, they have two thousand people on their feet stomping and clapping!" he told me with pride.

I was having a real conversation about wrestling and how it actually worked, and I was absorbing it like a sponge, processing information and filing it away in my brain as fast as I could. But while building a match from the ground up, telling a story, building emotion, and the all-important staple of Les's ideology, "calling it in the ring," were all things I would soon learn, these were concepts far too advanced for a neophyte like me to fully understand yet. If I wanted to run like the gladiators in the aforementioned fabled contest, I must first learn how to walk, and even before that, to crawl. ... So we turn our attention to the ring.

SPIN IT UP:
THE GAME, THE DOCUMENTARY, 2005

2005, early HWA days. I'm a young indie student/wrestler in training. It's hard to keep a job because inevitably they'll schedule me to work when I need to be at a show or at practice. Which one you think I showed up at? Wrestling was always the priority. (I wish Postmates/Grubhub and all that shit was a thing back then, seems like an ideal way to pay bills for an indie wrestler cuz you can do it anywhere/any time). One job I was able to keep for quite a while, however, was at a factory in Cincinnati. I'm still not quite exactly sure what we did, but my role was to hang pieces of metal of various sizes and shapes on hooks. Then they would move down the line and go through a series of treatments, maybe get painted? I think they were HVAC components, like air-conditioning-type-shit. I never asked. I just hauled the pallets up to the line and hung big-ass pieces of metal on hooks from 11:00 p.m. to 7:00 a.m., Sunday through Thursday. That's why I was able to keep that job for so long. I could train weekdays in the evenings, even have time to lift weights after, and still

make it to work. I had Friday and Saturday nights off to be at shows, setting up the
ring and wrestling. I got really good at setting up the ring, becoming something of the
point man for ring construction.

Back to the album we're spinning up: "Dreams," a big single off this record, was
getting heavy airplay at the time. I was bummed when they took away my porta
CD player. I guess it was so that If I was about to be ran over by a forklift I would
it coming, which was probably a good idea in retrospect, and I still had the radio.

I had some F'n cool coworkers, and they would blast the local hip-hop station
all night long. I remember that R. Kelly *Trapped in the Closet* thing was going on a
the time, which I couldn't stand at first, but after a while I was like, well, I'm invested
now. ... How'd this MFer get out of the closet?

I loved the track "Dreams." "Hate It or Love It" by The Game and 50 Cent was also
a big song at the time. I was persuaded to buy the album. I was, after all, making nine
bucks an hour at the time, a fortune for me. This album takes me back to that summer
in 2005. I was just starting to figure out wrestling. I was working my ass off, training in
the ring for hours nightly. I vividly remember pulling up the giant warehouse garage
door after practice to the balmy Ohio night air, putting *The Documentary* in the CD
player and pumping iron until it was time to go to work. "Dreams" is my favorite track
but "Church for Thugs" is a close second; that song pumps me the fuck up. "How We
Do" was a big hit from this record, but it's probably my least favorite song here. ...
Once a song hits me with an "up in the club," I'm usually out.

TRAINING

Here's the real peek behind the curtain. In the ring, Cody Hawk is commanding traffic amidst a circle of trainees. They're grabbing headlocks, hitting the ropes, slamming into each other with tackles, and taking hard back bumps. The reverberation of sound from the steel ring bouncing off the walls is still surprisingly loud. In between reps, Cody steps into the center of the ring to give instruction, and I struggle hard to hear what he's saying. Les is still talking in my right ear as I stare at the ring in awe. The secrets to how the sausage is made are being displayed right before my eyes ... the lost city of gold.

Les answers my questions, such as, How long does one train before getting to step in the ring for an actual match?

"Six months at least," he tells me, "That's the fastest we've ever had someone ready. You don't want anyone to see you while you're still green."

"Green" must mean inexperienced or not ready. Green, a picture of a klutzy, amateurish performance comes to my mind. ... Yeah, that must be what green means. "Bumps" must mean slams, falls, taking moves, from what I gather. The other word I keep hearing is "selling." I think I know what selling means; it seems pretty obvious. See, I'm figuring all this out. It means, like ... um ... acting like stuff hurts, like if a guy twists your arm, you act like, Shit, my arm hurts! I'm in pain! That's selling, right? Yeah, that's what selling means, I decide, satisfied. I begin to feel more comfortable. ... This is where I belong. I'm happier than a pig in shit, listening and observing.

The rest of the conversation with Les is a bit of blur, but I remember he brought up the down payment and financing options. For a lowly street rat like me, the numbers were so staggering my head started spinning. *Hoooold* yer horses! That was a splash of cold water in the face. Back in reality, Les was looking at me expectantly for my thoughts on what I've seen and heard thus far. I think I was able to awkwardly muster up an, "Uh, yeah, I'm saving money." Hardly convincing, I'm sure.

I was saving money, working as many of my six-buck-an-hour security gigs as possible. I believe the full cost of tuition was $3,000 – $2,500 if you paid up front. I did, in fact, know that already, a nugget of information I gleaned from going to the library and finding it on HWA's website. But I'd spent most of whatever money I had already by just putting enough gas in the truck to make the trip here. Even so, I'd paid little heed to the giant, flashing neon sign that read DO NOT PASS GO WITHOUT $2,500.

Dozens of interested parties who thought, Well, I can do that, probably came through every week. How many of their aspirations to do this for real came to a halt at this point in the conversation? I worried I'd be shown the door immediately. I wanted to grab Les by the collar and plead, "That's everyone else! They're not ME!" My God, man, you must understand! There was also the matter of my age. I wasn't 18, so despite my zeal, being broke and unable to sign any legal waivers was enough to wind the conversation down. The deal would not be closed today, the car would not be driven off the lot. Still, even though the entire place didn't drop to their knees and worship me, rejoicing "THE CHOSEN ONE HAS ARRIVED!" when I walked in, Les, had given me plenty of time and graciously said I could stay and watch the rest of practice before he retired to his office. Left on my own now, I lingered, a fly on the wall, careful not to get too close.

Cody was all business. He spoke with certainty, demonstrating techniques and bluntly correcting poor execution. There was little wasted movement, a serious training session. Two trainees performed a drill with full intensity, audible exertion, scowls on faces as their bodies collided into the ropes, bounced off the mat and slammed into each other. Two fresh guys replaced them seamlessly and attacked the drill. The frenzy of action slowed to a stop as Cody took the center of the ring and held court, a dissertation about throwing punches.

I'm all ears. I've seen millions of punches thrown over the years watching wrestling, but how does it really work? One of the eternal questions of the young wrestling fan. Cody instructed one trainee to close his eyes, and he did, hands at his sides. Cody proceeded to unleash of barrage of punches to his face, savagely, one after the other. Haymakers, jabs, rights, lefts and finally a brutal-looking kick with the ball of the foot right to the sternum.

The dude didn't flinch, didn't feel a thing. ... *Whooooaaaa.* Cody moved around the circle, one student at a time, they all closed their eyes and he teed off with strikes right to their faces! Every punch and kick looked like it could smash a bulletproof windshield, but they had no effect on the students. They were all a mirage. It was a powerful demonstration.

One student asks a question, and Cody answered with another demonstration, "My dropkick is very light," he said, "Hold out your hand."

The guy held out his hand like a target and Cody effortlessly ripped off a beautiful dropkick, launching his body into the air horizontally and flipping around in mid-air. It was like he didn't even jump, he just levitated instantly, and his foot tapped the target about as hard as you tap someone on the shoulder. Light as a feather.

Next, Cody went back around the circle, delivering the same strikes, but this time he instructed the recipients to "sell" the blows. It all came together. Cody reared back and threw the punch with all the force in his body, grunting with effort. The instant he made contact, his opponent, his dance partner, snapped his head back, grimaced, and grabbed his nose as if it had been broken. The grandfather clock is now splayed open and I'm getting a close up look at how the gears inside work. *It's an illusion.*

After practice concluded, everyone sat on folding chairs and worn, cushioned seats, stained and dotted with cigarette burns, that had been pulled from the backs of '90s minivans, seatbelts and all. The students were all smiles, T-shirts matted with sweat as they untied their long bootlaces. They chatted about training, their lives, their jobs. One dude, Trevor, was a waiter and was relaying a story about a troublesome customer, and everyone laughed. They told stories about their roommates' drunken behavior the previous weekend and chicks they were going out with. They were living real lives, mild-mannered civilians by day, superhero wrestlers by night. This was a revelation. They talked about their recent matches, as a few were active wrestlers and had had some of their first real outings in the ring. Some had trained as long as a year to earn the opportunity to perform on an HWA event. What lives these guys lead! No school, no teachers. Goodfellas. Made Men. I'd have shot a guy and dumped the body in the Ohio River on the spot to be a part of this fraternity, one whose members' lives WERE wrestling.

Before I left that night, Cody said I could come by and help out at shows whenever I wanted. So for the rest of the year, I became a familiar but quiet presence at HWA, sweeping the floors, setting up chairs, hauling boards to and fro from the ring truck, selling cans of soda and candy bars during the show ... or my favorite gig, being security inside the barrier, where I just got to sit and watch the matches from the best seat in the house. I watched attentively, always listening. I was right in front of the fans, but I was basically invisible, sitting in the corner of the guardrails in my black T-shirt. I felt like a spy, undercover, gathering intel.

I would need more money to start training. Champing at the bit to get in the ring, I wanted to have enough cash in hand to start the minute I turned 18. On top of doing security at the arena and Riverbend, I started working as a third-shift cook at the Perkins restaurant on Beechmont Avenue. Somewhere around this time I just sort of stopped going to school. I didn't exactly plan it. I didn't get up and walk out of class one day. School just kinda disappeared, became irrelevant. Mario and I skipped school on a Friday, the kind of beautiful spring day you just can't bear to spend in a depressing high school prison. We went to the HWA show that night at the Montgomery County Fairgrounds. As a reward for dutifully selling tickets to the show, but in retrospect probably more just to have a little fun messing with me, I was put in the opening Battle Royal. I nearly pooped my pants.

You may as well have walked up to me and told me in two hours you're gonna main-event WrestleMania. Out by the ring truck, I pulled Mario aside and in a whisper, but unable to control my excitement, I told him, "Dude! *Shhhh*. ... Dude ... I'm in the *ruuummbblle*! ... SHHH." This was top-secret information. There could be guys from TMZ on the roof with long sports lenses about to blow this story wide open.

PICCADILLY DIPSHIT TO BE IN BATTLE ROYAL IN DAYTON, OH, IN FRONT OF 250 PEOPLE

Discretion was of the utmost importance, obviously. I borrowed some athletic pants from a student I had made friends with and went shirtless. Standing in line with the other wrestlers behind the curtain, I tried to look like I belonged, cool as a cucumber, just gonna do a few push-ups here, get my pump on, you know, no big deal. Nutha day, nutha dolla, babe.

When it was my turn, I burst through the curtain and immediately felt the eyes on me, naked and exposed. I made my way down the aisle with no idea what to do with any of my limbs. The ring was filled up with bodies. I slid under a turnbuckle and found some open real estate in the corner. I scowled at my opponents, my head on a swivel. Paroxysmal, fidgeting uncontrollably from head to toe. It might have appeared to anyone in the audience who was actually looking at me that I was having a seizure, but they didn't quite know just who the fuck they were looking at, did they?

As far as I was concerned, my body language, my expression informed of only one fact: I'm gonna win this thing. Twenty wrestlers grit their teeth and clench their fists. The bell rings, and 40 seconds later I hit the floor, going ass over teakettle, clutching the top rope for dear life, a clumsy panda falling out of a tree. I didn't know how to take a bump to the floor, in fact I knew how to do exactly zero of anything, so what I did in the ring for those 40 seconds I couldn't tell you, but after an experience like that, worrying about school would have been like Neo bothering to call in in sick for work the day after taking the red pill. I never went back.

By this point, HWA was no longer a WWE developmental territory. That relationship had ended shortly before I showed up on the doorstep. Around this time, Cody and a dude named Chad who worked at a TV station bought the company from Les. I don't know the details, and it would all get a little murky later, but an arrangement was made where Cody basically took over the Heartland Wrestling Association, becoming head trainer, booker, spiritual leader and overlord of all things HWA.

Cody started in the business with Les in 1996, a remarkable worker and loyal soldier. Les, suddenly with a full plate of WWE developmental talent to train in 2001, tasked Cody with running the practices for noncontracted HWA talent and students. Just like that, with a knack for teaching and a willingness to embrace and explore new ideas while staying true to the old-school principles of the Les Thatcher system, Cody Hawk found his true calling as a trainer.

Cody was from Dayton. At 6'2" with a long goatee tied at the end, bleached hair hanging out the back of the ever-present bandana tied around his forehead, he was an imposing figure for a greenhorn like myself. My first teacher and first boss, the sheer weight of the knowledge he possessed was intimidating. Mostly inexpressive, he was a shop foreman who taught passionately but with a sort of deadpan gravitas: Here's how to do the job; here's how to not get yourself killed. Poor behavior or even poor performance on an HWA show might result in a torrent of swearing, thrown furniture and the offender being told to "get the fuck out of my building." Nobody wanted to piss Cody off, and fits of rage were only occasional. For the most part, Cody had a long fuse, especially when it came to teaching in the ring, an area where he possessed incredible patience. He took great pride in molding lumps of clay into efficient soldiers, technically sound products ready to be rolled off the line and stamped with the HWA seal of quality.

It all started for me with back bumps: crawl, walk, run. Taking a back bump is the first thing you learned at HWA and the only thing you did for a while, learning how to attack the mat, breathe out, tuck your chin, pop your hips up, and slap the mat with both palms at the point of impact, evenly dispersing the impact across your shoulders, fingertip to fingertip. Once you've mastered doing it once, next comes doing a few in a row, rolling to your right, getting up in a tight clockwise circle, elbow, fist, knee. "Work left, turn right" was painted on the wall, and it meant, as I discovered, that we always work the left arm or leg of opponents, Irish whips are always left wrist to left wrist, and for positioning purposes, like a dance, we always turn to our right. I had never picked up on this detail in all my years watching.

Once you are proficient at taking a few perfect bumps in a row, you increase the number and the speed at which you fire them: Zero, five, ten, fifteen, twenty bumps in a row. It's arresting to the system at first. Every bump is like a tiny car crash. If you don't learn to expel your breath before you hit the mat, you'll notice the sensation of being hit in the chest with a baseball bat.

Every mechanism must fire at the exact same time, and it all must come together reflexively. You must be able to check everything off the list: palms down, breath out, chin tucked, everything, then attack! – all at once, in an instant, without thinking. As I write this, I could get up from my seat and take a back bump on the kitchen floor in an instant without thinking, like an activated Russian sleeper agent.

I would stand ringside and watch practice. In between drills I would come in and take my bumps, then return to the floor to watch the more experienced students doing cooler shit. Back bumps were all I was allowed to do for now. I graduated to doing 25 in a row, all perfect, a brutal and exhausting experience. I remember working at Perkins one night after practice. I couldn't turn my head. I was like one of those old rubber action figures, I had to comically shuffle my feet in a circle and turn my entire body back and forth between the grill and the pickup window all night.

Next came the basic front flip bump, as you would perform taking a hip toss. Here's where Cody's patience came into play. Eager and aggressive as I was, I wasn't much of a flipper. The idea is to jump straight up, as high as you can, tuck your chin, flip in the air, and land flat in the same place where your feet just were. I would jump my ass up there as hard as I could and flip forward with all my strength, but for some reason my body, once airborne, would defy the laws of physics. I would float to the left, or the right, or backward, or end up facing the opposite direction somehow. I was like a drone that went haywire at takeoff. People put on helmets and protective eyewear when it came time for me to practice my flip bumps. There was no telling which direction I'd go. I grew frustrated, but Cody, ever sagacious, would calmly diagnose every mechanical problem with the bumps, rubbing his beard, working out the equation in his mind. Over and over, he'd tweak every little thing I did wrong until finally he told me ... probably mildly concussed ... to pick a spot on the wall and stay focused on it as I jumped straight up, and at the height of the jump, remain focused on that spot on the wall. Then and only then, finally, at the moment just before gravity takes over, tuck your chin hard.

It worked!

I started doing flip bumps that weren't totally out of control. Not perfect, but that will do for now. I've never been good at flipping and I don't plan to start now. Maybe when I'm in my 50s I'll start busting out my Funksault. Even early on when I started wrestling matches, I'd take standard suplexes, and no matter how hard I tried, instead of going straight over the top 12 to 6, I'd somehow go over at like 2 to 8 or 3 to 9, like somebody was suplexing a giant F'n frisbee.

Next came learning how to lock up, but not even in the ring, still not a part of regular practice. I was brought to an open space on the floor for a lesson with an overachieving wrestler named "High IQ" Quentin Lee, a somewhat portly, bookish type, smarter and more mature than most of us. He had an actual real job with a 401k and shit. He taught me how to circle. Your opponent takes a step in, you take a step, he steps back, you step back, follow him to the right, to the left, always remaining perfectly equidistant from each other and the center of the ring, synchronized. Locking up was different than I was used to from amateur wrestling. I finally got the signal from Quentin, his subtle slap to his shoulder that I'd noticed Ric Flair do a million times. I quickly learned that in pro wrestling, the collar and elbow tie-up always means left hand on the collar, right hand on the elbow. From amateur wrestling, I was so used to coming in and grabbing the back of my opponent's head with my right hand that it was a hard habit to break at first. Opposite, awkward.

Eventually I'd get to be in the ring and learn things like how to grab a headlock or, with my one new back-bumping skill, I could start taking tackles. I started learning to run the ropes. It's all footwork. You have to take the exact number of exaggerated steps on each pass. The goal is to be able to do it with your eyes closed. Everyone's step count is a little different. Mine was about two and three-quarters steps rope-to-rope, turning on my pivot foot and snatching the top rope with my right hand, pulling it under my armpit at a precise moment, my hip hits the middle rope, my weight still underneath me as I redirect because I don't wanna fall to the floor in the case of a turnbuckle breaking, as I'm warned. I think I was about two and a quarter steps in the WCW ring. That was another really cool thing about training at HWA. The remnants of the Developmental days that were left behind, cool shit like ring aprons from SummerSlam and shit, an announce desk from Thunder, but the important thing, the real blessing, was that HWA had an ACTUAL WWE ring, the 20-footer with real ropes, as well as two ACTUAL WCW rings, much stiffer, 18-footers, with shorter, cable ropes. WWE had acquired these and sent them to Cincinnati after the Monday Night Wars, which I had watched play out on TV, ended.

I initially started in the WWE ring, but that thing was super-hard to maintain. It would get all wobbly and shit. I think they sold it. I spent most of my time at HWA in the WCW ring, which was far more practical to travel with. We kept one at the gym and the other in the ring truck to haul to shows on weekends. I became an expert on that WCW ring. I knew every screw and bolt, every board, cable and giant metal hook. As I became Cody's most diligent student, he made me the point man on ring crew, under the ring tightening cables, making sure the mats are taped together tightly and all the ropes were even in strength and flush. Sometimes Cody would rent the ring to other promoters or to nightclubs for random events like Foxy Boxing or whatever (which reminds me, YouTube Renée in Pillow Fight League. ... Excuse me, Renée the Ripper). On those days, Cody and I would bring the ring to the venue and set it up with just the two of us. We could do it really fast, too, and I'd make a little pocket money for that. To this day, if you dropped a WCW ring in my backyard, I bet I could have it up in no time.

As my abilities grew, Cody started to devise a character for me. "I'm gonna make you a stoner or a football player," he said. He eventually decided on a stoner football player. We had Tuesday night TV tapings every week. HWA aired an hour on some little local station on some night at 10:00 or 11:00 p.m. then. Cody decided to run what he called a Sunday showcase, a Sunday afternoon house show type of thing to provide a platform for less-experienced students or those not booked on TV to hone their craft. As it happened, this Sunday showcase, which maybe 15 people attended, would be the event where I'd have my first real match against a veteran Cincinnati wrestler named Gotti.

The age-old saying goes, "Always bring your gear, you never know," and I had already bought a pair of blue football pants in anticipation of this new character Cody had in mind that was obviously gonna pop the territory and drive big revenue. I was told by somebody, I don't remember who, that I would be in the third match, 15 minutes. My balls sucked up into my abdomen. I've never been more nervous. This was it. Fuck. Stay cool. I'd been training officially for about six months. Cody told Gotti, "Put him in stuff and let him get out." That's all we went to the ring with. I didn't expect any different. The backbone of HWA philosophy, and all I knew up to that point was "calling it in the ring."

"You got a name?" the ring announcer asked me. I'm sure I had thought of a million ideas, but I was drawing a blank. This was all happening fast, and I had nothing. I totally froze. A wrestler who went by the name Tack turned to Cody, "He's like the F'n guy from the movie, *Varsity Blues*, Jonathan Moxley!" In the movie the guy's name is Jonathan Moxon. So thankfully, he had actually messed it up. Cody gave the OK sign to the ring announcer. I was busy pissing my pants, so I didn't offer anything. Just like that, I had a name, a name I like to think I've defined as my own. The fact that women wearing whipped-cream bikinis are often lurking around every corner ready to accost me is purely a coincidence.

I sprinted to the ring for some reason, in wrestling shoes and football pants, and 15 minutes later I had a real professional wrestling match under my belt. I don't remember anything about it.

Soon came more matches, always with a more experienced wrestler. I'd go to the ring having no idea what was gonna happen. I'd listen and do what I was told. Nobody told me to do anything I didn't know how to do. There was nothing I hadn't been training and perfecting with endless repetition. Now that I wasn't just doing the moves in a gym and I was in front of people, I was learning on the fly the ebbs and flows of taking the audience on a ride. Everything is meant to garner a reaction, to bring them up, to take them down, to make them cheer, boo, get mad, or pop with joy. I was picking it up. Understanding. Stuff I already knew but didn't know I knew now became clear with the final and most important ingredient added into the mix: the audience.

Back at practice, I was learning more and more advanced things. Now I could move around the ring really well, hundreds of repetitions of various drills had dialed in my footwork and timing. The most reviled of these drills was one of Les's most infamous torture devices, the dreaded "Triple 5s." On the surface, this was a "blow-up drill," simply used to increase one's physical conditioning. We did at TON of conditioning at HWA, which I always attacked with enthusiasm. If there was one thing I knew for sure I could bring to the table, it was the ability to suffer. I'd keep going and going like the Energizer Bunny, no matter what hell I was put through, that much I could promise. After six months, I had developed some serious endurance. Matt Stryker had even taken to calling me Captain Cardio, which I was really proud of. Nevertheless, the Triple 5s were always ominous. It went like this: Irish whip your partner into the ropes, hanging on and sinking down your butt with your arm fully extended, pull him back and whip him to the other side the same way, five times. Your partner reverses and does the same to you, five times. After the fifth, you reverse him and send him off to run the ropes, do a drop down, then leapfrog him as he comes back. As soon as you land, turn and drop down again, leapfrog, repeat five times. When you land after a fifth leapfrog, take off and hit the ropes, step over your partner as he drops down, go under the leapfrog, repeat five times. Grab your partner and send him toward the buckle, he'll do an up and over in the corner, jumping and using his upper body strength to launch himself in the air landing behind you. He runs to the opposite buckle and you follow behind him, another up and over, repeat five times. Your partner sends you running across into the buckle and you do an up and over, repeat five times. It was an all-out, concentrated attack on your heart and lungs, every muscle in your body. There was just no way not to be blown up at the end of it, and that was the point, or at least part of the point.

One horrendous day in the summer, practice was torturous. Cody was pushing us really hard, running us to death with blow-up drills and intense wrestling. Suffocating in this sweatbox, we were hands on knees, gulping for air, doubled over, trying to stay upright as practice came to an end. Please let this be it, I hoped, I was ready to keel over. "Triple 5s," Cody said, smiling like Satan, rubbing his long goatee like F'n Jafar from *Aladdin*. OH, COME ON! I was heartbroken. WTF, dude? The first pair got into the ring, an ice rink by now, slippery with perspiration, and began. They completed the first part, moving in quicksand and slipping a bunch, but when they got to the drop-down/leapfrogs the whole thing fell apart. One guy came crashing down balls first onto his partner's head. They landed in a heap. Cody yelled, "Stop! Get the fuck out of the ring. You're gonna hurt each other."

The mood in the room was tense. While this was going on, I took a few seconds to whisper in my partner's ear. He was less experienced than me, a good athlete but he was dying just like all of us. I knew the ring was slick and hazardous and we were both on our last gasps, but I thought we could get through it if we stayed under control. I sure as hell didn't wanna get kicked out of the ring and yelled at, and I didn't want anybody to ever see me hit the proverbial wall. I was competitive, and on top of that I was Captain Cardio, dammit!

"Take it one thing at a time," I whispered to my partner nervously, watching the ring, cringing at the Triple 5 hell we were about to enter. "We just gotta keep a good pace. Don't rush, follow my lead."

We entered the ring feeling like we were walking the plank. Cody looked annoyed. He's been disappointed already. Send in the next two wimps, I figured he was thinking.

Why is he so mad? I wondered. The door to the promised land, the land of success, of simply being able to call yourself a good professional wrestler, was closely guarded. The closer I got to it, the more intense things became, the more that was asked of me. It was still just a dream for me, this promised land, the actualization of being a good professional wrestler, but I was gonna get there no matter what, success or death. Fuck you, Cody.

I was on a pilgrimage. We began. First whip, nice pace, here we go ... one, two, drop, one, two, drop, OK, now reverse ... good ... easy pace, keep breathing, we got this. Entering phase two, welcome to flavor country. Drop down, get up, nice and easy, now leapfrog, land, soft landing, turn and drop down, smooth sailing. Five times. I stay relaxed, careful not to expend an extra ounce of precious energy. Every step, every movement, every breath is precisely timed and executed. Now I'm the guy running, coaching my partner as we pass each other, feel the beat, the pace, keeping the rhythm. It's like music. Moving to phase three, light on my feet, running corner to corner across the crocodile mile of a canvas like a cat burglar ... one, two, step, jump with both feet, lean my weight in the corner, explode out in one smooth motion, soft landing like a ninja. We're doing it! We're gonna make it. I run behind my partner as he plods toward the corner and encourage him, one, two, three, jump, one, two, three. He's barely getting any height and I'm sliding under him, marching him back to the other corner. He gets his feet up maybe two feet off the mat on his final up-and-over and I dive under, his feet barely clearing my head. WE DID IT!

I'm elated, pissed and vindicated. High on endorphins and a lack of oxygen, brother collapses in the ring and I lean over the ropes, holding myself up. Cody is laughing, pleased, as he begins to explain to the other students the difference between how the first two guys attempted to tackle this exercise and what my partner and I did. I must have done something right. I try to make sense of what Cody's saying, but my heart is beating like a bass drum in my chest, I've sweat out half my body weight, and I feel like I've been in a sauna way too long. I wanna crawl out the garage door into the fresh air. I don't get a gold star, but I feel some type of validation, then all of a sudden ... a lightbulb goes on above my head. I have learned what this drill, this shitty godforsaken fucking drill is really about.

One thing you hear early on in any wrestling school is that if it feels like you're moving too slow, that's probably just right. At first this may seem strange, but what it means is that when you're watching a highspot on TV, maybe Rey Mysterio and Psicosis doing some crazy head scissors, or Flair and Steamboat doing enough arm drags and hip tosses to make your head spin, they aren't moving as fast in real life as it seems on TV. If you get in the ring and just start moving a million miles an hour, not only are you gonna get blown up quicker, your timing will be off and the moves will get screwed up, or – worse yet – someone will get hurt. You don't wanna have what we call "happy feet," the jittery hallmark of a green wrestler. This principle holds true in many other sports as well. *Relax.* Dustin Rhodes, at 52, is still the fastest man in wrestling. When he hits the ropes with that velocity, leapfrogging, running, ducking and stopping on a dime, dropping to his knees to deliver his trademark Goldust punch, I'd be willing to bet he's at a resting heart rate. It's his footwork and timing, honed to perfection from decades of repetition, that make it look so smooth and so fast.

weekend he came down to Cincy to pick me up, and we drove the five hours north on I-75 with the sunroof open. I stayed at his apartment for a couple of days. It was 1997. I was 12, a potent mixture of testosterone, angst and trying-to-figure-out-what-the-fuck-was-going-on-in-the-world brewing inside me. I remember on this trip we went inside a sporting goods store. I had just started junior high wrestling and I was obsessed. All the other kids had nice ASICS gel headgear. I didn't have money to buy cool headgear so I wore some goofy-looking shit from the 1950s that the coaches gave me. It was uncomfortable and uncool, and it always fell off too. I remember lifting the nice, cool ASICS gel headgear while I was in that store in Detroit with my dad. If he would have known, he would have beaten me into a coma.

I'm not sure how I acquired *Around the Fur*. I'm gonna go ahead and say my dad bought it for me because it's a nicer story, but it's entirely possible I shoplifted that too, but let's go with the Disney version. ... Thanks, Dad, for buying me one of my favorite albums ever! ... See, that's just much better, isn't it?

Let's start with the cover art of *Around the Fur*, a photo of a chick in a bikini with a tattoo. I was 12, check! The opening track, the classic "My Own Summer," starts with just the most badass guitar lick (is it a lick?) I've ever heard. I used this song as the entrance music for my debut match in CZW, the first time I wrestled at the ECW arena (which when I was 12 was this mythical place, a castle built of bricks of cool), I would later use the Deftones' "Rocket Skates" as entrance music a time or two, though that's off a different album.

The title track is one of my favorites. Just *chill, chill, chill*, then *SPEAAK*! Going from highs to lows, heavy to mellow, slow to fast, is a hallmark of the Deftones' sound. In research for this piece, I went to Wikipedia and learned this album incorporates elements of new wave and something called shoegaze. ... Cool ... I also learned that upon its release some music critic named Robert Christgau dismissed this classic as a "dud." ... Listen here, Rob, you can go fornicate yourself on an iron stick! Call *Around the Fur* a dud to my face and I'll F'n headbutt you and put you in a Bulldog Choke until you apologize and write a sincere letter of apology to the Deftones. I'll even make you get that shit notarized just to really make it a pain in the ass. Fuck You.

"Be Quiet and Drive," the other big single here, is a classic, just a great song to listen to when you need some space. "Mascara," a spooky song that will affect you. "I'm all about her shade tonight." ... shudder. "Dai the Flu" is a beautiful, aggressive and tragic-sounding song, one of my all-time favorites. Chino, the Deftones' vocalist, is at his best here, displaying an array of emotions and range. "Headup," a collaboration with Max Cavalera of Soulfly/Sepultura is ... Just. The. Shit. Heavy. F'n. Metal. F'n Chino vocals mixed with classic Max vocals ... so unique. Put that shit on and get on a bench press ... guaranteed new PR. This album is me at 12, but also me today. It never gets old.

TAG MATCH

I learned how tag team matches worked and how to cut the ring off and build to a hot tag. We practiced calling a false tag on the fly over and over, with the heel on the outside, briefly grabbing the ref's attention and the babyface making the tag behind the ref's back. The heel in the ring dragging him back to enemy territory and the babyface on the outside grabbing the baton seamlessly and distracting the ref, himself now in a rage, trying to push past the ref, insisting that there was a tag. This gives the opportunity for both bad guys to double-team the good guy in peril illegally, building the heat to a fever pitch. Every player on the board must be in total synchronization with one another. A simple, old-school tactic that's still beautiful when executed to perfection.

A goofy-looking kid the same age as me named Jimmy Turner joined HWA. He had trained with Shark Boy and had some experience on shows. Cody immediately paired us together as a tag team with the stoner football player motif. It was a great fit. I was starting to figure things out, and Jimmy was better than me at that point. Now, we had a gimmick to lean on, which is useful when you're just starting out. Since we weren't good enough yet to just go out and have banger matches with our wrestling skills alone, we could, as the old rule of thumb states, "work the gimmick" while we listened to the veterans in the ring and continued to learn our craft.

We had a lot of fun with it. We called ourselves Necessary Roughness, dressed in crop-top practice jerseys and football pants, black smudges under our eyes. We'd come out to Sammy Hagar's "Mas Tequila," a takeoff on that song from *Jock Jams*, running to the ring, shoulder-bumping each other like juveniles who just got done smashing Red Bulls and shotgunning beers in the back of a pickup truck at a Kenny Chesney concert.

We were given a cheerleader, the stunning Jenelle Sinclair, who later married my buddy Brian, who wrestled under "The Buffalo Bad Boy" Brian Jennings. They're actually expecting their first child just a few weeks before Renée is due. Jenny, with the varsity cheer squad outfit, completed the act. Two hyper buffoons doing the evil hot chick's bidding. People hated us. They would stand up and hurl lewd insults at us, while Jimmy and I ran around hitting the ropes and chest bumping, spiking footballs, doing the *Dumb and Dumber* high-five where we miss each other.

Jenny was actually the star. Women in the crowd became incensed at the sight of her. The shit they would yell at her isn't fit for print, even in this book. That's how much they hated her. It was great because it helped people really get into our matches. We'd bump around like ping-pong balls for the babyfaces. Every time we got an advantage, we'd do some Keystone Cops shit and look like dummies, then toward the finish Jenny would throw brass knuckles into the ring or distract the ref or some such thing, and for that key moment, we would all magically become a well-oiled heel unit and steal the victory.

Jimmy and I would celebrate like Mojo Rawley and Gronk doing shots of Goldschläger at a pool party, and Jenny would parade around in her tiny skirt with a snide rich-girl look on her face. It drove the people insane. Les couldn't stand us. One time he came to a show with Harley Race. Suffice to say, Harley did not enjoy our presentation that evening. Cody had taken over, but Les's name was still synonymous with HWA, and he was absolutely mortified. I'd be willing to bet he's still mad about it to this day.

We became a signature part of the shows, and with our improving skills we started having better and better matches. Jimmy and I would stay for hours after practice to experiment, inventing new double-team moves and sitting around studying wrestling tapes. We had a really good thing going on for about six months — learning, growing, having fun. We were transforming from a couple of goofs into a real tag team.

It all unraveled very quickly, however. Jimmy got a girlfriend and, just like that, it was over. He brought her with us on a road trip to Atlanta for NWA Wildside, and it was puppy love. Soon he started missing practices to hang out with her, then missing shows. Then I never saw him again. I was pretty pissed, but I didn't have time to worry about anyone who didn't have the singular focus that I did.

Girlfriends? I thought. There's no time for girlfriends!

Fuck him then. I quickly resolved to move on without Jimmy. Stryker made me my first pair of trunks, and I bought a pair of used Highspots boots from somebody in the locker room for 75 bucks. I had already started letting my hair get wild, and I just let it keep growing because wrestlers have long hair, I guess. With so much time spent in the weight room, my physique was really starting to get put together. That, coupled with the trunks, boots and long hair, and I dare say I was starting to look like a real pro wrestler.

After being burned by my partner, I became only more obsessed with working harder than everyone. I refused to miss a practice for two years until one day, I came back to Cody's trailer in Dayton, where I was staying after working a double shift at the factory. Bleary eyed, I took an hourlong nap and got ready to leave for training, when Cody said, "You know, it's OK if you miss one practice, dude," and ordered me back to bed.

I was now embarking on a singles run as a babyface at HWA. Although I was improved greatly in the ring, nobody really had any reason to like me, and I didn't really have a character. I just came out all pumped up and generic as fuck, basically the same as the Necessary Roughness thing except I didn't intentionally make myself look stupid. The guys with more tenure and actual characters who the crowd could buy into were on top, and I wanted to be in those cool main-event matches. I was having good matches, getting better and constantly trying new shit, but I felt there was some sort of ceiling I had reached. I was just a random guy.

I needed a hook. That came in the form of a heel turn. I blasted Cody, our top babyface, in the skull with a belt. The tried-and-true student vs. teacher angle. I had a chip on my shoulder at this point, the kid who first walked in the door long left behind, that life gone. I had dedicated my existence to becoming something new entirely, and that dedication had paid off. I was feeling myself a little. I F'n told you I could do it!, I thought. Fuck you.

I wanted to step up and take a swing at the top guys. Cody and I embarked on a great story, filled with bitterness and hatred, where we beat the holy shit out of each other. In an attempt to make the heat look as real as possible, we got into a locker-room-clearing brawl that tore up the entire arena, smashing holes in the wall and destroying equipment. It went on for an awkwardly long time … intense, realistic stuff. I was legitimately hated, and I loved it. I got off on it. I had turned my back on the home team. Cody was the heart and soul of the promotion, loved and respected.

They remembered me as the kid selling sodas; they had no respect for me. Now I was gonna turn around and shove it up their asses.

We went on to have a bloody steel cage match at a show called CyberClash because it was broadcast on the internet for 10 bucks, which was a new concept and felt like a big deal at the time. Les even came out for it. Stepping into a cage for the first time, on the biggest show, as the top bad guy in the promotion, in the match the people came to see, was the coolest moment of my life up to that point.

As I stood in the center of the cage, sneering, middle finger in the air, Piccadilly was a distant memory. I had left every naysayer, every bully, every asshole teacher, every cop, every last one of 'em, in the dust. As far as I was concerned, I was the king of the world. I was 20 years old.

FLICK PICK: LAW ABIDING CITIZEN, 2009
JAMIE FOXX, GERARD BUTLER

Law Abiding Citizen is a thriller and a mindfuck, one protagonist, one antagonist ... or is it? Which is which? Jamie Foxx plays a DA who cuts a deal with a murderer. The problem is, this man murdered Gerard Butler's family. Clyde Shelton (Butler) is much more than just an honorable family man, as we find out, and he wants justice, not a deal. This film makes you ask questions: What would you do if you were in Clyde's shoes? What if it were your family? What is true justice? Is Clyde a vigilante? A hero? ... Or is he no better than the men he's extracting revenge against? Which ... is ... EVERYBODY. Clyde puts the whole F'n system on trial. You will root for Foxx, you will root for Clyde, you will be shocked, appalled and taken on a ride. I don't want to spoil anything, but I implore you to pop some popcorn, toss some Milk Duds and Reese's Pieces in the bowl (I love movie theater snacks), close the blinds, put your phone on airplane mode and watch *Law Abiding Citizen*. If you're anything like me, you will not be disappointed.

HOME AWAY FROM HOME: TORONTO

As I've mentioned, my wife is Canadian. I love Canada. I've had so many great times up there. Renée was born and raised in Toronto. Her family all still live there, so we're there a lot. At least we were before the pandemic. (Aren't you sick of every single thing you try to say coming out with a COVID-era asterisk attached?) Renée is a very proud Torontonian and lived and worked for a long time right in the heart of the action, so she makes a great tour guide. This gave me a whole new appreciation for this town.

My favorite spot is Horseshoe Tavern, a place with a rich history and a secret, glory-hole-esque pick up window in the wall for the A&W Burgers. We've spent a lot of time walking along Queens Quay looking at the water or Trinity Bellwoods. Toronto in the summer is beautiful. I've biked half that goddamn city. So many cool streets and eclectic neighborhoods. My favorite bar, around Queen and Ossington, was called Lipstick and Dynamite. Notable mention: Sweaty Betty's.

Toronto is a melting pot, like many places. Great restaurants and the best street meat, but no matter where I am in Canada my favorite shit is Tim Horton's. I can't get it all the time so it's like a treat for me. I was doing a movie called *Cagefighter*, and we filmed in Regina, Saskatchewan. Every day they came to me and asked what I wanted to eat. Sushi? There's a fancy steakhouse in town? Steamed chicken breast on a bed of greens under a chocolate fountain? Every time my answer was the same: "You know what I want."

"Tim Hortons?" they'd sigh.

"Hell, yeah," I confirm.

I miss Toronto. I can't wait to go back. It's a hotbed for wrestling, and the fans are great. We did TV at the Air Canada Centre, which felt to me like a Borg cube from Star Trek. Cold and utilitarian.

I loved the Ricoh Coliseum, where we did house shows. Renée's brother Erik does sound for concerts and told me the Ricoh has shitty acoustics. "Low roof and a big concrete floor," he said. Still, I liked the Ricoh better, even though I almost crashed into a streetcar more than once trying to find the entrance to that place. Maybe I liked it better just because I liked house shows better, but the Ricoh had a personality. Actually, I had one of my favorite matches in WWE at the Ricoh. ...

TORONTO, RICOH COLISEUM
MARCH 12, 2016

At least one of my favorites that existed on television. In WWE, during the time I was there, the majority of your week was untelevised. You'd wrestle matches on house shows around the country or international tours. After the brand split in 2016, your typical domestic schedule was reduced to four days a week: three house shows, one TV show. It occurs to me that by doing it that way, 75 percent of all the wrestling you did, 75 percent of your career, would basically have never happened. It's kinda weird to think about.

House shows were just wrestling shows. A night at the matches. Often in smaller towns in older buildings, buildings with character. I think of that little building in White Plains, New York, the West Texas loops, that little hockey rink in Barrie, Ontario. I loved those atmospheres. I wrestled Cena and A. J. Styles in front of a hot, standing-room-only Palm Springs crowd in some kind of carpeted event room where I swear to God there was a bar mitzvah going on next door.

Of course, we did the major venues, MSG, the O2 in London, the Forum in L.A., but I always had a soft spot for house shows that had a vintage, old-school vibe. It's nice to feel like a rock star, but I always savored the feeling of just being a "rassler." When I first started on the road, they hadn't even started using the stage with the ramp and the screens at house shows, just a curtain. I kind of liked that better. Eventually to enhance the live-event experience, they would bring in a host who would kind of vamp with the audience before showtime. They would lead trivia games on the screen. I did not care for that. Play some fuckin' AC/DC and open the doors. You're overthinking this shit. Don't distract the children with all the lights and screens, just let them walk in the door and see the ring for the first time. That's the magic.

I was coming off a hot PPV main event in Cleveland with Roman and Brock Lesnar, a triple-threat match where the winner got the title shot at Mania. That's one of my favorite matches too. Michael Hayes told me afterward, "You had 'em! They thought you had it won!"

I did not, in fact, have it won, but I was still pumped. Afterward, we were in Brock's dressing room, and Paul Heyman said, "That right there, that could have been the main event of WrestleMania."

I genuinely appreciated the praise, though I doubted my paycheck would reflect that. That show was still a ways away and there was a gap to bridge. As it happened, I would get the title shot after all, at a Network special called Roadblock, three weeks before WrestleMania, at the Ricoh.

I remember standing ringside at TV talking with Hunter and Michael. Vince had booked the match with no plan. He had just told Hunter, "Figure out how to get out of it. I look forward to watching it."

HHH was taking the belt to Mania against Roman. I was taking the L for sure, but I was going into a thing with Brock, so I couldn't just get Pedigreed and left for dead in Toronto. Bit of a tricky booking situation. How does everyone come out looking good? That was the question we mulled over.

"Well, isn't it obvious?" I asked. "We go sixty. Broadway, baby."

Hunter and Michael laughed that off immediately. For real. A 60-minute time-limit draw. What's so funny? I was at least half serious. I would've done it.

Internally, there was something in the air about the match.

Pat Patterson came up to me and gave me the classic, "Do you know who was just talking about you?"

Sigh. "Who, Pat?"

"Nobody! That's who!" before laughing uproariously and saying, "Oh! My God! I can't wait to watch that match!"

There was some kind of understanding, something that went unsaid about what we would do on the night. Pat knew. It would be a classic, old-school kind of wrestling match. The Ric Flairs and Harley Races, the kings of the Broadway, of calling it in the ring, had seemed to have passed that torch to HHH. They called him a ring general. That's what you aspire to be when you walk into training on your first day. Those are the guys you study. They say this guy is good. I had worked with H before, of course, when we did Shield vs. Evolution, in a couple of badass six-mans on PPV that went all over the building, but those matches were a different animal.

I was in the middle of the most ridiculous run of consecutive shows, wrestling long matches most every night. I was run down and pulverized. I was starting to go braindead and giving less and less fucks every day, but I basically lived in the ring at this point. My confidence that I could bend any audience to my will was high. Little red wagons and shit aside, when I'm in my element and the bell rings, I know exactly who I am and what I'm capable of. I ponder HHH, this … ring general. Let's find out just how good this motherfucker really is.

I thought back to HWA. My penultimate match with Cody Hawk. It was right before I left for Puerto Rico. Cody wasn't sure what the finish should be, so he told me he would decide in the ring, after 60 minutes. We did the finish in overtime; 63 minutes had elapsed. We went to the ring without a winner planned and not one single iota of a spot called. It felt like my final test. If I completed this task satisfactorily, I would be a legitimate professional wrestler. That's all I ever wanted, really, just to cross the barrier from the crowd to the ring at the Red Barn.

Now, in 2016, I'm this jet-setting cartoon character who doesn't know what time zone he's in, shaking hands and kissing babies, talking in corporate buzzwords on morning radio. This was a chance to get back to the original goal. To be a professional wrestler. "Train hard and master your craft," I remembered. This wouldn't be about gaudy Mania entrances, who had what belt, or any of that shit. There would be ego involved, but this would be all about the craft.

Friday night, the night before Roadblock, I would be in the main event of the house show in Montreal. Toronto is drivable, under six hours. I was riding with R-Truth and Swag, who were on early. I instructed them to go on and get to the next town instead of waiting all night for me. I would catch an early morning flight. At the end of the night, I peeled off my sweaty shirt and threw a hoodie on before catching a ride to the Fairfield Inn by the airport, and I noticed they have a bar. I've never seen a Fairfield with a bar. Score. I sat down a few minutes before closing time and pounded a couple drinks. I set my alarm, lay down and got two hours of sleep. The next morning, I landed in Toronto and made my way to a Holiday Inn Ronnie and Swag staked out the night before. I dropped my bags in my room before meeting a Suburban downstairs that would take me to a department store for an autograph signing. For hours, I signed a simple "DA" on 8x10s, action figures and foam belts, taking pictures and meeting the Toronto faithful.

I returned to the room and tried to squeeze in a short power nap. I met Truth downstairs. He was sitting in the SUV, Bluetooth in, lost in creativity, working on a rap album. I sat in the passenger seat and went to YouTube on my phone. I played some bootleg footage of the most recent HHH singles matches and began visualizing potential scenarios as Swag hopped in the car. We were by the airport. The drive to the venue took a long time, a lot of traffic. I was in no rush. When we got close to arena, finally getting off the Gardiner Expressway, we grabbed food and supplies. There's a little shopping center I know with a Goodlife Fitness not far. There's a Starbucks right there and a few restaurants. We stocked up on all necessary provisions. Truth figured I'd be in a hurry to get to the building. I tell him it's cool, I still gotta hit the LCBO. There's one right across the parking lot. I walked in and picked up a bottle of Jack for later. It's going on 6:00 p.m. A short time later, we arrived at the Ricoh, fans crowded around the garage entrance, screaming and holding signs. We pulled inside through the door in the brick wall. We found an empty locker room space and I chilled. It was 6:30 p.m. I waited. I waited for it.

This Network special was cool. It was like a hybrid PPV/house show. We would have announcers, the fancy black barricades and the whole camera crew, but limited hoopla. Unspectacular house show entrance ramp, long walk down the aisle. A little more poorly lit, it would resemble the classic footage, the darkened, smoky arena with one light hanging over the ring.

I loved it.

Finally, Michael finds me. "Hunter's in his dressing room," he tells me.

He looks a little nervous. A sign that it's time to start putting this thing together. I wasn't gonna make the first move.

The lack of conversation between Benoit and Regal, Les and Cody's voices in my head. The religion I was brought up on that matches were to be called in the ring. It was still ingrained in me. Where I started, getting caught going over your highspots before a show, or even talking about a match beforehand, was viewed as a sign of weakness. I knew Michael would find me, but if he didn't, I was prepared to walk right to the ring.

There is a weird, old-school ego thing that goes on between "call it in the ring"-minded guys, and it's admittedly stupid. Neither guy is gonna want to be the first to get too excited or have an idea. Both will just be like, Sure, whatever, we'll figure it out. Even though you are working together, there is still some kind of weird chess-game battle going on. Nobody wants to make the first move. This is what was happening tonight. That's the way I wanted it.

This scenario felt specifically tailored for my particular sensibilities, a gift from the gods of wrestling. An actual Mania main event would be pre-planned and produced to the hilt, rehearsed move-for-move with all kinds of run-ins and bells and whistles. While that's great and all, that's not what I set out to do as a teenager. If Hunter was really the shit, then I wanted to go out there and call it in the ring with him. If he's supposed to be the new measuring stick, then fuck it, let's see what's up.

I walked into Hunter's dressing room and sat down. We split a stack of special-event posters to autograph. He was relaxed.

"What do you wanna do?" he asks.

"I dunno, what do you wanna do?" I return.

He doesn't have a real answer. He chews gum. The game is afoot. We sit next to each other and sign posters for another 30 minutes, making idle conversation, not talking about the match at all. The mood intensifies every time Michael pops his head in, looking for something to write down. It's a full-on game of chicken that finally ends in a draw. Doors are open, and the show is about to begin. We need a finish. It's immediately clear we're on the same page and see the story the same way. There will be a false finish where HHH barely gets a foot under the bottom rope and referee John Cone seemingly counts three before waving it off. As close as you can possibly get.

I think of a spot I did on *Raw* recently where I kinda tightrope-walked the railing and delivered an elbow drop on my opponent through the announce table. If HHH just moved, I figured I could crash through the table. That would be my demise. Perfect finish. I left to go get dressed, as if I even really needed to, and to start getting loose. I returned a short time later. There were a couple quick possible bullet-point moments called, a few maybe this's and maybe that's, but I left a few minutes later and wouldn't see Hunter again until we locked up.

I was in the hole-in-the-wall locker room we had found, listening to "History of Bad Men" by the Melvins when I wondered if I knew how to do a Sharpshooter. I sought out a body. I think it was one of the FTR guys who I had lie on the floor in the training room while I applied it. I knew that I knew, I just wanted to double-check because I never do it. Of course I knew how. Duh. I texted Nattie and mentioned that if the situation presented itself, I might wanna bust out her finisher later. As I suspected she would, Nattie approved with glee.

The abbreviated card of this Network special went by fast, and all of a sudden, it was time. Kinda snuck up on me. That's what you get when you show up to the building so late. I walked down the hallways of the Ricoh in my scummy outfit, tossing on the same leather jacket I walked into the building with as HHH made his grand entrance. I could hear it, the shitty acoustics reverberating through the walls, Motörhead and the water spitting and all that. I was sure he looked like a superstar, all impossibly muscular and chiseled of granite.

A camera catches me as I turn a corner and head into Gorilla. It warms my heart to see Pat here. He has come to Toronto just to watch this match in person. His presence justifies my confidence. I wonder what Les and Cody would think right now. ... Would their confidence in me be the same? I see Pat's smile and feel his firm hand grab my shoulder as I pass. Pat knew. I pause at the curtain. Drop into a push-up position and complete one hindu pushup, pop up and stretch my hands over my head. Scotty Armstrong, producer, timing the show, looks at me and says, "Thirty-eight minutes from right now."

I think it was 38. "Don't we own the network?" I ask.

Scotty laughs. My music hits, the familiar "*RRRRRR*" I hear every night. I walk. It's a long aisle.

The storyline has been set up to be a sort of "this rogue might hijack WrestleMania" kinda thing. It's pretty cool. If I win, shit, I'm the champ. I'm main-eventing Mania, Brock, H and Roman can sort it out for themselves. Of course, nobody truly believed that was gonna happen. It was my job to make them believe, if only for a moment. I think I held some hope deep down that Vince was gonna wake up on the jet, be pissed at himself for falling asleep and be like, "Fuck it, we're gonna *shaaake* things *uuuupp.*"

But I knew what my job tonight was. Get HHH over as a defending World Champion and try to look like a million dollars in the process. To this day, I don't think I've ever looked like a million dollars, but I've looked good a few times. However much money it takes to hit your credit limit, run out of cash, and pass out during a lap dance at a strip club, I've looked that many dollars good at least.

I'm where I need to be. It's real to me at this point as I walk. Fuck this guy. Big Bad HHH. Where you from again? Please. Oh, sorry, am I supposed to be more intimidated by the 108 world titles you booked yourself to win or your physique? I saw those ads you did with Ronnie Coleman for that creatine shit, you guys looked good. But you ever been hit over the head with a five-pound weight in a sock? Before we talk about you being a ring general, I just wanna mention that the sexual tension between me and Steph in those interviews was just good acting. She's a hell of a performer. You're supposed to be so much better than me, but I'm just not buying it. If I'm such a fucking cockroach, then stomp me out, man. Do it. I fucking dare you. The Game? Dude, get the fuck out of here with that. You ain't shit.

Ring introductions. I expect to be treated by many like a street rat. I don't seek any approval from the audience at this point in the show. I don't need to. I'll have them later. The crowd is enamored with HHH's presence, as I knew they would be. HHH on what feels like a special event for the crowd is cool. He's a big-PPV, Mania-only guy. They see my ass every time we come to town. Extra big-star bonus? Something must be up. Hybrid house show/PPV energy. Tonight is weird, man. We both get boos and cheers. It's a soup of reactions with those weird acoustics. I love it. I'm in no rush.

The bell rings. There are dueling chants of "Let's-Go-Ambrose" and "Tri-ple-H." All I'm concerned with is what my opponent is gonna do. Make a move. We start slow like I knew we would. I beckon HHH to the center of the ring and he goes all Flair with the headlock to the hammerlock. I take a tackle, AHA! I knew it! I see it in his eyes. This is what I was hoping for, HHH with a hard-on, out to prove a li'l sumthin. The crowd gets a little restless early, it's expected. This tempo is unusual, old-school. We just keep staring each other down between exchanges, going back and forth, setting the pace. Don't let the crowd start calling your match for you. We get to work. We wrestle, work over body parts, bump and sell. Calling shit back and forth, improvising, sometimes communicating without words.

Later, the crowd is on fire as I climb the turnbuckle and drop a diving elbow to the floor onto my boy H. We're having a hell of a match, super-fun, everything I could have asked for. I lie on my back after the impact and give a little crotch chop/"suck it" deal, as sleazy as I can make it. It's fitting. This dude was always making dick jokes. Like we're sitting at TVs at ringside, a bunch of people going over the main event segment and Hunter's there, he's asked his opinion and he makes a dick joke. Everybody laughs cuz they're supposed to. Then another *South Park* kinda joke. Then more laughter, then another fucking stupid DX joke that I might have laughed at when I was F'n 12 and you guys were cool. I was always like: WTF?! Why does everyone put these jokes over? We've got work to do!!!

It appears, ever so briefly, that I may shock the world and hijack WrestleMania. I have HHH prone on the announce table and start pounding the piss out of his eyebrow with my fists. I'm in fifth gear, smelling blood. I'm invincible, but inevitably I will fly too close to the sun ... and get burned. That time is now. I crash through the table as the crafty old pro simply rolls out of the way.

HHH slides into the ring to take the count-out victory. There's surely no getting up after that catastrophe. Nah, fuck it. I ain't going down like this. "Six ... seven ..." the ref counts as I crawl from the wreckage, physically damaged beyond repair, but mentally undeterred. "Eight ... nine ..." I manage to bring myself to my feet and with every bit of will I have, slide into the ring, and beat the count. An act of defiance that spits in the face of my rival and gives me one last moral victory. I knew HHH was waiting in the ring, ready to put a slug in my skull. I knew I'd eat a Pedigree as soon as I made it in. Fuck him. He's gonna have to kill me. I went out on my shield. The Ricoh has seen something special.

Pat was overjoyed. Hunter was blown up. I had another town to make.

I stood soaked in sweat and talked with Tex, Renée's dad, backstage. He's a concert promoter and is always around the venues in Toronto. It's that time in the magical afterglow after an event, the house lights come up and the crew is tearing down. Guys are dangling from the ceiling, attached to ropes by carabiners. The sound of the wooden boards of the ring clacking as they're stacked, of road cases being moved around. The smell of spilled beer and stale popcorn.

I shower and jump in the SUV with Truth and Swag. I sit in the backseat drinking as we sit in traffic. Buffalo and Jenny had driven up and were in the audience too. They meet us at the hotel bar. There's no other patrons or fans. I can just chill and hang out with my friends in peace. I'm tired and happy. It's a great night.

The next morning, it's a painful walk from my bed to the shower, where I stand under water turned up as hot as I can stand it for 20 minutes. Gotta prime these muscles to get back to work. Then it's back in the car for a drive to Erie, Pennsylvania, for a spot show where I'd wrestle yet another main event, thank God against Brodie, who I know will take care of me. I'm feeling like Homer Simpson after he failed to successfully jump Springfield Gorge. Then it's a drive to Pittsburgh for TV where I see Hunter. He's real beat up, but the pride is evident in his face. That twinkle in his eye you never get to see, almost like he had reconnected with a little part of himself, that part of him that just wanted to be a "rassler."

Vince loved it. Steph was really stoked about it too. Pat can't stop talking about it. He's asking people in catering: "Oh! My god! Did you see that match?!" This all makes me feel good.

I'm proud every time somebody comes up to tell me how much they enjoyed watching it, that it felt really unique.

That match doesn't have any historical significance and will probably just be another one lost in the annals of time. I doubt you'll find that shit on Peacock or whatever, but I hope the people that were there have fond memories of it. Maybe it was the first show they brought their kids to, or it was just a fun night out with the gang drinking giant cans of Molson Canadian and watching some wrestling. A night at the matches. Maybe some kid got a blow job in the parking lot. I'd like to think so.

I'd go on to wrestle Hunter a few more times, in places like Belgium and the UK. We always had dope matches. Turns out that HHH kid can work. He's just gotta do something about those skinny calves.

2008 CHUNK

2008, SOME BAR, SOMEWHERE IN OHIO

"Staple it to my cheek," this guy says.

He's backstage, holding a staple gun and wants me to staple a dollar bill to his face in the ring tonight. Sure, buddy. I was wrestling a guy named Drake Younger. He was affable, but I didn't know anything about him other than he seemed from our conversation to be something of a hardcore stylist.

"Yeah, if you want," I tell him, though I have no intention of using a staple gun. Truth be told, I didn't even really wanna be there, on a Tuesday night in some dive in front of 50 people. I don't even know why I still do shows like this ... what's the point? Just trudging along aimlessly because it's the only thing I know how to do. Everyone on the card is wearing gothic face paint and falling on their heads, attempting moves they have no idea how to properly execute. They are all dressed like Jeff Hardy. I am depressed. Nonetheless, I go out for my match with this Drake. I enjoy wrestling, at least, and I took off work for this. The few bucks I make tonight will barely cover my gas, but I'm here — might as well grab my guitar and go bang out a tune. We're having a fun match. This Drake dude's easy to work with ... he sells his ass off. It gets a little wild. We fight all over the place, calling shit on the fly. Drake does a Cactus Flip off the bar ... the crowd is into it. I start coming to life, lost in the moment. I am happy. In the ring, I hit Drake in the head with a stop sign and that staple gun falls out of his shorts onto the dingy mat. There's a flyer stuck to Drake's sweaty back advertising 2 for 1 margarita night or something. I look at the staple gun. I look at the flyer. Eh, why not? I grab my opponent around the chin and place the flyer to his cheek, raise the staple gun above my head like a scepter and hear a collective "WTF" from the audience. I place the proverbial barrel on his face, grit my teeth and use all the might in my bicep to squeeze the trigger. There is a satisfying *CLICKCLACK*. I've heard plenty of *OOOHS* and *AAAHS*, plenty of pops, cheering, or booing. Plenty of whatever desired response I wanted to elicit from an audience. This was a particular reaction I had never garnered before, however. It was a different energy. It was … disgust, shock, revulsion. Cover-your-eyes-and-look-away-type shit, I couldn't really put my finger on it, but I liked it. It was a new feeling, a small hit of a new drug pumping through my veins for the first time. As I got in the truck to drive home in the snow that night, still feeling good, I didn't think much of it. Tonight was just a lark. I had no idea I was already addicted.

In 2008 I was carrying a lot of baggage. Four years ago, I had peeled out of the driveway and hit the road without looking back. But old demons had been clinging to the vehicle's undercarriage the whole time and were catching up with me, as well as new ones I met along the way that were chasing me down, visible in the rearview mirror. I just kept my blinders on and gunned the accelerator like always. Now my transmission was shot and I was on the side of the road in the middle of a barren desert with a full tank of gas that couldn't take me anywhere. Not that I knew which direction to go anyway. There was nothing in sight.

I'd bought into everything. I did everything I was supposed to do. "Train hard and master your craft." What a load of shit.

I did it all, waking up in the middle of the night to drink protein shakes, flexing in the 8x10s. Bringing stacks of video tapes to the post office, sending them out to any promotion on earth whose address I could find at the library. I once called Tommy Dreamer nonstop for 48 hours straight until he picked up and wouldn't leave him alone until he booked me in a dark match. About a dozen different people at WWE told me I was hired over the years, but none of them ever called me back. Terry Taylor told me he was taking over talent relations at TNA, and I was gonna be the first guy he got hired. That was two years ago; still haven't heard from him. Puerto Rico dried up. … They waited until I went home for Christmas to tell me they couldn't afford to bring me back, but they would still be sending the $3,000 they owed me. I didn't expect I'd ever see that money and I never did. I couldn't get booked anywhere I wanted to work, and on top of that, HWA shut down over some money shit. HWA had been my home and the only source of stability I'd ever had in my life. It messed me up. I was angry, bitter and confused.

For a while, I didn't panic. With the lack of wrestling opportunities present, I had time to make some cash at a real job and I ended up with a gig as a personal trainer. I enjoyed helping people get into shape and made a lot of friends at the gym. I'd work all day from morning to evening, working out in between clients, then I'd train till 11:00 p.m., at Sacan Martial Arts, where I'd discovered submission grappling. After that I'd go back to the flophouse apartment I shared with Ricker, who's now wrestling for NXT under the name L.A. Knight. Back then he called himself Dick Rick. From here, Buffalo, who lived across the street, would come over with a six pack and we'd discuss what trouble to get into that night. Maybe we'd go to a dive up the street called the Back Door or go to whatever bar where it was ladies' night. Sometimes I'd get talked into going to a nightclub called Metropolis, which I hated. It was always packed with girls, but it was a dance club and I sure as hell don't dance. To this day I'd rather get a root canal than go to one of those clubs on the Strip. I like a comfortable stool and jukebox. Often the party came to us. That apartment was a beacon for an endless procession of stupidity and destruction. I think people liked to come over because you could trash our place and we wouldn't notice. I didn't have a bed. I slept on a blanket on the floor, which was fine because I hardly ever slept.

To say Buffalo is a die-hard Buffalo Bills fan would be quite the understatement. His apartment, with so much Bills memorabilia, looked like the stadium gift shop: everything from the glasses and coasters to the shower curtain and the toilet paper sported the Bills logo. The funny thing to me was how he could love something so much that brought out such profuse and uncontrollable rage in him. It was a paradox. If he loved the Bills so much, why did he get so angry when he watched them play? Why did he call them such horrible names? It seemed exhausting to be brimming with so much hate for the duration of a whole game, but every Sunday during the season he managed to scream obscenities for four quarters straight without taking a breath, vocal chords strained, veins popping out of his forehead, steam coming out of his ears. I feared his head would pop off. It was like a scene from *Total Recall*. The first time I witnessed this phenomenon I thought maybe he had taken some acid and was hallucinating, storming the beaches at Normandy in his mind, fighting off a regime of lizard people. No, turns out he was just watching the first two minutes of a meaningless regular-season game. That's passion for the game. So when we started a flag football team, Buffalo naturally nominated himself captain and insisted on playing quarterback.

He took it very seriously. He wore one of those little things on his arm with plays written on it and would yell at us for running routes incorrectly. "*RIIICKKKERR! UP AND OUT, GODDAMNIT! UP. AND. OUT!*" One time I let a TD slip through my fingers, and before I could even get back to the bench, he was assaulting me with a 9-iron he had inexplicably acquired. On game nights when everybody was back at the apartment drinking beer and hanging out, Buffalo would make us sit down and review the game tape Ricker had on his camcorder. He would swear at the TV, pausing and rewinding, dressing us down for our incompetence at the top of his lungs. After we lost enough games, he started developing a twitch. One time the opposing team intercepted a pass and ran it back to the end zone. The guy spiked the ball, and since it was the ball we brought, Buffalo took this as the ultimate sign of disrespect and a donnybrook broke out, which actually served to finally bring us together as a team. We had recruited Mario to play for us, and the poor guy ended up carried off the field with a broken nose and a concussion.

For the time being, I had enough to distract me from the fact that my career was basically nonexistent. Then I got let go from the gym because I wasn't an actual certified trainer, and everything changed. A new manager came in and said I had to get this expensive certification to stay on. I can get it, I told him, no problem. I didn't have nearly enough money for it, but I certainly wouldn't if they fired me, I argued. I didn't like that guy. Now I was back to working shitty temp-agency jobs at warehouses and factories. I couldn't even afford a membership at the gym where I had just been walking around like I owned the place.

I used to date this girl who it turned out had a pretty serious drug problem. It didn't seem like a problem to me at the time. ... It just meant she always had drugs. She introduced me to snorting Klonopin, which is a terrible idea and, needless to say, not a useful skill. Now that I had nothing to do some days but sit on the floor, staring at the wall waiting for promoters to get back to me, it seemed like as good a way as any to pass the time. I couldn't afford any coke, but I'd sit there with the six-pack of Milwaukee's Best that I would get for $3.49 from the Pony Keg and stare at that wall getting dialed the fuck in. I would cut promos in my head. When shit got really good, I'd be walking around in a circle in my little empty room, practically foaming at the mouth, spitting and swearing at my reflection against the streetlights in the window. I would write stuff down in a little notebook: lines, concepts, phrases, ideas. I had a platform now.

That dude Chad had the rights to the HWA name, and he was trying to get something started. It wasn't even remotely the same thing, but it was something. A dude named Tatum was in on it, and he was running weekly shows at the Sorg Opera House in Middletown, Ohio. An aptly named city, it's halfway between Cincinnati and Dayton. The Sorg was for sure haunted. I didn't need to take the ghost tour I was offered to see that. An opera theater that held regular screenings of *The Rocky Horror Picture Show* but didn't have much else going on, The Sorg, being in the heart of downtown in a town that wasn't really Cincinnati and not really Dayton, was happy to have anybody wanting to run any type of show there. These shows didn't draw well, anywhere from 15 to 100 people max, mostly friends of the wrestlers who probably got in for free, but I was happy to have a forum to unleash my frustration, particularly because they did a little weekly recap video and put it on YouTube, which was still kind of a new tool at the time and would open up a world of possibilities.

I started cutting promos every week. The dark and creepy Sorg ambience matched my mood. I felt like a human cockroach, surviving under a rock. Once a week I'd scurry out from the shadows into the light to stab someone in the face with a fork, as I had recently taken to doing, then I'd reach deep down into my guts, pulling out all my pain and torment, verbally displaying it on the table for the world to see. I was turning inward. Instead of running away from, ignoring, or attempting to dull the negativity and pain, be it past or present, self-inflicted or not, I embraced it. I lived in it, let it transform me. New life began, crawling from the primordial ooze and taking over my body. I would push my scratchy, drug-addled voice to its limit and an exploding, molten river of emotional instability would scorch anything in its path.

I didn't even care if the camera was on. I was living this, electricity and venom running through my veins as I tried on my new skin. I had died in that dilapidated Opera House in squalor and obscurity and had been reborn to see the world with new eyes. Fuck 'em all. What is "making it"? I don't need anybody's permission to be me. I don't care what anybody thinks about me. The entire world in and out of this business either hates me or doesn't give a fuck about me anyway. They can't stop me from creating. I'll create the art as it should be and it can be as good as anything out there, whether there's five or five thousand people watching. You're not better than me, with your money and your contracts and your fancy lights and TV. Fuck you. I liked the idea of this YouTube. Nobody might ever see what I do today, but a decade or two from now when I'm dead and gone it might be like an obscure LP someone finds in a record store. It'll exist out there forever for someone to appreciate. I still had my orange spray-painted MOX jacket I'd made on the roof in Puerto Rico. I still wore trunks and boots, but I had started wearing this creepy rubber old-man mask. He had a bald head, a mustache and smoked a cigar. My mom had gotten it for me for Halloween when I was a kid. It was the only one the store had left. All the popular characters and bright, colorful masks were gone, but this thing was so strange it was surprisingly effective at being disturbing. Some fans would laugh and try to make fun of me at first, coming to the ring in a stupid rubber mask ... that is, until the violence began. I would make the whole scene uncomfortable and leave people feeling weird. Not so funny when there's attempted murder going on in front of you.

I devised a story where Jake Crist, a tremendous worker and one of my favorite opponents, beat me by kicking me in the head an egregious amount of times. I didn't actually know anything about post-concussion syndrome at the time. I was raised on the "walk it off" method of injury treatment my entire athletic life, but I think that's the concept I kind of stumbled on to. The need to avenge both the loss and the traumatic brain injury I was still feeling the effects of in storyline, visible in every promo I did, spurred me on in a vicious pilgrimage to cripple my adversary. I wasn't trying to do some lame shit like pin a babyface and take his belt. I spent months literally trying to murder him. I was playing with dark, gritty concepts and getting fully lost in the narrative. This story was as real to me as anything else in the world ... maybe more so. Cashing checks at the gas station and staring at dead-eyed coworkers in the break room was like living in a world of robotic monotony. Back in wrestling, now things were alive, luminescent and real. I could feel all of it. I took pleasure in my fingernails scraping at the bottom floor of society, coming up bloody and dirty.

I took a long run one night with my portable CD player. Four miles from the apartment, a general idea came to me under the moonlight. I heard a couple of sentences echoing in my brain, but it was more of a concept or a theme than it was some fabricated, word-for-word speech. I saw it. I didn't know exactly how it would come out, but I knew I had the promo of a lifetime. I loaded that bullet in the chamber for now. I had just the place to unload it. I had another booking coming up with a group called Insanity Pro Wrestling, 90 miles west in Indianapolis. They ran a good show and I'd worked for them here and there over the years, but a few months back when I was really down and still working at the gym, I got a call from a guy named Dan. He had an idea for the top program at IPW: me and a guy named Drake Younger. I remembered Drake. I was just happy to hear from anyone at that point and I agreed to come in.

I may have wrestled here at the Salvation Army Community Center at Fountain Square in Indianapolis before, but after my recent evolution, or maybe devolution, to my baser instincts, I was, for all intents and purposes, a brand-new creature. I walked in as something like an adolescent carnivore – dangerous, aggressive, but without its legs fully underneath it yet, new to the world, gaining confidence and testing the boundaries of its environment. That would soon change. We quickly moved to set up a main event with me and Drake for the IPW championship. Here, we executed the first key moment in the story. Drake, our protagonist and hometown hero, pinned me clean in a fairly fought and contested straight-up wrestling match. That set the table. As the crowd cheered and the referee handed him the belt, I heard the people in the audience.

"Loser!" they taunted me. "Go home, weirdo!"

They loved Drake. Nobody loved me. Why not? I tried really hard. I didn't break any rules. I did it your way ... what's your problem with me? He's supposed to be better than me cuz he pinned my shoulders to the mat for three F'n seconds? And who are you people? What makes you so special? I don't need your love. You're no better than me, and neither is this motherfucker! I lambast Drake, and pull a fork from my boot. I proceed to maim him, mercilessly and repeatedly, tearing at the flesh on his face with my weapon. There's blood, a lot of blood. Officials finally break up the attack; Drake is in bad shape. It's an unpleasant scene.

I move through the curtain to backstage with a camera in pursuit. I'm covered in my adversary's blood. It's on my face, in my hair, streaked down my chest, dried and sticky. I smell of iron. A backstage interviewer approaches, attempting to ask me questions. I'm in my own world, waving my fork at the camera and too close to her face for comfort, wielding it like a conductor's baton as I assess tonight's situation in staccato prose.

She attempts to leave, and I fear I have offended her. I'm just trying to answer her questions. I ask her, "Did I lose?"

I explain that I don't feel like I lost. It was a good night, an exciting night, an adrenaline-fueled, high-stakes title match. "I felt ALIIIVE!" I tell the camera.

I don't even mind that I got cut in the head. I don't mind that I cut Drake Younger's head cuz I just like ... to feeeel reaaally really alive. I like to drive really fast. I like it when I feel blood pouring out of my head and I hear it hit the canvas with the little sound that blood makes when it hits the canvas. I like to feel my fingernails, and this thing here digging into the forehead of somebody else. I like to feel when it hurts a little bit cuz I like to feel alive. I like to go to bars and bang really ugly girls. I just like to ... I'm just a sick guy. I'm really ... I'm really a dirty guy, but I really love it cuz I really love feeling alive. In December, Drake Younger, if you've got any balls, we're gonna dance again for the world title and you're gonna feel more alive than you've ever felt in your life. ... But as much time passes bell to bell, you're gonna wish you were dead for Every. Single. Second. Of it.

I chase the cameraman away. Somewhere in this moment, in this rambling, incoherent excuse for a promo, some final piece of a puzzle clicked into place. In that place where you lose yourself and find yourself*. This creature had reached full maturity. I was now a fully formed entity.

The girl in this promo was actually my friend, the illustrious Jill Shields, one of my favorite people. She did an exceptional job of looking terrified, mostly because she had never met me nor done anything like this before, and she was actually terrified.

The program with Drake was a success, and our matches became more outrageous and violent each month. I was finding a real groove, developing a style that suited both my character and personality. A polished product off the HWA line, now repurposed with a rubber mask and thumbtacks sticking out of its back, wielding sharp weapons.

At an afterparty after one IPW show, we sat around drinking and watching the previous month's show on DVD, so much smoke hanging in the air even the neighbors were probably high. I was feeling good, and not just cuz I had a good ecstasy hookup in Indianapolis. I wasn't creating work that I hoped somebody would appreciate some day while I was lying in a gutter. I was doing stuff people were enjoying in the here and now, and they kept coming back for more.

The angle at IPW was hot, and on top of that, it was leading to more opportunities. Through the magic of YouTube, I was gaining a small amount of something I'd never had before ... buzz. At every show, I'd meet somebody new who wanted me to come work for them. Soon, I was crisscrossing all over the Midwest, getting speeding tickets, couch surfing, stabbing faces, cutting promos and generally freaking people out.

Then the signal came. Through the night sky. A homing beacon. From the Northeast. The mother ship was calling me home somehow, to a place I'd never been.

Somebody popped in another DVD, "Check this out, maaynn," Drake said excitedly. It was CZW.

---

* *Point Break* quote

JACKSONVILLE MARRIOTT, MARCH 7, 2021 1:21 P.M.

Tonight is the first exploding barbwire deathmatch to take place on American PPV, the first time a match of this type has been seen on American soil in 20 years, there has never been a successful attempt in the US. These matches were made famous in Japan by the legendary Atsushi Onita. They look really cool, this match can bring an element of danger and suspense unlike any other. There's a whole lot that can go wrong. The prospect of being severely burned by the pyrotechnic explosive charges or maimed by razor sharp barbwire notwithstanding, I'm mostly worried that something could go wrong logistically and leave us looking silly with our dicks in our hands. This whole concept is quite ridiculous, over the top but like....so cool... historically most of these matches are kinda shit. While it's gone unsaid, myself and Kenny Omega are endeavoring to have the greatest exploding barbwire death match of all time, about 9 hours from now. We are diametrically opposed people on the surface but we have a commonality. We're mad scientists, obsessed with our artistic vision. Kenny like me will feel compelled in the moment to risk his body for the sake of the piece of work we are painting, to create something truly memorable, to imprint indelible pictures, feelings and emotions in the fans' minds. I can feel the buzz, anticipation around the hotel this week is high, the fans are excited.... tonight while it's never easy to main event a stacked AEW PPV, this is one of those times when you know you've captured everyone's imaginations. Tonight they're here to see the main event. The eyes of the entire wrestling world will be on us, curiosity abound with the promise of seeing something you've never seen before. Sitting here comfortably on this couch right now this match feels like a freezing cold swimming pool, I can't imagine wanting to jump into that it seems truly awful...but I know when the time comes.... I will be in my element. Our lawyers have been trying to secure the rights to X's Wild Thing, Onita's trademark walkout music for my entrance tonight but I think we've run out of time...Tonight after 29 minutes of stylized ultra violence a new hero will be made, Eddie Kingston my rival and former friend will run into the burning building sacrificing himself for me. I told him months ago he was already a babyface we just gotta wait for the right moment where you finally show your true colors, the fans already know deep down he's a good guy, he's just too proud to admit it, this should be melodramatic, gonzo storytelling at its finest.

JACKSONVILLE MARRIOTT, MARCH 9, 2021, 6:16 P.M.

It was all so perfect...I'm handcuffed, beaten to a bloody pulp, left for dead in the center of the ring. The bad guys have gotten out of dodge, the world championship safely in their grasp. The plan has been executed to perfection, Jon Moxley is about to be blown to kingdom come. I roll over and look weakly at the screen on the stage. I see a clock counting down to zero, the final explosion set to go off at the 30-minute mark is less than a minute from detonation. I resign myself to my fate. Eddie Kingston appears from the tunnel, fighting through anyone standing in his way. They plead with him that it's too dangerous, *the whole thing's about to blow!* He rushes into the ring anyway, and desperately tries to revive me, to drag my dead weight to safety.

"Wake up Mox, Wake the fuck up!"

"You stupid MFer, I knew you were gonna get yourself killed!"

But it's too late. The clock winds down, we have less than 10 seconds now.... without thinking, instinctively Eddie performs the most heroic and selfless act we've ever seen. He throws his body on top of mine to shield me from the blast, sacrificing his own well-being, his career, for mine. The eyes of the world are glued to the heart wrenching, awe inspiring scene unfolding. Eddie covers his head, closes his eyes, thinks of his mother. He says a prayer...3....2. . .*my oldest friend*...1.... . .

...?...

...uh?...1!!. . .??

What the Hell was that? I can't even continue this right now. I might head down to the lobby and ask for a bottle of Scotch and a handgun so I can blow my brains out.

LAS VEGAS, MARCH 13 2021 2:22 P.M.

If you've read this far, by now you're probably familiar with the infamous explosion, or lack thereof — the finale that capped off AEW's Revolution PPV. If you're not, I'll catch you up real quick, though I can't imagine there's anybody on the planet that didn't hear about it. ... I'm sure President Biden was briefed by his advisors first thing in the morning. ... No doubt there were villagers in rural East Africa sitting around the campfire laughing at the tale, astronauts on the International Space Station probably shared some freeze-dried ice cream as they lamented the news from Earth.

The son-of-a-bitch bomb didn't go off. Well, then ... shit. The clock struck zero. I closed my eyes, took a deep breath and held it so as not to inhale any of the smoke and debris that was surely about to fill the ring. I couldn't cover my ears cuz I was handcuffed. I just hoped I didn't bust an eardrum or go deaf, which might sound silly in retrospect but I was expecting some '90s action-movie-explosion-type shit. ... Instead, I heard a long *hiiiiiiiisssss,* that sounded like a lawn sprinkler, and a *pffffffftt* ... a few sparklers. I think I saw some smoke in my peripheral vision.

I lay under Eddie for about 15 seconds before asking ...

"Was that it?"

"I don't know," Eddie answered, still motionless, on top of me.

"Huh," I said, "I think the explosion sucked. ... I'm not really sure what to do."

After another 10 seconds, I wondered aloud, "Maybe it looked good?"

The crowd must be in stunned silence, that's it. ... But as if on cue, I heard the audience boo and begin chanting, "That was stupid!"

"Oh, no, yeah, it definitely sucked," I told Eddie as I wondered what our response should be. Talk about getting caught with your pants down. We were lying there motionless. I was physically and emotionally spent. ... I felt like the kid in *American Pie* who blows his load early. I wanna explain to the audience how this has never happened to me before, it's just cause you're so hot I couldn't control myself. Except it's the lack of loads being blown that has upset the audience in this instance. What to do? Hmmm ... I'm reminded of the episode of *Friends* where Ross tried to put the moves on his cousin. Time stood still.

Say something clever. ... OK, it doesn't have to be clever, just has to be words ... any words will do ... Oh my god, this is the longest that anyone has not talked ever!

The doctor was out now, and I begged him to mercifully get Eddie out of here. Eddie is between a rock and a hard place. Should he keep selling it like he took a big concussive blast? They're telling Doc on the headset that we should just keep lying there, but I've had enough. I yelled at Doc to get some people out here and get Eddie the fuck outta here, at least. The ring has now filled up with people all feigning concern. They're supposed to be tending to the victims of this creative tragedy, but they all just look confused.

The audience is confused as well, and rightfully so. The drama had built to a perfect crescendo, Eddie's big hero moment, the final 10 seconds before the dud explosion were incredible suspense, and then it all disappeared in an instant. Now it's just awkward. Fuuuuuucckkk! We were right there! The Slinky got all the way down the stairs and came to a halt on the bottom step. ... I'm so embarrassed. The audience isn't stupid. They must know what we were going for ... that shit was supposed to look like Krakatoa, but instead it looked like a volcano I made in fourth-grade science class. We'd have been better off shaking up a six-pack of root beer or dropping some Mentos into a two-liter of Pepsi. How we gonna explain this? I sit there deflated, feeling the eyes staring at me. I'm at a loss.

"TK says cut a promo," referee Aubrey Edwards told me. "You gotta try and save this shit."

A microphone appears on the mat before my feet. My old friend the live mic. Its presence brings me comfort ... confidence wells up inside me to some degree. ... I reason that it's not so bad. It is what it is ... like being caught jerking off. There's really no way to explain it away. Imagine you're caught with your pants around your ankles. ... You recoil into a standing fetal position. "Dude, get outta here!" You desperately try to stammer out an excuse but there is none. ... We see the box of Kleenex and the bottle of Jergens, dude, it's sitting right there. Hey, we all do it, nothing to be ashamed of. Obviously, I didn't plan for you to have to see this, but it happened, let's just never speak of this again and move on. ... Even though I look like a 13-year-old over here clutching the November issue of *Dirty Sluts* magazine with shame and terror in my eyes.

Everyone in the world told us that we couldn't trust fireworks, and a match like that was only gonna be as good as the special effects turned out. I learned one valuable lesson from this experience: Exploding barbwire death matches rule. You may ask yourself, Why would I wanna be involved in such a transgressive concept in the first place?

I guess you could say it all started in one of my homes away from home.

HOME AWAY FROM HOME: PHILADELPHIA

The City of Brotherly Love. Except a lot of people are mean. Not really mean, it's just a city with people who take no shit and don't suffer fools. I felt at home in Philly immediately. I stayed in Manayunk, a super-hilly neighborhood. Sketchy as all hell driving in the wintertime. I think of the arena, Flyers games, Dev's Grandma's Italian stuffing, dive bars that look like somebody's house. I never had a dog in the fight about which place delivered the best cheesesteak. ... Those conversations between proud Philadelphians can get tense. I thought they were all pretty good, but, boy, did I fall in love with Wawa.

JOKE CLAUDIO TOLD ME:

SOMEBODY JUST THREW A JAR OF MAYONNAISE AT ME AND I WAS LIKE, "WHAT THE HELLMANN!?"

I woke up on the floor in a room I had never been in before. I had no idea where I was. The room was basically empty, a shelf full of books and little else. Light shone through the blinds as I opened my eyes. I was laying on my side in a sort of vegetative, caveman-trapped-in-a-block-of-ice-coming-back-to-life state. I had all my clothes on as far as I could tell, including my shoes ... no need to panic. I tried to make out the titles of the books on the shelf before bothering with trying to move. A bunch of graphic novels ... maybe I'll get up and take a look.

I roll over and am slightly startled to see a very pretty girl staring at me, propped up on an elbow, smiling with excitement, her eyes about 12 inches from mine.

"Hey," she says.

I pause briefly to think. I've never seen this woman before in my life. I don't move a muscle. I make a decision on how to respond.

"What's up?" I reply with vocal cords that sound like an old exhaust pipe.

"So, you were pretty out of control last night," she says. She's fully clothed. I didn't sleep with her. I feel pretty good. The sun is shining outside. What happened last night? I remember yesterday. ... We walked to the Tower, a local bar, in the afternoon. Other than that, I got nothing. She has brought me a coffee. Alright! I sit up and drink it. She's very nice. She asks me, "How are you feeling?"

"Not bad" I reply.

She attempts to have sex with me. She succeeds. She begins to fill me in on the events of the last 12 hours. We're still at Dahmer's house, where we started. That's good. I learn a fight broke out and David (who wrestled under a mask as OMG) got taken away in an ambulance because he punched a window and sliced up his arm.

That doesn't sound good. Hopefully he's out of the hospital by now because he's got a Thumbtack Kickpads match today. Today is the Tournament of Death.

I had been staying at Dahmer's place, a house in Jersey just over the bridge from Philly, as I would sometimes, with Sami Callihan and Chrissy Rivera. I'd come out so Sami and I could spend the week going to all the many different wrestling schools in the area to train. TOD was tomorrow, and everyone coming into town had congregated for something like a Fourth of July cookout for psychotics. Apparently, as this gracious woman who has taken it upon herself to take care of me all night and make sure I didn't kill myself or anyone else explains, I was out of my goddamn mind all night. I remember the Tower. The Phillies game was on; they were giving me Yuenglings, but it was early and we were just kind of killing time waiting for the Midwest car to get there, plus I could drink like a thousand beers and it would mostly just serve to make me better at pool. Somebody must have slipped me something. Or I took something on purpose, I don't know. I would take all kinds of random shit back then. I had reached a point where I didn't care about the future or anyone else's definition of success. I was living for the here and now, performing in electric, bright plasma-red technicolor. I wanted to tell stories loudly, aggressively and unapologetically. I wanted to revel in sadism. I wanted to shock and disturb audiences. I wanted to have filthy drunk sex with every aspect of deathmatch wrestling and really put the focus on the details. That is to say, I don't care about the model with big fake tits. I wanna smell the armpits of the cute, homeless chick.

I got kicked out of the Tower. Sami claims I threw a glass in the first five minutes I was there. Possible, but doesn't really sound like me. He took me back to the house and put guards on me, but I kept escaping back to the bar. That kinda sounds like me. David claimed I dropped an elbow on him into a dumpster or something, so everyone got kicked out, definitely me. In any case, we were back at the house and all parties agree I was on autopilot. The lights on, nobody home. Allegedly, somebody played a Chikara DVD and I hurled a beer bottle at Dahmer's TV yelling, "Fuck Mike Quackenbush!" Why was I throwing shit? At some point I was told the plan was to get some coke into my system to snap me out of it. I was cornered and pinned against a wall like King Kong in chains, long enough for a coaster with a couple lines on it to be placed under my nose.

As the story goes, a rolled-up dollar bill was positioned in my nostril and carefully aimed at the tip of a snowy trail. All they had to do was get me to snort it upward, but (allegedly) I burst into laughter and exhaled so much air through my nose and mouth that it blew all the blow (that's fun to say) all over the place. Grant, a.k.a. Danny Havoc, was still mad at me the next day for wasting good cocaine. I pleaded with him that I didn't remember and it was an accident. I don't think he ever forgave me.

Ultimately, I was placed in a full-body bear costume and left to rampage through the house, screaming obscenities while onlookers took shelter behind furniture so as not to get swiped in the face by a paw. When this wild animal wandered into the backyard to forage in the grass, one poor bystander was hit by a running dropkick that was described to me as an assault by a cross between Doug Furnas and a 6'2" Teletubby on Meth. Many just enjoyed the show and took Polaroids. Luckily, only the cops showed up and nobody called animal control.

I make some small talk with my new friend, laugh at all my comrades' misfortunes the previous evening, and lament my own embarrassing behavior. Oh, well. IT'S A NEW DAY! Good day so far. I carefully walk down the stairs, careful not to step on anyone who may have been passed out, curled up like a cat on the steps. I enter the living room. A beer-can tornado had hit South Jersey, an F3 at least.

All is quiet. I'm hungry. I rifle through the cupboards and find a slightly out-of-date box of Wheaties. Score. The Breakfast of Champions. I walk out onto the back porch and observe the smoldering wreckage in the yard as I munch handfuls of cereal. What surprises are in store for today? I wonder. On this, the day of the Tournament of Death. This is my first.

I'm mostly just concerned with putting on a show, a performance supercharged with aggression and adrenaline. Savoring the taste of pain and blood, my own or not, swirling it around on my palate like a fine Pinot noir. Could there be a better way to spend a beautiful day? What are you gonna do, golf? Are you even breathing? I'm pumped ... tinges of that electricity that's already idling in your veins first thing in the morning on a day like today. I could have never guessed that by the time the sun went down someone would be actually dead.

SPIN IT UP:
JENNY LEWIS WITH THE WATSON TWINS, RABBIT FUR COAT, 2006

I first listened to this album when Renée, who was kind of secretly my new girlfriend at the time, put it on in the car on a drive from Seattle to Portland after a *Monday Night Raw*. We stayed at a Quality Inn in Downtown Portland. A dead body would not have looked out of place in the creepy pool. Nonetheless, we had a great time that night pulling Coors Lights from the mini-fridge and jamming tunes into the wee hours. Jenny Lewis is a bad bitch, an amazing musician. On this album she is joined by the Watson Twins, and the three of them harmonize together beautifully to create a folksy masterpiece. This is another one of those albums that take me to a specific time and place. My favorite song here, I think, is "Rise Up With Fists!" ... The sound of Jenny Lewis's voice always just makes me feel good.

MORE CZW

I still didn't consider myself a deathmatch wrestler. I was just upping the intensity and creativity of my matches and not being a little bitch about it, all this pretentious "learning to work" shit. Fuck you. You learn how to work. It was 10 million tackles, drop down hip-tosses and comebacks later and I was bored. Still, as I stood on the balcony at the arena in Philadelphia, watching four guys waddle around a ring littered with debris, somewhere deep in the back of my mind, maybe Les's voice echoed, "Those guys down in Louisville hitting each other over the head with lightbulbs and frying pans and every other thing ..." Because all I could think as I watched four giant toddlers roll around on their butts occasionally tapping each other over the head with weapons was, "These guys don't know how to work." And that's exactly what Les would have said. These types of pursuits, I was taught, were for wrestlers with no ability, for idiots. The art of professional wrestling, the whole point, was to NOT get hurt.

Nonetheless, as I continued to observe, I couldn't help but notice the bloodthirsty crowd in a frenzy. Wasn't THAT the whole point, to get the crowd? The more CZW I saw, the more I began to question the dogma I was brought up on, the incontrovertible truth that this was garbage wrestling. What I began to see was the work of tremendous athletes, fearlessly blending every conceivable influence, and taking it to another level with every F'n shooting star press, brainbuster, piledriver and springboard goddamn triple gainer off of, onto, into or through any perilous contraption you can imagine.

At this time, CZW was stacked with talent. A diverse roster of innovative junior heavyweights, hard-hitting brawlers, crazy characters and borderline masochists. They even had a student from their school who was supposed to be good, named Adam or Mike or Michael Cole, Adam Coats or something, but he never turned out to be anything.

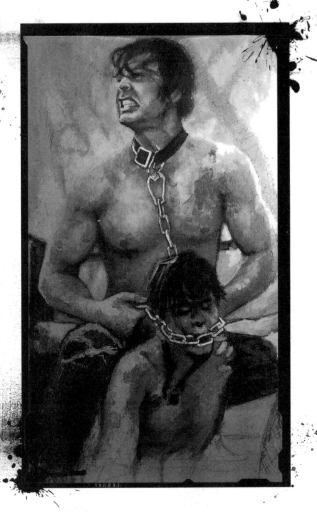

While I wasn't initially interested in becoming a deathmatch wrester per se, what I was interested in was taking all these dangerous and exciting elements that the crowds ate up and making some sense of it all. One might say that CZW in 2009 was best enjoyed in highlight form. The best moments were incredible, but imagine if you took those highlights, along with this intense atmosphere, this aesthetic, and sprinkled in a little psychology, a dash more storytelling. Then you'd really be cooking with gas. I would use my brain. Still, easier said than done.

The CZW crowd was unique. For one thing, it was a Philadelphia crowd, a hotbed for wrestling since the dawn of time. Philly fans have always been notoriously brutal. For another, it was a post-ECW, post-Attitude Era Philly crowd that had been watching

CZW push the limits of ultraviolence even further than its predecessors for years, so needless to say, they had seen just about everything.

Upon debuting, I immediately formed an alliance with Sami Callihan, who I knew from Ohio. We had already started tagging over the last year. Sami was super-creative. He was really into horror movies and knew how to edit videos and stuff like that. Since I was wearing rubber masks to the ring and getting weirder and stabbier, my standard dinner fork had graduated to a giant barbecue pitmaster fork. It was a perfect fit.

Sami was also going through an acid-wash phase, which worked because I got all my clothes from Goodwill. We were called the Switchblade Conspiracy, usually just referred to as the Switchblades, which sounds much better. I'm not sure exactly where the "conspiracy" came from. Grant once told me he was gonna form a group with a name of equal cleverness called Infantslaughter Babystomp. Sami and I were both so motivated and both so aggressive, it didn't matter what you called us. Nobody could match our intensity. We complemented each other perfectly and made a tremendous team: two pissed-off kids, a pair of hyenas who migrated in from Ohio. They hated us. I mean, they F'n hated us at first. They thought we were pussies. I knew this because that's what they called us. This is good, I thought. This, I can work with.

CZW was now my highest-profile gig and quickly becoming my favorite place to work.

Not because they paid me anything more than I could drink or snort in the 14 hours I'd spend in Philly, not because I loved working in the ECW arena, which even today maintains a certain romance for me, and not because I loved the intensity of the environment and the new palette of ultraviolent colors with which I had to paint. CZW, as strange as it may sound, brought me a sense of normalcy, of family. And for a time, I felt some stability once again.

We called ourselves Team 74. We were the Midwest car. There would be many iterations, but generally, Rob "Ego" Anthony, wrestling under a mask as Egotistico Fantastico, would pick up the van in Chicago and drive east to Indianapolis, picking up the "Naptown Dragons," which consisted of Drake, Scotty Vortekz and OMG, before driving east. I would find a ride to drop me off at an exit on I-70 in Dayton, where I would be picked up. In actuality, 74 runs from Indy to Cincinnati, making our name a misnomer but it stuck. On those early trips, Dan was with us, and a dude named Carter who could do a shooting star leg drop. He also did that shit Pac does but instead of the top rope he would do it off of a chair, which was mindblowing. Ego once had a developmental contract with WWE, stationed at FCW. I found his stories about how that system worked interesting because it sounded like an F'n nightmare to me.

Upon jumping in the van the first time, Ego was the only guy I didn't know, but by pure coincidence we had a connection that made us fast friends. His roommate in Tampa was a guy named The Bad Seed, an HWA alum who I had once shared an apartment with, along with a strange dude we just called Gimmick who slept in a tent in the living room. The Bad Seed was a character. Intense, perpetually miserable, juiced up and obsessed with Metallica, he demanded quiet at all times. He would stay locked in his room only to emerge screaming, eyes bugging out of his head, face as red as a tomato should the decibel level reach anything above a conversational tone.

Constant concern he might try to kill us in our sleep aside, we had both concluded, in our separate experiences living with The Bad Seed, that he was just too impossible not to fuck with. We traded Bad Seed stories for hundreds of miles. Ego would start behind the wheel then Dan would take over, driving through the night, blasting Tech N9ne and smoking Swisher Sweets to stay awake. You got whatever sleep you could get. I learned an underrated wrestler trick: Always have earplugs with you.

When it was finally time to get on the Pennsylvania Turnpike, little David would usually take over. OMG, who listened to ska and never stopped smiling or telling aggressive jokes, was often called Little David by the other guys, especially by Scotty. Scotty was the exact same size as David but he wielded what he called a "pimp hand" and exhibited the corresponding behavioral traits of such an evolutionary advantage.

In the early days, Drake didn't have a valid license. I actually didn't either, after so many speeding tickets in so many states, but I didn't know it at the time. Arriving in Philadelphia, we'd weave through the streets, using something Ego had called a "Garmin," the first GPS I'd ever seen. We'd eventually arrive at the arena in the morning, pulling into the razor-wire-fenced enclosure and parking to get a couple of hours' rest.

Around noon, the parking lot would begin filling up with tailgating SUVs, barbecues and coolers of beer. This is where I first met Grant. He was discerning. He thought before he spoke, and the gears in his head were always clearly working. While everything around him was often just nonsense, Grant was a constant anchor of logic. I immediately loved him.

Rick Clark would arrive. Heavyset with a thick Jersey accent, Rick was a superfan who was beloved by the crew. He'd open up the back of his SUV and reveal a command center, always stocked with Yuenglings and Jack, the CZW equivalent of a green room. The most popular feature of the Rick Clark mobile was something called Kush, a highly potent type of marijuana Rick could acquire. It was spotted purple and blue and looked more like some giant mushrooms from *Alice in Wonderland* than weed to me.

A circle would be formed and a multicolored glass bowl passed around. Scotty would get very excited for this ritual, like a kid on Christmas morning, "Yo, pass me that ish, son," Scotty would say, speaking in his peculiar Naptown dialect, strangely beautiful blond hair blowing in the breeze. Smiling and high as all hell, he looked like something off the cover of a romance novel … if the novel was about a guy from Indiana that robbed a liquor store to fund his dogfighting operation. One time only, I tried this Kush, so as not to be rude, then I stood comatose for the next 90 minutes or so, regretting that decision terribly.

Beers and laughs would be had, a casual atmosphere. By late afternoon, as more wrestlers and fans arrived, the energy changed, excitement growing. Evening draws close. … Soon it will be game time.

My foot begins to tap now as wrestlers begin to disperse, getting inside their heads. Ideas are exchanged. Inside, guys are trying out moves in the ring, barbwire is being stapled to boards, panes of glass brought in on dollies. The fans are now waiting in line out front, buzz in the air. Final preparations are made, music and lights tested, merchandise laid out, the smell of hot dogs, pizza and pretzels fresh from the oven.

"You got a CD case?" I am asked. A signal that our coke has arrived from New York. I return to the parking lot, now deserted, and join a couple others inside a car. I sit in the passenger seat and do a couple quick lines off of a Soundgarden CD case. It's F'n showtime. I walk back into the arena and begin to transform, now inhabiting the mental space I will need to be in when I walk through the curtain tonight.

In the locker room, I sit on a folding chair and pull another chair up to face me. I take a plastic sheath full of rectangular razorblades and slide one out with my thumb. I carefully squeeze it with my fingers, bending it in half and breaking it. I take one half and use a pair of scissors to cut two tiny pieces off, just the way I like them, a proprietary design. I press the tip of my finger to them and they stick. I gently place them onto a piece of white tape with the sharpest edges exposed. I cut the tape in two places and wrap them up securely like a couple of swaddled infants. I put them to bed, gently resting them in an empty Altoids tin for later, just in case.

Eddie Kingston walks in the door. He is angry with someone, telling people someone is a motherfucker.

Frank Talent, a sweet old man and crusty representative of the athletic commission, comes into the locker room to gather us all around for his regular speech, stressing the safety rules and regulations. He tells us to have a good show. Everyone applauds.

The sound of ring announcer Larry Legend's unmistakable baritone comes over the speakers, and the show begins.

I have butterflies.

Hours later, post-show adrenaline is high. Chairs are collected, floors are swept, thin envelopes of cash are passed out. Outside, the Rick Clark mobile is back. Rick is still hyped, giving high-fives as wrestlers and friends talk about whatever craziness went down that night. The Midwest car is loaded and pulls into the gas station around the corner to fill up. With a surplus of cash now, we load up on things like cigarettes, snacks and energy drinks. Scotty buys a couple of grape White Owls. We park at a diner, still just up the street from the arena. On the other side of the street is Nickels Tavern, a local, very Philly, very dive bar. Some people enjoy a quiet meal at the diner, while I, along with whoever chooses to follow me across the street, go to Nickels, which by now is already packed with degenerates basking in the afterglow of all of tonight's insanity and bloodletting.

At closing time, Team 74 reconvenes and hits the road with whoever is sober behind the wheel, possibly Dan, who is irritable by now. His negative energy is not well received and he is fucked with mercilessly. Drake and I insist we stop at Tony Luke's really quick on the way out to pick up cheesesteaks, an argument ensues. We stop at Tony Luke's. I stand outside the pick-up window ordering, giggly, beer-drunk and sleep-deprived, adrenaline slowly fading. I pass out in the back seat before we're out of Philly. When I wake up, we're somewhere around Pittsburgh pulling into a rest stop on the PA Turnpike. I am refreshed. Getting up, I notice my shirt sticking to the seat like it was superglued. Dried, sticky blood. I get rid of that shirt and put on a hoodie, walking into the cool morning air. The rest of the team is passed out or trudging zombie-like into the rest area to take a piss. I'm in a good mood. I go in and grab a coffee, ready to take over behind the wheel. I adjust my seat to a perfect chill, cruising position, pull out onto the Turnpike and bring us through PA, West Virginia and into Ohio, alone with my thoughts, winding through the hills, watching trees and fields roll by, classic rock on the radio. Later when the sun is up, the rest of the van stirs awake, conversations are had reflecting on the events of this month's CZW excursion.

Scotty calls Little David a bitch. David aggressively protests this statement, and Drake laughs uproariously. Jokes are made and the mood is light as we pull over at an arbitrarily chosen exit off I-70 in Dayton, where I'll get out, handing the keys to Ego. Bro hugs, fist bumps, sarcastic insults and goodbyes are exchanged before the van pulls back on the highway to continue east. See y'all next time. I look around and pause. ... I take a few steps in no particular direction. Shit! I forgot to call somebody for a ride.

"T-O-D?"

That's what Zandig said. John Zandig, CZW owner, founder and something of a cult icon himself. Zandig was like a mob boss. The don, 6'2", 260 pounds but with a larger-than-life quality ... bald head with a big gold earring and a muscle gut. I hadn't really had much conversation with him — he mostly passed messages through intermediaries. I had come back through the curtain at the arena, adrenaline pumping, puddles of blood still forming in my eye sockets. People were congratulating me. It was dizzying. I was so excited I didn't know which way to walk: proud, happy, smiling, breathing hard, high on brutality and the crowd's subsequent reaction. I ended up standing in the locker room. I was a sitting duck. In the state I was in, I could have been talked into riding a motorcycle through the jungle, naked, covered in honey after signing over my 401k and agreeing to sell Herbalife products.

My arm had been tied off with a rubber hose and a measured, potent shot of CZW was active in my bloodstream. Dan came running up to me, wide-eyed.

"Say yes," he told me.

"Huh?" I asked.

He had just come running from the balcony where he'd been watching the show with the boss. ... "Zandig's gonna talk to you. Say yes."

"Huh?"

Sure enough, Zandig came squeezing his big-ass shoulders through the door a few seconds later. There was a smile on his face, the don was pleased. His eyes locked on mine as he came toward me and stopped. "T-O-D?" he said. I was a goddamn sitting duck. He was asking me to participate in the upcoming Tournament of Death, based on the performance I'd just had.

I found it interesting that so many prominent deathmatch wrestlers, with names such as The Necro Butcher and Mad Man Pondo, while seemingly so violent and unsavory on the outside, were so often such sweet guys out of the ring. Likewise, while the guys who were known for taking the most ridiculous, death-defying bumps and doing the most vile things to their bodies for the sake of entertainment might be regarded as dumbasses or nutcases by outsiders, in reality guys like Grant and "Sick" Nick Mondo, for example, are two of the most intelligent and well-spoken people I've ever met.

The best example of a gnarly, intimidating individual who one might assume spends his nights beating people to death with his bare hands outside roadhouses the cops have just raided, but is really just a big ol' teddy bear who would give you the shirt off his back, was Marvin Lambert, a.k.a. Brain Damage, RIP.

Marvin was often referred to as "the Ultraviolent Terminator." He was huge, 6'4", 275 pounds, heavily tattooed and pierced, and he wore MMA gloves and baggy military-looking pants into the ring. His shtick was that he would punch people in the face as hard as he could and mostly didn't sell anything. The crowd loved him. Damage performances were usually one-way traffic; he just beat the fuck out of people. While he was by no means Nick Bockwinkel, he wasn't asked to be, and on the night of our first one-on-one encounter, I didn't need him to be. I just needed him to do what he did best. I knew the crowd would delight in him pounding this newcomer, this little punk-ass friend of Sami's, this pussy from Ohio, into hamburger meat. I knew cuz they told me.

The story was simple: Damage had a bazooka in each hand, while I was holding pea shooters. I would give them what they wanted, for a time, absorbing a hellacious beating, but I would not back down, frustrating them. Then I'd get beat up some more, and they would be satisfied that I would soon be destroyed. Then, still not backing down, I would gain the advantage with tactics and skill, which would *reeeally* piss them off.

I would employ basic psychology, things like working a body part, a novel concept at CZW. When I got Damage to sell, after weathering the storm and picking him apart, the crowd would be indignant, I figured. The fact that this pussy was still standing and Damage was hurt would spit in the face of all their logic and understanding of the laws of the universe. It would become a fight. Damage would have to earn it. They would worry. This wasn't what was supposed to happen, but it was happening.

The simple, easy-to-understand arithmetic being displayed right in front of their eyes would be hard to ignore. When the time was right, I would fall victim to my opponent's physical superiority and they would breathe a sigh of relief. They'll wanna chalk this close call up to some freak occurrence, an off-night for their hero, but they'll never look at me the same way again.

We called very little. I had quickly grown to love Damage, but I didn't trust he would remember anything if we planned too much. Damage was motivated; he had a specific and effective act, but it wasn't every day he was asked to have a fairly routine singles match, and he wanted to prove he could work. He told me people didn't think he could have a good match, and this was music to my ears.

"Just trust me," I told him. "All you have to do is what you always do."

In the ring, I would be in his ear at all times.

"Just listen," I assured him, as the moment drew closer. I saw the whole thing in my head. I instructed him to just beat the shit out of me ... keep coming forward and not sell anything until the time was right.

He did everything perfectly. He was a heavy guy, and as I suspected he might, he got blown up. He fought through that shit valiantly, listened to every word I said, and was there for every cue. He was the best goddamn Brain Damage he could be, and now he had an example to prove to whoever he wanted to that he could work a good match. The highlight of the match was Damage punching me in the face with a right hand that exploded my head into a plume of red mist, electrifying the audience. It looked like a snuff film.

Afterward, Damage was in tears. He wrapped his big arms around me and sobbed into my neck, as deep and heartfelt as I've ever been hugged by anybody. He thanked me so profusely I thought maybe he would owe me a Wookiee life debt and would be my sidekick forever from this point on, which would have been cool with me. Damage's manager, a nice dude named Billy Gram who looked like Alice Cooper's evil twin, also sincerely expressed his thanks for my help with what Marvin accomplished tonight. For some reason they really were out to prove something. I loved that.

"T-O-D?" One question, three letters. I wasn't booked on TOD, didn't expect to be asked. While I was a decidedly non-PG wrestler, I still didn't consider myself an official, card-carrying deathmatch guy. If I said yes, there would be no turning back. The moment hung in the air for a lifetime as I considered the implications. Zandig didn't say another word, he just stared at me expectantly. I saw my reflection behind him in a mirror off to my right. The bandage on my head that looked like a Japanese flag was glued to my forehead, raccoon-like red circles framed the whites of my eyes. I realized, there's no decision here. I already was a deathmatch wrestler. "I'm in," I said.

A smile I couldn't wipe off my face. A new shot of adrenaline hit me, one last sharp downhill on a roller coaster I didn't see coming. Zandig, smiling, simply nodded, shook my hand, and walked away. I'm buzzing. I head to the parking lot still in my trunks. I need a beer and a cigarette.

Somewhere in Ohio, Les is reading an article by the light of his bedside lamp. He pauses and looks up, takes his reading glasses off. He has a terrible feeling. A pang in his gut. "Did I hear something?" he wonders. He scans the room. *Naaah*, it's just my imagination. He turns the light off and goes to bed.

SPIN IT UP:
SHOOTER JENNINGS, THE OTHER LIFE, 2013

Shooter Jennings was kind of the official soundtrack of our lives for a group of the boys in WWE at a certain point in time. Shooter is the son of the legendary Waylon Jennings and carries on his dad's tradition of "outlaw" country proudly, but he's not a one-trick pony, Shooter can rock, roll, strum or sing any style of tune. Don't put Shooter in a box! He's an artist, a storyteller, a spinner of yarns.

The appeal for us was very logical. ... See, life on the road as a country singer ain't that much different than life on the road as a wrestler, and I think we were drawn to a lot of country songs on the road because of the parallels. The tales of Willie Nelson, Waylon, Johnny Cash, Hank Williams and many other storytellers seemed to be narrating our lives as we were living them. ... Some of the boys away from their wives, and maybe multiple kids at home. We were beat-up, tired, driving 350 miles in between shots, bleary eyed, pulling into the La Quinta in Branson, Missouri, on speed at 6:00 a.m., those F'n Froot Loops at the continental breakfast looking like a mirage in the desert, drinking whiskey in the back of a van, getting in fights at truck stops, nervously trying to hide the smell of weed from the Border Patrol stop outside Laredo your woman left you, your dog just died, all that type of shit. ... I was first introduced to Shooter's music by my good friend and frequent riding partner Joe Hennig, a former WWE superstar (even I can't help saying "superstar" instead of "wrestler" when it's preceded by WWE, WTF?). Joe is the son of the legendary Curt Hennig, aka Mr. Perfect. He was good friends with Shooter, and they bonded over the pressures and expectations of following in their fathers' footsteps. It was hard to pick one Shooter album as a Spin It Up. I guess I could have included two; it's my F'n book. It was a close race between this and *Electric Rodeo*. The tracks "Gone to Carolina," "Some Rowdy Women," "Little White Lines," and especially "Hair of the Dog," which many drunk WWE (fuck!) superstars have sung at the top of their lungs at the crack of dawn while rolling into a town to entertain the local folk that evening. But in the end, I had to pick *The Other Life* because of the track "Outlaw You." Shooter explained to Joe what this song was about: his Dad, Waylon, was the shit, the original outlaw, and this song is kind of a "fuck you" to commercialized country singers and how record labels have tried to sell the image the original outlaws created. I won't try to tell that whole story here ... maybe Shooter will write his own book.

I love "The White Trash Song." It's a great way to start your day. "Wild and Lonesome," a duet between Shooter and Patty Griffin, is as beautiful as any song I've ever heard.

"The Gunslinger" was one of our favorites, listening to it we created a secret handshake that was something of a mixture of a cheers, a hang ten and throwing back a shot. When I did Make-A-Wish visits, I would often show the secret handshake to the kid. I would tell them to watch out for the signal after Roman and I defeated the bad guys that night. The memories of looking out into the front row as the Make-A-Wish kids proudly displayed the weird hang ten/problem drinker signal we created, smiles on their faces, are some of my favorite memories. They were on the team. This is why we do this.

Renée and I got to see Shooter play at the Whiskey a Go Go in L.A. once. We hung out a little backstage and I was able to express to him how much his music had meant to the locker room over the years. I hope he understood the depth of my sentiments, but he might have been way too stoned, which would be even better in a way. One time Joe and I drove from Lubbock to San Antonio, listening to this album the whole way, and we counted 42 F'n deer on the side of the road. I didn't hit one

TOURNAMENT OF DEATH

We wound through the woods, a caravan. Three cars en route to an undisclosed location. Chrissy Rivera was driving. Sami was in the passenger seat. I sat in the back looking out the window as we passed mossy trees and dense forest. It became darker the deeper we got.

"I don't think I've ever been to Delaware," I had said as we loaded the cars back at Dahmer's house before setting out. We drove down I-95 and crossed the state line. Now it was some real *Hansel and Gretel* meets *Mortal Kombat* shit. I didn't know if we we're gonna come up on a house made of candy and some witch was gonna try to cook me, or if Scorpion was gonna jump out from a tree and shoot that shit out of his hand while aiming at my head. Somewhere in between, maybe. To grandmother's house we go, for a tournament that gathers warriors from all over the world, who will bludgeon each other in combat until only one remains.

Tension in the car. I wouldn't say I was nervous, but there was a certain gravity hanging over the day. It hovered over the caravan as we pushed further into the woods.

"Where in the hell are we going?" Sami said. "This is crazy, man, it's like something out of a movie."

I didn't disagree. I just kept looking out the window.

Finally, we see daylight and round a bend, coming into a clearing on a slight incline. We've reached our destination. Far from the prying eyes of athletic commissions or rules and regulations of any sort. We've arrived at the site of Tournament of Death VIII. There was no turning back. I had no idea what to expect.

The annual Tournament of Death, featuring the most extreme, bloody, violent and shocking matches in North America, took place in Delaware to avoid interference from sanctioning bodies. In a place like the arena in Philly, for example, the use of fire or fluorescent light tubes would be off limits and ... well, for our purposes today, that is just unacceptable. TOD 8 was held at a property in the country conveniently owned by D. J. Hyde's parents.

We parked beside the house, where cars were gathering and bodies were milling about. In the distance, I could see the ring in the middle of a huge field surrounded by trees on all sides. It was like a huge swath of forest had been cleared for the sole purpose of this event. In a few hours, the field would be filled with vehicles and fans, tailgating, barbecues, beer drinking, clouds of pot smoke, probably a good amount of psychedelic use. Ultraviolent Woodstock. Deathmatch fans, I would learn, are not only unique, but some of the best fans in the world. They truly appreciated the efforts and sacrifices of the participants, and once you were in, you were in. Being such a niche style of entertainment, there was a family atmosphere, and these fans all gathered on this day to have fun.

I walked toward the ring and the curtains that had been set up to create a makeshift backstage area. I noticed, laid out across the grass, dozens of bundles of tubes, stacked glass panes, ladders, tables and water cooler jugs duct-taped to long handles to create comical *American Gladiators*-like weapons (they could be surprisingly crowd pleasing). I see "Scrawny" Shawny Kernaghan, an unsung CZW hero who worked harder than anybody on show days, power walking back and forth with spools of barbwire and other TOD paraphernalia, hammering, sawing, fastening together light tubes into a huge log-cabin formation and creating all kinds of apparatuses meant to be destroyed by the impact of a human body with its supple flesh, or wielded in such a way as to maim.

Today, in the first round, I would continue my series with Brain Damage. This time the fans expected that I would for sure get the absolute trouncing of a lifetime. I survived an encounter with Brain Damage in a more traditional setting, but now all bets were off. We were at TOD. ... This would be unfettered ultraviolence. This was Damage's world, and I'd be out of my element. The story would be the same, but this time the gore and intensity would reach another level. I'd surprise them yet again. Sami had a brilliant idea for the finish in which, at the apex of the action, Sami and the new recruit to our little group, a student named Joe Gacy who Sami had taken under his wing, would run interference. Zandig was very hesitant at first. Traditionally, all finishes at TOD should be ridiculous highlight-reel bumps that elicited a chorus of air horns, a trademark of the CZW crowd.

Air horns sounded when they saw something particularly crazy, a sign they liked what they were seeing. A traditional distraction finish from TV wrestling had no place here. I was hesitant at first, too, but the Switchblades were so despised by the audience at this point that when I visualized it, I knew this would work. It would be the last thing they expected and would get tremendous heat.

When you do shit like this every other match, it quickly becomes lame. The fans feel cheated and you get the wrong kind of heat. But this type of thing never happens in a TOD. It's actually out of the ordinary, an affront to every reason we've gathered in this field. This will work, I decided, but it would be up to me to make sure we got the RIGHT kind of heat, to tell the story perfectly. I had to let the audience blow their load before they realized they were with a hooker. If they are left with blue balls, nobody wins. If they see Damage massacre me in such a way that the police should be called, if not for the fact that we're in the middle of nowhere and I went running like a scalded dog, they would be euphoric. Told you he was a pussy. When we stole a shitty three count and advanced to the next round, and they realized this beautiful woman at the bar hadn't actually been interested them, they would be too stoked about the experience to care for long. They'd call their friends and tell them what happened. They'd just leave that one detail out.

While matches in TOD were only limited by your imagination and how much bodily harm you were willing to risk, opening-round matches often had fun, cheeky themes. Since I had a penchant for stabbing people in the face with a fork, our match was called a Dining Room Deathmatch, with an emphasis on cutlery and other sharp items. We started the match by sitting down across from each other at a finely appointed dinner table with a cake topped with hundreds of thumbtacks, which I'm sure a fan made. To class it up further, we had a real grandfather clock in the corner that Gacy would eventually take a bump into.

A brawl quickly broke out and I went toe to toe with Damage. Then he took over, smashing dinner plates over my head, which made a great sound. When I went to return the favor, in a happy accident, I flung the goddamn thing right by his head, which made me look like quite a dork. The crowd, who was waiting for any little thing to confirm I was a pussy, jumped all over it. You couldn't have planned that more perfectly. The brawl continued. Now Damage and I had a chemistry, same as before, he just kept coming forward, no-selling everything. I'd give him four or five shots for every one I endured. ... Honey badger versus grizzly. I won't back down. I'm in his face, but I'm on the backpedal for the duration of the match, getting hung over the top rope with a belt around my throat, getting gouged with a saw blade taped to a plastic baseball bat (another Item I'm sure was a gift from a fan) and eventually getting suplexed into the ring from outside through a glass windshield wrapped in barbwire and light tubes.

Still, I refused to die and attempted to exchange fisticuffs with the Terminator, a brazen but foolish move. I lost this gamble and got a package piledriver on my head, just like last time. We were right back where we were before. Only this time I kicked out. *The nerve of this little shit to kick out. Would you just kill him already?* Damage is ready to oblige. After all, this time, it's Tournament of Death.

Damage rolled out and retrieved a weapon from under the apron, raising it high over his head as he circled the ring for all to see. He's got a skill saw.

"*What the fuck is that? What the fuck? Whhhhat the fuck is that?*" I hear a panicked fan ask aloud, her voice getting higher and higher. The bloodthirsty crowd is practically salivating.

"That's a fucking electric saw!" someone replied.

Dead to rights, I'm on my knees and Damage stands behind me with the saw buzzing in his hand. He grabs me by the hair and jerks my head up. I feel like I'm about to be waterboarded.

The lamb is about to be slaughtered in sacrifice. The crowd rejoices.

He lifts the saw and places the blade right above my eyebrows, the mechanism does the work, sawing back and forth on my flesh.

I'm being electrocuted. Justifiably freaking the fuck out, one last burst of survival adrenaline brings me back to life, I try desperately to escape Damage's clutches to no avail. He snatches me up and once again drives the blade into my face as rivers of blood flow from my face to the sea.

I burst from the ring like I'm escaping a burning building and try to get as far the fuck away from it as I can. I've been finally exposed as the coward they've always known I was.

Cheering, euphoria, chants of C-Z-W and airhorns echo in the festival atmosphere. All is right in the world.

Joe Gacy shows up and grabs the audience's attention with the sound of a chainsaw, standing in the aisle. Sami appears as if from nowhere and whacks Billy Gram at ringside with a kendo stick in a drive-by. Sami enters the ring and bangs the stick on the mat like he's got a flare and he's trying to get the T. rex's attention. He does and Damage charges him with the saw in the corner. As soon as Damage puts his sights on the intended distraction, I appear, slide in behind his hips, grab him by the belt and roll the monster up with every goddamn bit of wrestling savvy I have for a one, two, three.

I pop up in celebration, a bundle of nerves and adrenaline, none of my body parts work correctly. I literally fall out of the ring. The heat is nuclear. They are pissed. "Bullshit!" they chant. Sami and I escape, and Gacy, left for dead, is killed by Damage with the grandfather clock. As the hero leaves to applause, the crowd takes a breath, as they have seen a hell of a fight. It's the good kind of heat. A success. The Switchblades are still the hottest heels in the company. Damage looks like a monster, and not only did this crowd get everything they wanted, they will never doubt me again.

Soon after, I enter the ring in a sort of shellshocked, oblivious state for a hastily thrown-together three-way dance in the second round with Scotty Vortekz and Nick Gage. I take a piledriver on the top of my head through a bundle of light tubes from Gage for the finish. All the preliminaries are done and the finals set. Joy and relief. I survived. My work is done. That was fun! As I peel off my bloody jeans, assessing the day, I'm already coming up with ideas for next time. For now, it's time to relax, heal up these wounds and be a spectator for the rest of the show. But as it turned out, my night was not over.

The finals of TOD VIII were Nick Gage against Thumbtack Jack. Nick "FN" Gage, king of ultraviolence, with his immutable, in-your-face, expletive-laced verbal style, was in the early stages of becoming a cult icon. Jack was an import from Germany, with a hot act based around sickening visuals. Earlier this evening he'd had a hypodermic needle stuck through both cheeks. The ring was set up with the classic 200-light-tube look ... tubes attached upright to the ropes every 6 inches or so, all around the ring. There were bundles, panes. A lot of F'n glass, man.

I was happy to be watching safely from afar with a Yuengling. With the final, ultraviolent battlefield all set up and ready to go, there was electricity in the air. This should be good. I had walked slightly uphill to the entrance gate a few hundred feet away, shirtless, in a pair of gym shorts and goofy Payless sneakers. Out of the sight of fans, it was a good view. The match starts and the action builds slowly. I chat with a few people and pop another Yuengling. I see a crash of tube glass and hear some horns go off, but I can't really see what just happened.

I take a few steps forward and look closer, taking another sip of my beer. A few seconds later, I hear panic and commotion coming from the backstage area. Slightly concerned, I start to walk that direction. In my peripheral vision I see that Thumbtack Jack is alone in the ring, kicking tubes, seemingly at a loss. I sense confusion in the crowd. I feel bad energy. As I continue walking toward the curtain, I see Sami burst out in a panic. "Mox, GO!" … I continue to stroll. "MOX, GO FIGHT JACK NOW!" Sami screams, motioning toward the ring. It's all in slow motion as my brain pieces together what is happening in a matter of seconds. I'm now at a jog. Everyone around me seems to be panicking. Still in slow motion. Nicky must be hurt.

Minutes into the finals of TOD and Axl Rose just walked off stage. We could have a riot on our hands. This is not good. Jack's out there alone. Probably doesn't know what's going on. Am I going to the ring right now? Seems that I am. As I round the corner, Shawny appears in a full super-slo-mo panic, pointing me toward the ring with an exaggerated motion like a third base coach telling me to turn the corner and head for home plate. Guess I'm going to the ring. As I pass Shawny, I hear him behind me, "Do you want a shirt?"

"I'm good," my autopilot replies. Time to call it in the ring.

Jack meets me at the curtain, I throttle him by the throat and he asks in his German accent, "What is going on?"

I instruct him to hit me with shit and he obliges. I fling him toward a bunch of light tubes, feed in, and begin getting smashed with them one after another while I try to assess the situation and formulate a plan. Boy, I'd love to grab a chinlock right now. Into the ring we go. Buying more time, I eat a light tube headbutt sandwich. I'm sent into a pane and realize the situation I'm in when I slip on the mat and barely make contact with it. All the broken tubes and dust littering the ring sent my feet right out from under me. Now rolling over to get up and do it again, I realize I'm a human Taipei fist being dipped in glass, and I'm wearing nothing but shorts. All I see is white. I feel like I'm in a giant snow globe. I feel the hundreds of little cuts all over my body. Too late to back out now. I destroy the pane this time by spearing it with my face as hard as I can.

After about a minute of killing time, taking abuse, the heels run in and gang up on Jack. Then all the babyfaces come out and run off the heels and everyone beats up D. J. All the good guys celebrate, Jack is presented with the trophy, everyone chants "C-Z-W" … *yada yada yada* … crowd goes home happy, no riot having ensued.

But the night is STILL not over yet.

Last I had seen Nicky, he was wearing a white Chicago Bulls home jersey. Now when I saw him backstage, clutching his arm to his side as hard as he could, I thought he had changed into a red away jersey. Then I realized it was the same white jersey, but it was literally soaked in blood, sopping wet. The crowd was asked to not go anywhere so that we could get an ambulance in here as quick as possible. This was a dire situation. There was only concern for the health and wellbeing of their hero. What the fuck kinda directions you gonna give an ambulance? And how long is that gonna take? I wondered. Somebody must have been thinking the same thing because soon after that, a helicopter was touching down in the middle of this deranged circus to airlift Nicky outta there. I can't imagine what the scene must have looked like to them from the air. In a closing scene straight out of Hollywood, Nicky was stretchered into the copter as the sun went down and the whole crowd chanted "Nick FN Gage!"

What a F'n wild day. Grant and I walked up to D. J.'s parents' house to take painful post-light-tube showers that left their poor bathroom looking like a scene from Carrie. We loaded the car and I drank beers in the back, twitching and fidgeting, pulling little pieces of glass out of my skin that were barely bigger than grains of sand. I still have chunky scars all over my legs from that day.

Even though in actuality I didn't really do anything, jumping into the ring without hesitation, basically naked, when CZW was in crisis, earned me a whole new level of respect. Zandig even went out of his way to say thank you on CZW's website, saying something about how I was still a piece-of-shit heel, but he respected my guts. My next appearance at the arena, I'd be met with an ovation instead of the usual "Fuck you, you pussy," treatment.

We awaited word about Nicky's condition, but at the moment we weren't all that concerned, he was in good hands. He'd even been trying to convince them to let him go back to the ring. In a few days we would see the footage. Nicky took a shitcan bump through the top and middle rope through the vertical tubes and when he did, it sliced his armpit wide open. He landed on his ass, took one look at it, chicken winged his arm to his side and power walked outta there. He knew instantly he was fucked up. It's absolutely horrifying. Turns out there are a lot of major veins and arteries in your armpit. This was a worst-case scenario. He could have bled to death easily if he hadn't got help in time. In fact ... he did. We found out Nick Gage was legally dead for seven minutes in that helicopter.

JOKE CLAUDIO TOLD ME:

BECAUSE OF QUARANTINE
I'M MAKING ONLY
INSIDE JOKES.

"What if we started the match that way?" I ask.

Jimmy Jacobs was my opponent in an "I Quit" match that night. He smiled and thought it over. I have suggested Jimmy start the match by appearing in the balcony. From there, he'll jump off the railing and take me out with a crossbody before I know what hit me, from the ceiling into the ring. I assure him I will catch him. Jimmy knows I'll catch him. He trusts me, that's not the issue. Our issue is traditional thinking tells you that starting a match with such a bang would leave you nowhere to go. I know that logic. I understand that logic. I've heard all the analogies.

"Fuck it, let's do it," Jimmy said. Gabe Sapolsky had been the one to tell us that we were free to do a spot on the balcony if we so chose. I just didn't wanna have to deal with getting all the way up there just for one spot. This was an elegant solution. We tell Gabe our plan.

"Then what?" he asks.

"Then we have our match" Jimmy replies.

Tonight is the first Dragon Gate USA IPPV, broadcast live. I feel that Jimmy and I have driven a lot of the interest in this show. We've been involved in a vicious feud, and the war of words has escalated. It's deeply personal. Jimmy would later tell me that for quite a while he thought I really hated him. For three or four minutes at a time, in promos Jill filmed for me on her camcorder, I probably did. I remember snorting a line about the size of a pool noodle at an afterparty in Indianapolis and yelling to her, "Get your camera! It's time!"

It's been a great rivalry that will culminate tonight when he stabs me in the dick with a metal spike. That was Jimmy's idea ... he didn't know if I would like it. I loved it. If I'm gonna say, "I quit," it's cuz I'm getting stabbed in the dick with a metal spike. Jimmy bled like a fuckin' pig. I loved that "I Quit" match.

2009

I'd started working for Gabe in 2009. There was a thing called the Jeff Peterson Memorial Cup in Florida. It would be four teams of four, each representing a different indie promotion in a 16-man tournament. There was to be a team from CZW, and it ended up being Team 74: Scotty, Drake, Ego and me. There was no pressure. We had a fun trip, driving down to the Sunshine State for some wrestling. We barely had enough money between us to make the trip. I had to pull some sleight-of-hand shit with the lady at a tollbooth just to get us to the show. The first night took place at an armory, and when we got there, we realized Gabe Sapolsky, former booker at ROH, was booking the tournament. He gave a little speech beforehand about how so many people had moved on from the indies to WWE, and it was time for a new generation to step up.

In reality, he was scouting talent for his new venture, a promotion called Evolve. I didn't know him, and I doubted he knew who I was, but before the show he asked me if I'd cut a pre-match promo for him. I obliged and was led by a camera guy to a little empty room, basically a closet. I proceeded to spit some shit off the top of my head about how I wasn't here to make friends with anybody, to-hell-with-sportsmanship kinda thing. I then went out and had a good match with a guy named Brad Attitude. This was a pure wrestling tournament and it was stacked with talent. The team format gave us a sense of CZW pride. If y'all think all we do is stab each other with shit and fall on light tubes, we're about to show you a thing or two, motherfucker. We were Team CZW. We all cheered each other on like a family.

The next night I had another cool match with Silas Young, but before that Gabe came up to me in the locker room and asked me if I could be in Philadelphia in one week's time. He was also the booker for Dragon Gate USA. They had a deal where they did PPVs that would air later on cable. PPV? Cable? These were big words for me when Gabe asked if I could make the show. I didn't know shit about Dragon Gate, and I didn't know how I would get to Philadelphia, but I knew that Gabe was the guy who gave the first major exposure to guys like Bryan, Punk and Samoa Joe. He was like the ultimate PR guy for his talent. He had been so into the promo I did off the top of my head the day before that he decided he needed to start using me immediately.

With Gabe pushing my shit, more people would see it than ever before. It would be like putting out music on a real record label.

"I'll be there," I answered without hesitation.

I was standing outside by myself after my match, smoking a cigarette, feeling good, enjoying the warm weather and looking at the night sky. This had been such a fun weekend: good friends, good matches, good times. I thought about how I might get to Philadelphia next weekend, then I was hit with a premonition. Clear as day. Unequivocal. I was going to WWE. I don't know how I knew. Maybe my confidence was such at the time that I could see exactly how the dominos were about to fall, but I think it was a legit premonition from the future. You might not believe me, and I don't give a tiny rat's ass if you do or not. It was a moment of clairvoyance. I saw abstract images that came into focus and became reality years later. "Holy shit," I thought to myself. I was a little shocked. I didn't expect that. That can't be right. I would go on to tell myself it was my imagination and forget about it. It was barely a year later that WWE called me.

There are only three guys on the planet who know what it was like to be in The Shield. Nobody can put on a T-shirt and join The Shield. The Shield does not recruit, there is no revolving door. There is and will only ever be one incarnation of the Shield: Me, Seth Rollins and Roman Reigns. It's an incredible thing to be a part of something so much bigger than yourself, something that takes on a life of its own. Something that will never truly belong to WWE. It was our baby. In creating The Shield, we created a monster. It didn't come to life in a creative meeting. It came to life before your very eyes, evolving and growing into something that captured fans' imaginations all over the world, something they could believe in. That's the kind of thing you wouldn't trade for the world.

Initially conceived as three guys whose primary focus was to guard CM Punk's WWE Championship, The Shield quickly formed a separate identity. The Punk thing was just a germ of an idea, a single-cell organism that might exist on WWE television. That's all we ever asked for while we were sitting in Tampa, the chips on our shoulders growing by the day. All we wanted was a small crack in the door so we could kick it open.

With the Foley thing scrapped, I remained patient for a while, sitting at *Raw* and *SmackDown!* every week awaiting my opportunity. I did dark matches and live events. Traveling on house-show loops was fun. I had a few really hot matches with Zack Ryder, who was on fire at the time and getting bigger reactions than anyone I'd been in the ring with up to that point. It was intoxicating, feeling that energy night after night. It was also a great opportunity for me to show I could jump right in and tear it up with a guy the crowd treated like a legit superstar. I can tell you for a fact,

because I was there, that for a minute they had it with Ryder, he was over as all hell. Of course, being WWE, it wouldn't be long before they went out of their way to fuck it up for reasons I can't explain. I'll tell you one thing about Zack Ryder, too: No matter what, he always maintained the best spray tan in the game. Respect.

After a couple months, frustration began to set in. NXT had started at Full Sail, so now I had three TVs a week at which to sit around and do nothing. I existed in a strange purgatory, not on the main roster, not part of NXT. I still had to report to FCW, but I was on the road every week. Hunter would always just tell me to be patient ... they were waiting for the right thing. I'd seen him be brutally honest with talent before and surmised he had no reason to lie to me. I chose to take him at his word and hung in there. I heard some rumored ideas. I even pitched a lot of my own to the writers in long, detailed emails.

Despite that, I wondered if my ship had sailed. I actually started to feel like I was becoming a joke. I could sense it in the dismissive way I was spoken to at TVs. Resentment grew. I did not like sitting on the sidelines. With no creative outlet, I started to lose it. I battled paranoia. I just needed something, anything. Just give me a fucking mic and an angle, I'll do the rest. I longed for a tiny crack in the door, but it remained tightly shut for seven months.

I didn't like the way I felt.

By the fall of 2012, I was ready to burn the whole fucking place down.

Seth had his own issues. He was NXT champion, but perceived attitude problems had threatened his job. He had been, as Joey so memorably put it, "a cunt hair away from being fired."

The two top guys in developmental had become anti-office. Our situation had bred an us-against-the-world mentality already. If they think Seth has an attitude, good, fuck 'em, he should have an attitude. If I make them uncomfortable, if they don't like the fact I won't kiss anybody's ass, good, then they can all suck my dick from the back.

I remember one time at Full Sail in the early days of the NXT tapings, Hunter treated everyone to a motivational video piece on the big screen in the auditorium where talent meetings took place. There's a million versions of this video on YouTube, inspirational clips accompanied by the audio of a famous speech by a guy named Eric Thomas. He tells a story about a guru who brought a guy out to the beach and took him so far out in the water he started drowning. He asked him, "When you were underwater, what did you wanna do?" The guy said, "I wanted to breathe."

Long story short, the moral of the story is you'll only be successful when you want to succeed as badly as you want to breathe. Of course, Hunter gives a little speech after the video plays. I appreciated the sentiment. There's a lot of truth in it, but for me, a guy who had sacrificed immeasurably for the sake of the art and suffered long and hard by that point, it was like yeah, no shit, what do you think I've been doing for the last eight years? In fact, what do you think we've been doing down here in Florida all this time? Getting F'n tans? We were down there busting our asses, day in, day out, and no matter how much great work we produced, we were made to feel like WWE's redheaded stepchildren. I wondered what Hunter was really trying to say with that video. Was there a subliminal message? Was it that if you really wanna succeed, you have to do more than work hard, bust your ass, or be good at what you do? Or was it that you have to be willing to lie, kiss ass, politic, throw people under the bus and stab them in the back? If you really want it, you have to be willing to sell yourself out entirely, get down on your knees and blow somebody for it and be perfectly happy looking at yourself in the mirror? If that's the case, you can take all your brass rings and shove them up your ass for somebody else to fish out. I'm not interested.

Darkness hung over me everywhere I went. Until finally, a ray of light peeked through the clouds.

The first we heard of it was in October: rumors, rumblings, some kind of angle involving new callups. Could be bad. Could be good. Could be some jobber shit, but it was something. Interests were piqued. Me, Seth, Roman and Big E were all in Atlanta for the Hell in a Cell PPV. If there was truth to these rumors, this mystery angle would likely involve some or all of us — we didn't know who. We didn't even know what it was, but we speculated we might all be in a group together. We were getting little bits and pieces of intel, enough that we learned that whatever was going down wasn't gonna go down tonight, after all.

Speculation was it would have been something to do with the Hell in a Cell main event, CM Punk vs. Ryback. I think it was the next day that we learned whatever this was, it would not involve Big E. He had his own angle coming up, but this other thing was real. Nobody really told us anything. We weren't sat down and told, "You guys are gonna be a three-man group called The Shield" or anything like that. We were left in the dark to wait for instructions. Our excitement grew and our imaginations ran wild.

Seth and I were already a team in a lot of ways. After working so closely as opponents, training, riding and surviving day-to-day in the trenches of FCW. The us-against-the-world mentality had been brewing within us for a long time now. Things were different back then for a new guy. A developmental prospect on the road would be under a microscope. One mistake, one missed handshake, one social faux pas could ruin your career. Jackals were always lurking. The locker room culture would change for the better over the next few years, but back then, remnants of a previous era remained.

I was told heat was inevitable, just don't give anyone any bullets. They can't shoot you if you don't give them any. Not the most welcoming environment. There were stories of new talent being forced to drink until they puked and stuff like that. I hate that type of bully shit.

In December of 2011, to throw us a bone, Johnny Ace sent Seth and I up on some house-show loops. I would go first. In Ft. Myers, Florida, on my first night, I worked with a pre-Yes! Movement Daniel Bryan, and we tore it up. What I remember most was sitting in the locker room beforehand and Bryan coming up to me, his head on a swivel, looking around to make sure we were alone. He told me in almost a whisper, "Don't ask anybody for advice." Reason being, if you did and were given stupid or bad advice, everyone would be watching the next time to make sure you did what you were advised to do. If you didn't follow it, you would get heat. I heeded Bryan's words. Most young guys would approach the top guys and say things like, "Did you see my match, sir? Anything I can work on?" That's just not my style. No good could come of that. That small conversation with Bryan gave me better insight into the Machiavellian shit that went on up there.

More house-show loops came for us, and Seth and I would compare notes when we got back. Joey would read us the producers' reports that were sent to the office. We were doing a great job and getting glowing reviews, but the more we went up on the road, the more we felt like outsiders. Heat was in fact, inevitable. The word going around was that Seth was cocky. I was not particularly well-liked either, not by a longshot. Seth came back from a loop once and we sat down at Four Square Burgers in Tampa with Juice to hear all about it. Seth had learned that I had major heat. How the fuck is that? For what? Ooooh, right, now I get it. I had been on a loop the previous week and on the first night, I got stiffed really bad, knocked completely fuckin' stupid and barely finished the match in a total punch-drunk haze. I have no memory of what happened next because I was concussed, but when we got to the back, allegedly, I, a nobody from FCW, proceeded to motherfuck my opponent about it, in front of a locker room full of WWE stars. You can imagine how this may have been received by some.

I didn't even know I had been concussed until the next morning when I realized I'd been totally out of it all night and couldn't remember any of the match. No big deal, shit happens. We had a great match the next night, and I didn't think anything of it, but gossip happens. Third- and fourth-hand stories get blown out of proportion, and before you know it, your reputation precedes you.

Seth told me another story once about some guys who obviously didn't like him trying to get him to drink with them. Not in a friendly, "Dude, let's have a beer" way, but in a "Hey, we think you're cocky, so we're gonna try and make you do a bunch of shots to prove you're one of the boys" bully way. Seth's not a drinker. My fucking blood boiled. That's my boy. I did not care for that at all. This kinda shit brought us together. What were all these guys' problems anyway? *Fuck 'em*, we thought. When we get our chance, we'll just outwork and outperform all of them. They can't stop us, but it seemed like that's exactly what the whole world was trying to do. Our pitches to creative went ignored. Dr. Tom had been fired. Rob MacIntyre had been fired. FCW was in the midst of a hostile takeover, and operations were set to move to Orlando.

It appeared to be now or never.

If this was our shot, we'd likely only get one, which was fine with us.

We had lost all semblance of patience.

By the time we sat in a car talking about what this thing might be, brainstorming ideas, we had some serious attitudes. Together, with a common cause and shared experience, frustration and anger simmering under the surface, we were even more combustible.

Nobody had any idea the incendiary ingredients they were playing with.

Then ... they went and gave us a heater.

First time I met Roman was my third day at FCW with that weird mock show put on for the office types. He was known as Leakee then, jacked up, ripped, great hair, the whole deal, moved around the ring really well too. The guy sitting next to me mentioned who some of this Leakee's relatives were. "They love him," he said.

I wondered where on the family tree he was in relation to Matty. Standing around outside later I asked as much. "He's my brother," Roman told me. This gave us a connection right away. Matty, after leaving WWE, had come back to HWA and worked with me a few times as RO-Z. After a match we had in Dayton, Cody told me Matty came back through the curtain, looked at him and said matter-of-factly, "He's gonna get a contract." At 20 years old working with a real-life WWE star, fresh off TV, that was a huge boost for my confidence. I never forgot it.

Ambrose and Rollins were names already becoming inextricably tied together. It wouldn't have been a big shock to anybody if we had come up together in some form. We were beginning to understand, from what little we were told, that we would be in some way affiliated with CM Punk. If it was true, that would seem to be a fit. Punk's presentation was anti-establishment, and we all had indie street cred. Roman was a football player, from a family cemented in WWE legend. On the surface, the parallels might not have been obvious, but from the moment we all began to realize that whatever this was gonna be, it was gonna be us three, it felt right. I can't explain why. Although, I remember talking with Seth and we realized something. I think the reason we had such great chemistry as opponents and later as partners was because we were totally different. We brought different things to the table. ... I remember we realized, what's the one thing we're missing? A big-ass goddamn powerhouse Samoan.

Roman had a young daughter and a family to provide for. Living in a rented townhouse, he'd been paying his dues in developmental for two years. All his eggs were in this basket, and he wasn't interested in waiting around any longer. He was ready to reach out and take it. His loyalty was to his family, therefore his loyalty would also lie with us, because if we were gonna make a run at the top of the hill, if we were gonna throw up our middle fingers and go after the money, Roman was gonna ride with us.

Y'all fucked up and gave us a heater.

The concept of this angle, what this group was supposed to be, was still vague. We held tight. Joey was really tight with Punk back then, and he pulled the three of us into the front lobby of the FCW Arena for a top-secret briefing. We all stood at the concession stand, and Joey confirmed we would be coming in with Punk, in the main-event storyline. We looked around at the PPV posters lining the walls. There were no more specifics given. The most important thing, as Joey explained, was that we stick together, at all times. We would be a threat. We would make a lot of enemies. There would be attempts to infiltrate us, to pull us apart. This was our shot ... it was us against the world. We must maintain our solidarity in face of this challenge. We would have each other's backs. We would ride together, room together, train together. Fight and stand our ground together. All for one, one for all.

As we turned around to leave, walking down the hall toward the door leading back out to the gym, Joey caught the first glimpse: a silhouette of Ambrose, Rollins and Reigns, shoulder to shoulder. "Stop!" he said, he stared at us with a grin on his face, taking it in. "This. ... I like this."

INDIANAPOLIS, NOVEMBER 11, 2012

"You wanna hear it?" Seth says, behind the wheel of a rented Chevy Malibu. We're heading from the airport to the TV hotel in Downtown Indianapolis. He has gotten some intel. He knows what our name is. I didn't even know we were gonna have a name. All I know for sure is that some shit is supposed to go down tomorrow night, at Survivor Series. My palms sweat and I fidget in the passenger seat. Do I wanna hear this? I cringe. I brace myself. Roman's head pops up in between us from the backseat. "It's ... The Shield," Seth annunciates slowly.

"The Shield?" I ask.

"The Shield," he confirms. Silence lingers. I try this on for size. I stare ahead and repeat it in my head a few times. I visualize it in print: The Shield.

"Like the show?"

"Yeah."

"What's that?"

"It's a cop show."

"Yeah, it's pretty good."

"The guy from *The Commish*."

Nothing.

"Dude, you've never seen *The Commish? Commish rules.*"

"I think he was also The Thing."

"Yeah, that movie sucked."

Silence in the car again.

The Shield.

I finally come to a conclusion.

"It's not bad. I kinda like it," I say.

"Sounds pretty dope," Roman says.

"It's not bad," Seth agrees.

We ride on, we're all excited. The moment we've all been waiting for is 24 hours away.

This was our shot.

Was his name Michael Chiklis? I wonder.

Roman pops his head up again, "Wasn't that the shit in *The Avengers*? Are people gonna think we're trying to be superheroes or something?"

We briefly consider this.

Nah, it's not a problem, we decide.

It's not bad. The Shield.

BROOKLYN, DECEMBER 15, 2012

It's WWE's first ever show at the Barclays Center, TLC on PPV. The most intriguing entree of the night will be The Shield's first official match, a Tables, Ladders and Chairs match against Ryback, Kane and Daniel Bryan. The last month has been a whirlwind, a dizzying amount of travel, photo shoots, and main-event segments on TV. We got over. Real quick. They were going with it. We were brought in for a tour of Titan Towers. It was like we were being given the keys to the castle. They led us to a big-ass room full of merchandise, toys, shirts and every other F'n thing and said, "Take whatever you want, we'll ship it to you." This is like some childhood fever-dream shit. I grabbed a bunch of DVDs, but I ended up leaving them in the apartment with Cass when I took off to Vegas. After we got done working out in the gym, which was straight out of a 1987 issue of *Muscle and Fitness*, quads blasted, pecs decked, The Fink appeared as if from nowhere to congratulate us on how well we were doing. It was like, of course, we're in magical WWE land and The Fink just lives here.

We had stood in a recording booth like the Shirelles and performed the lines "Sierra, Hotel, India, Echo, Lima, Delta." We were getting a real Jim Johnston original theme. It was all moving very fast. It wouldn't be long before they'd be sending us to signings at shopping malls and we'd be walking into throngs of screaming teenage girls. A month ago, we were nobodies, and all of a sudden we're the fucking Backstreet Boys.

We've been creating what The Shield would eventually become on the fly, making it up as we went along. That first night at Survivor Series, our mission was to destroy Ryback. After he hit his finisher on then-WWE champ CM Punk, but before he could make a cover. Punk had put it in our ear that people might be in Ryback's ear telling him not to sell for us. As would be the case in these scenarios going forward, our philosophy was, there's three of us and one of him. Of course, Ryback is a sweetheart, but our mindset was this guy was standing in our way. We were seeing red, velociraptors locked on target. The instant we were let loose from our pens, we sprinted from the back of the arena, fangs out, and descended on the ring in a hurricane of steel-toed boots and fists. Seth and I were practically falling over each other to get to this guy, driven mad by hunger.

We beat the fuck out of Ryback. I remember pulling his foot out from underneath him when he tried to get up, we completely smothered him. Earlier in the day, workshopping the best way to put this big bastard through a table, I remember saying something about maybe we could do a kind of Dudley-style power bomb. From there, we created the Shield Triple Power Bomb. Initially just a pragmatic solution to serve our purposes for the night, it would become our trademark and the most destructive weapon in the game. The first night they gave us black turtlenecks to go with our pants and heavy boots. By now we had started wearing tactical vests and raiding army surplus stores for anything that looked cool. We ordered lighter combat boots from 511 Tactical that made us faster and more nimble. We had morphed into this paramilitary SWAT team. We looked fucking cool, man.

On that first night they had actual riot shields for us, big plastic monstrosities with "Shield" actually printed on them. The excitement of our debut must have briefly clouded my judgement because I was actually pretty into them for a minute. I was like, I can fuck somebody up with this. I remember Fit Finlay showing us the proper stance and posture to correctly use the shields. Luckily when Vince saw them, from 40 feet away, he yelled something like, "If you guys are so badass, do you need those?"

"Fuck, no, we don't!" I screamed and we all agreed. The shields were never spoken of again. Thank God, cuz if we had come out with those goofy-ass things you might not be reading this book. Somebody for sure would have tripped and fell trying to get in the ring with such a cumbersome instrument, and that for sure would have been me.

For the last few weeks, we'd been doing run-ins and developing the Shield style of attack. We were just PASTING motherfuckers in those days. It was us against them ... fuck 'em. If anybody had any thoughts about making some sort of an impromptu comeback to save some face, those thoughts would quickly go out the window. If you threw Seth off your back, I was on your leg. If you got ahold of Roman, Seth and I would have our claws sunk into you. You'd have to swat us out of your hair like bats, and if you managed to do that and took your eye off Roman you'd get run over by a train.

We didn't give anyone any room to breathe. We were pros ... we never hurt anybody, but there were a lot of busted lips, black eyes and bruises. It wouldn't take long for the higher-ups to privately give us the blessing to be as physical as necessary, despite the complaints, of which there were many. This emboldened us further. What we were doing was working.

I remember when we put a shellacking on The Rock in San Jose. When we made it back into Gorilla you could hear a pin drop. Awkward silence. We looked at the monitor on the wall and saw the highest grossing movie star in the world face first on the mat, coughing up blood. I think every single producer, writer, referee and hot dog vendor within 100 yards was scared for their job in that moment. We stood close together and shared looks with each other. I leaned into to Roman while we watched Rocky mix the blood with his spit to make it look better. It shined fluorescent red on the mat.

"That's F'n awesome," I whispered in his ear, "That's money, *baaabbby.*"

I swear to God, nobody in Gorilla said a single word for several minutes, until Rocky came back through the curtain, looking a little shellshocked. He was swarmed by offerings of towels and Fiji water. His eyes darted around, searching, and locked onto us, he pushed through the crowd, came right over, and a big smile broke out on his face. He thanked us and shook our hands, explaining to the concerned parties something about the cold air and blood vessels in his lungs. Happens all the time, he said. Rock was happy. A Tsunami-sized wave of relief washed over Gorilla. Guys were shaking hands and grabbing each other by the shoulders, overcome with joy as if nuclear war had just been narrowly avoided.

Our operations were obviously serving the interests of Punk and Paul Heyman, but they would always disavow all knowledge of our actions. In those early days, we stayed close with them. Sometimes we'd ride on Punk's bus. One time Paul jumped in a van with us on a drive from Philly to Pittsburgh after *Raw.* He boasted that he never fell asleep. Ten minutes into the ride, he had nodded off in the front seat, snoring. We hit the first stop on the turnpike and Paul went up to the Starbucks and ordered eight venti iced coffees with cream. Two for each of us. That's a lot of F'n caffeine. I remember sitting in the backseat, nursing my first giant beverage when I noticed Paul had sucked down his first before we hardly got back on the highway. He transformed in a matter of minutes, electric shocks practically visibly sparking around him as he launched into four hours of a Paul E. TED Talk about the business, draining his second gargantuan iced coffee at a clip.

We never heard anything about longer-term plans. Everything was day-to-day. We had expected our affiliation with Punk and Heyman would continue after they were outed as having hired us as mercenaries, but we were getting signs otherwise. I wasn't there for any of the initial conversations about Punk having a group, so I can't speak to what exactly that original vision was. I do know, however, that Hunter had his own vision. With the Death Star under construction in Orlando, and having taken charge of the developmental system, Hunter saw the Shield as an opportunity to bring three guys up from his freshly rebranded NXT who could make an impact. We could sense we were in the middle of something, but we didn't want to be pulled in either direction or serve anybody's motivations. This was our baby now.

It was an intense time. We didn't trust anybody. Our dreams were in reach. ... We were on a high-speed bullet train, the world passing by us in a blur. It was vital we didn't let anybody throw it off the tracks. We wouldn't let anybody screw this up for us. We had the hot hand and we were raking in chips, but the stakes of the game were about to get even higher.

If I remember correctly, it was an injury to Punk that forced a change in the card. We were standing on the ramp before *SmackDown!* in Charleston, South Carolina, when we learned our first match was the next week, on PPV. It would be a six-man TLC match. There would be a lot of elements at play, six players and a lot of inanimate objects. There would be no soft opening for The Shield's official in-ring debut. We'd debut on a live PPV before a sold-out New York crowd. We had to steal the show. This would be make or break. You've never seen three happier guys in your life.

We had only had one actual match as a team, the night before the PPV, in Wilkes-Barre, Pennsylvania. We'd spent most of the afternoon at the ring for what they called a rehearsal with Kane, Bryan and Ryback bandying about ideas and staring at ladders. It was only mildly productive. By showtime, all our minds on the next night, we rushed out for a regular six-man tag. Having come through the crowd for all our appearances thus far, and being positioned as an invading force that wouldn't be welcome in the locker room, we decided it made sense to enter the same way for the match. Michael Hayes agreed and got it approved. Our signature entrance was born.

After weeks of chaotic special forces operations and attacks, finding ourselves in a basic tag match was a jarring change of pace. We had never actually wrestled as a team before, and it felt like we were a band rushed on stage for our first performance together, instruments barely tuned, a set list thrown together, getting a feel for each other's presence on stage.

Roman was all instinct. It was in his blood, like a baby turtle who knows to make its way to the ocean. He was always where he needed to be ... his timing was there. He kept his ears open at all times. Over the next year he would improve literally every night. Seth and I could practically read each other's minds. It was a basic wrestling-school six-man and we got through it in 10 minutes. It felt like it lasted 30 seconds. A quick little test drive in the parking lot. Tomorrow, we would get her out on the highway and see what she could do.

The beauty of The Shield in those days was that we were three complete unknowns. Facing all-star teams of WWE superstars, it would appear on paper that we were outgunned. The secret to our success was that we were like the old Soviet hockey teams. We played a system. We always got the puck to the open man ... we were a machine. We pushed the pace and made our opponents try to keep up until they eventually broke. The idea being that the great team will prevail over the collection of great individuals. This was the strategy we brought to TLC: divide and conquer, isolate, create two-on-one situations, overwhelm. Michael Cole would refer to this as "the numbers game" or our "pack mentality." This principle would be the story of the match and the backbone of countless kick-ass Shield six-mans in the future.

Another hallmark of Shield matches that fans might not know is that they always seemed to be put together at the last minute. *Raw, SmackDown!*, PPV, whatever it was, it always seemed like no matter how early everyone sat down to talk about a match, nothing would really get hammered out until the 11th hour. I can picture Michael Hayes, running up to us with a pen and an empty yellow legal pad, begging us to give him something to write down. Roman and Seth are bent over at the waist by the makeup table drenching their hair in conditioner; Tommy the producer is screaming at us "Shield, we gotta go now!" Entering from the top of the arena meant we had to head up at least ten minutes beforehand. Those last couple of minutes before we ran down the hallway, flanked by security, following the lead of either Sassy or John Marx, who have already scouted the route, were always chaotic. As soon as we left, we would be cut off from communication to Gorilla, save for maybe a poorly translated message over a headset that left us more confused. Last-second details, changes in times or commercial breaks, sometimes even finishes, would be shouted down the hallway as we looked back over our shoulders and gave thumbs up, whether we heard correctly or not.

"Did you hear what he said?"

"Nope."

Tommy would be jogging beside us with waters and gum. We would run up flight after flight of stairs, getting a good pre-match blowout of the lungs and raising the heart rate. Sometimes we'd have a good spot to chill and stay loose while we made sure that no matter what happened, at least the three of us were all on the same page. If we had to go into a public area on the concourse, it would be complete pandemonium. The procession would bulldoze through hysterical fans taking a piss or getting a hot dog, caught off guard that their seats had just become front row. We would often be herded into janitors' closets and tight spaces of the sort. We spent a lot of time in janitors' closets.

This night in Brooklyn would be typical Shield.

I remember riding a bus into an elevator. We descended into the bottom of the brand-spanking-new Barclays Center. After we exited, the bus would spin around on a giant turntable and drive back into the elevator to ascend again. An elevator big enough to hold a bus?! That shit blew my mind. I don't remember much about the next few hours, other than that when we arrived, either Hunter or Vince or both didn't like what we had come up with the previous day for our match. I don't even remember what that was, but we were back at square one, trying to come up with a finish that appeased everybody.

Once that was out of the way, the six of us sat in the production meeting room with Michael. A lot of ideas got thrown around. Tension was rising ... we could feel the hands of the clock ticking, getting ever closer to showtime as we tried to piece this thing together. As soon as it seemed like we were really getting somewhere, The Shield was taken away to do a promo. It took *foooooreeeever*. I remember the three of us standing in this little room holding scripts just bursting at the seams. We wanted to get out of there and get back to what we were doing. Before we knew it, we were up. It was time.

It was a blur of time and space, guys with headsets and security as we moved through hallways and stairwells. "We have The Shield. We're on the move," I hear.

In an elevator, packed shoulder to shoulder with all those accompanying us, we stood in a tight huddle and went over everything, or at least what we hoped was everything. We hadn't seen or talked to our opponents in quite some time. There was no producer here. We were on our own. This is the most important night in all our lives. Make or break. Stress level is high. This thing was far from nailed down. We never got that one satisfactory all six guys get together, go over it and make sure they're all on the same page moment. In the future, we'd rarely if ever get those, but after tonight we'd never need one.

We established fail-safes and planned for alternate scenarios.

We emerged into some kind of not-yet-open-for-business bar/lounge area. Security went outside to clear the pathway, leaving us alone in the quiet. All the radio chatter and chaotic energy gone, just the three of us in the room, we made peace with our situation. Fed up with having to think so much, I remember blurting out, "Fuck it!!"

We are confident.

At this point, whatever happens happens. Our attitude is, This match is gonna be fucking sick no matter what. We are gonna make it fucking work. The chips on our shoulders are now weaponized.

We are a team.

Nobody is nervous.

"Sierra, Hotel ..." we hear out in the arena. "Is that our music?" Seth asks.

"I dunno" I answer.

"GO, GO, GO!" the headsets yell at us. We assume that's our music. We've never heard it before.

Emerging at the top of the steps among 16,000 fans felt like opening the hatch on a plane you were about to jump out of. An indescribable "WHOOOOOOSSSHH" of adrenaline. No turning back now, we jump without hesitation and begin our descent, faces of screaming fans rushing by us, paratroopers preparing to land in a war zone, as soon as our boots hit the ground we will be in the heat of combat. Everything is on the line. All we have is our will, our guts and each other.

This match is still my favorite match we ever had. There's a rawness to it, a purity. The stakes were so high and so real. None of us had ever seen a PPV check in our lives. There were no houses, no Range Rovers, no Teslas, no 2015 Dodge Rams. We had been given the chance to put our money where our mouths were. We would step up to the plate without fear and knock it out of the park.

Years from now, being live on PPV, in a packed arena on the big stage would become old hat. I'd struggle to manufacture adrenaline. On this day, however, it was the most electric experience of my life. This is what we've been waiting for all this time sitting down in FCW: the lights, the crowd, the *oohs* and *ahhhs*. The New York crowd was deafening. Being front-and-center in the WWE ring on PPV, I had a flashback to when we were in high school and used to go to Buffalo Wild Wings to watch PPVs. Attendance was only for paying customers. I would order a soda because that's all I had enough money for and refill it five or six times throughout the show. The whole place would cheer and boo and go nuts for title changes. I would always leave on a high, walking home in a fantasy world where the patrons of BW3s were watching me on the screen.

The brawl began the moment we got over the barricade. The action built and we cut a hell of a pace. We never slowed down. Every time a babyface was taken out, they'd be replaced by a fresh house of fire. Every time a Shield member was about to be taken out, another one would be there for the save. Kane, Bryan and Ryback were all fucking tremendous. The six of us were magically and thankfully all on the exact same wavelength the entire match. Everything hit right on the money.

We employ our strategy, continually gaining a numbers advantage through all the ebbs and flows. A Shield pride takes over in the gray area where storyline meets reality. We feel like the best team in the world. These guys can't beat us ... they're not even a real team.

When we have the advantage, we dissect our opposition, carnivores tearing flesh off the carcass of our prey. When we lose the advantage, we bump our asses off. Seth and I bounce around the ring like rubber balls. Every time the heroes, the established WWE stars, seem to really gather momentum, here comes another fucking Shield guy. The numbers are even, but it seems there's just too many of us.

For all much of the audience knew, we were just extras in some storyline. The big question coming into TLC was: Are these guys for real? As the match unfolded, with every save, with every double team, that question was getting answered. We were winning, so the reaction and next logical question was: Jesus, who the fuck ARE these guys?

We command the ring. Acutely aware of where our partners are at all times. Implicit trust in one another.

I am happy to utilize chairs. I bring the Necro Butcher chair bodyslam to WWE, delivering two to Bryan. I give Kane a Lita-inspired DDT, driving his thick, masked head into a chair. I'm in the zone, feeling it. We've been riding the wave of the hot crowd ... it almost seems too good to be true. About the time Seth and I are positioning Bryan for a double superplex off a table propped up on the top turnbuckle, we feel and hear the crowd. We know this is the shit.

We attempt the same superplex on Kane, but he knocks me down and sends Seth careening to the floor, before bouncing off that table and sailing his big ass through the air with a vintage Flying Cow like it was 1998. The match is a wild and exhausting sprint. Complete chaos. We Triple Power Bomb Ryback through a table again, but there's Bryan diving through the ropes and kicking the piss out of all of us. Bryan puts me in the Yes Lock, then Seth, then Roman, but there's just too many of these Shield guys. I convince Kane to Chokeslam me through an open chair. He's reluctant at first, but I assure him I'll be fine. I see the people stand up as Kane Goozles me; they see it coming. I destroy the chair. Roman makes the save. Too many of 'em. Ryback seems to have it in the bag and hits his finish in the middle, but ... too many goddamn Shield guys.

In a spontaneous moment of explosive physicality, Roman spears Kane through the barricade. We bury him in rubble, taking him off the board. We lure Ryback away from the ring. He launches Seth from a ladder 15 feet to the floor. Seth takes a gnarly bump and smokes his head on a table. Ryback stands triumphant for a moment. I got one! he thinks. It's too late, though, it's already over. Roman and I have Bryan two-on-one in the ring. No help is coming for him. He's eaten alive. I feed Bryan up to Roman sitting on the top turnbuckle for a Super Bomb through a table in the middle of the ring. Roman makes the cover. I play defense, but I know there's no need. It's checkmate.

It's an emphatic statement.

Coming through in the clutch like we did, we were made. Soon, Shield six-mans would become must-see TV. We would become an even more well-oiled machine, tearing the house down every night all over the country against every all-star combination you could think of. Even the guys who didn't like us eventually came around. Instead of feeling threatened by The Shield, now they wanted to work with us. We were having killer match after killer match, and making our opponents look great. We would go on a long undefeated streak in six-man tags. The writers kept trying to beat us. We refused time after time, standing our ground together. It got downright awkward sometimes, but we had strength in solidarity. We knew the equity in what we had built and were not willing to give it away.

I remember in February we were gearing up for a PPV match with Ryback, Sheamus and John Cena. Cena was going to the main event at Mania. We were hot, we were fresh. If we went out there with Cena and took the fuckin' *schmootz* and got pinned like everybody else, we would then become everybody else. It would kill us. I remember after the go-home *Raw*, being in the car with an uneasy feeling in my stomach.

"I ain't fucking doing it," I said. "Whether they fire us or we get Cena'd and killed off, it's all the same. We're dead either way."

"Hell, no," Seth said. "They're not beating us."

"Nah, dawg," Roman concurred.

Eventually, after months and months we couldn't delay the inevitable any longer and on *SmackDown!*, we lost a six-man tag for the first time. On free TV. Thinking back on it now, I still think we could have gotten way more out of that undefeated streak. But writers gonna write. Fittingly, and upon our insistence, it would be Bryan that scored the game-winner.

At Barclays, we were pumped up, fist bumping and savoring victory both literal and figurative as we made our way through the curtain. There was so much to come, and it would come at us fast. Headlining Europe tours, opening the show in Wales and, jumping in a helicopter to London while *Raw* was already on the air, we landed and walked straight up to the concourse for a six-man we'd have to call on the fly with Kane, Bryan and The Undertaker.

Our first WrestleMania, I remember walking out into the open air of the stadium, staged under an awning. Before our music hit, with nothing playing on the speakers, I felt the reverberation of the giant human mass buzzing in my bones. We would get our first real contracts. As a team, we decided to not draw any attention to the matter and milk those developmental contracts, double-dipping for as long as possible. We'd get our regular weekly checks, plus payoffs for house shows, TVs, PPV checks AND a free rental car.

After Europe, we landed on a Monday afternoon with the Blue Tour, but instead of getting a day off before *SmackDown!*, we were picked up by a bus and taken to *Raw* immediately. We walked into Nationwide Arena in Columbus, Ohio, and tore the house down in yet another six-man main event. Afterward, the jig was up. We were brought into an office and we expected to sign our standard low-downside guarantees. By this time however, we were an established main-event act. We were the workhorses they were relying on more and more. Vince rewarded us by giving us more than double the standard downside, increasing every year for three years.

Ultimately, that didn't matter, because being on the road Friday to Tuesday every week for the next two years, we always crushed our downside, but up to that point we had been nickel-and-diming, splitting express deal rooms on Priceline between the three of us. I didn't mind sleeping on the floor. ... I was good at it. As far as we knew, this could end at any moment. When we walked out of that office, we were walking on air. They stuffed us in a car service to shuttle us to somewhere in Michigan for *SmackDown!* As we relaxed in the Suburban, we felt a huge sense of victory. We had taken the hill and the money. Together, we had gotten to the honey hole.

That was all in the near future.

Back in Brooklyn, the babyfaces, the first all-star team we ever defeated, are all separated by at least 100 feet when the match ends. Divided and conquered. Roman and I pick up Seth, and the three of us leave together in the same camera shot, no man left behind. All the final pieces that made up The Shield fell into place, and it happened in real time. Three guys, all totally different, who believed in themselves and each other. Three guys from different backgrounds who brought something different to the table came together as a team with a common goal. Three guys with attitudes, powered by the only fuel I've ever known: hunger, anger, frustration, and a drive to take down all who sought to stand in their way. We became unstoppable.

LAS VEGAS, MARCH 23, 2021, 6:58 A.M.

My hips hurt, especially the left one. WTF, my *hips*? If there was ever a sign of getting old, this must be it. I've never really had trouble with my knees, either. In fact, I've violently twisted and torqued my lower limbs in enough directions they shouldn't even be attached to my body anymore. Swelling and pain comes, of course, but it always vanishes like it was never there … a little too expediently, I've often thought, suspiciously, like I'm freakin' made of elastic. That was then, this is now. I'm sitting downstairs this morning, sipping a coffee. Wife and dogs are still in bed. The sun is freshly risen, and I listen to the birds chirping outside as I write. A great feature of this house is the greenery in the backyard. We have a lot of trees, so we get all kinds of birds … lots of hummingbirds, sometimes a roadrunner wanders in. We have one big-ass tree, native to the Mediterranean. God bless whoever got that sumbitch to grow in the desert. I put a chew in … maybe the nicotine will somehow magically make my knees stop aching and create lubrication in my hips … my newfound problems that seemed to surface at the exact moment I turned 35.

I gotta train at 8:00 a.m. with Gil, a little earlier than usual as I have to fly to Jacksonville at 2:00 p.m., and I wanna get something in before I sit on a plane all day. I usually train in the morning and wake up two hours prior because it takes my creaky body at least an hour to loosen up and become operable. I'll arrive in Jacksonville just before midnight and rent a car. This new Marriott we're staying at is 45 minutes from the airport, so I'll be in my room about 1:00 a.m. I will call Renée and put *Family Guy* or *Friends* on the TV in the background, as has been my habit in hotels for years. One of them is usually on around that time. I'll sit down and try to write. If uninspired, I'll just read a little, or I'll play with promos in my head ... probably sip a cocktail. I'll consider having a hot shower to loosen up my neck, which will be immobile by that time, and soothe the rest of my aching muscles, but I won't, cuz then I'd have to get up.

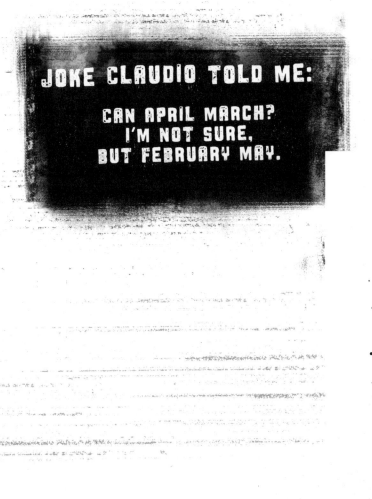

JOKE CLAUDIO TOLD ME:

CAN APRIL MARCH?
I'M NOT SURE,
BUT FEBRUARY MAY.

JANUARY 2019

First I heard of Tony Khan was from Chris Jericho. I hadn't talked with Chris in some time about anything that didn't involve Sasquatch, lake monsters or UFOs. I did know he had been doing a lot of stuff outside WWE. He wrestled for New Japan and even had his own cruise now. After our New Year's Day hike, I mentioned to Renée that I was gonna hit up Jericho and get the lay of the land from his perspective. I hadn't been on the indies since 2011, and the whole landscape outside WWE had changed dramatically in eight years. I never made dick on the indies, but now a lot of folks were making good money. There were groups with TV; there was something called GCW now. These days everyone can stream. Guess DVDs aren't a thing anymore.

Before I left CZW, Drake, Nick Gage and I had a three-way light tube fest in front of 50 rabid Lumberton, North Carolina, fans at a weird bought show, sacrificing pints of blood for the sole purpose of putting out a hot seller on Smart Mark Video. Everything's different. I'm F'n Rip Van Winkle. There seemed to be a lot of cross promotion now. It was a little overwhelming trying to make sense of it all.

I figured Jericho could give me a good look at who might be totally full of shit. I also just wanted to talk to another wrestler. I hadn't breathed a word about my plans to anyone but my wife, and I didn't feel I could talk about it with anybody in WWE. Chris is one of the smartest guys in the business and somebody I trust, so I was curious about what the reaction would be when I told him I was planning to walk across a bridge I knew full well would likely blow up behind me.

I sent Jericho a text on the afternoon of January 1 to hit me up. I never heard back. He's a busy dude … probably on tour or some shit. I saw some stuff about this new AEW thing over the next couple weeks. I thought it was just another indie. I saw some guys I see on all these other shows ... that Pentagon dude. It looked like they were bringing in Jericho for a big show — that's cool. I didn't think it was anything out of the ordinary. Seems like there's like 200 companies, and they all have three letters. I had too many of my own problems at hand to go sorting through them all. For now, I was just focused on getting to the finish line.

It was a few weeks later. I was riding in the back seat with Hennig and Bo on the way to Memphis for *Raw*. I had to text Jenna Loeb from TR about something, and scrolling through the Js in my phone right next to her name was "Jericho NEW." Now I remember. The MFer had changed his number a few months back, and I had texted his old one. I texted Chris's current number the same message I had before, and about 30 seconds later he hit me back. We decided to talk the next day.

Jericho called me while I was in the hotel room, dreading having to go to *Raw* that afternoon. This would be a conversation of the highest kayfabe, we agreed before I finally dropped my bombshell along with three or four minutes of the reasoning that had brought me here. I half expected Jericho to try to talk me off the ledge. ... For all I knew he was gearing up for a return at the Royal Rumble. Without hesitation he just said, "Yeah, that's why I left," before going into some of his own creative frustrations.

I volleyed back some more of my own baggage, which he returned with more of his own. The conversation quickly escalated into a full-blown bitching-about-WWE session, the kind that can only take place between two people who have worked there. We talked for almost an hour before he mentioned this AEW thing. He explained to me that this is a real thing and he's signed a deal there. There's real money. Real backing. These people aren't stupid, and they're trying to do it right. There is a guy named Tony Khan. "They're gonna make a go of it" he says. "This is what I'm doing for the next three years."

This is a lot to process.

My initial reaction is, I want to be a part of it. I try to quell my excitement, but it's just so nice to talk about new possibilities instead of how I'm gonna buttfuck a corpse in seg six tonight. Just make sure you finish in four minutes, and Vince wants to see a lot of brains.

Cody Rhodes is involved. I know Cody. Jericho asks if he can have Cody call me. I agree. This remains top-secret-security-clearance-level shit. Cody calls me as I'm pulling into the garage for TV. I go to an empty staircase in the concourse and call back. Cody explains to me what's happening with AEW. I listen. There is much more infrastructure in place then they're letting on. There's talk of network television. I'm filled in on what exactly AEW is … this guy Tony Khan again. It's mostly just a pleasant catch-up conversation. There's only so much to talk about. I still have almost four months left with WWE, and AEW ain't even gonna run a show till May. As it would turn out, 25 days after my WWE contract expired. Where?

"Wait, what MGM?"

"Vegas."

Pretty fuckin' interesting.

MAY 2019

It wasn't as easy of a decision to sign with AEW as you might think. The last few months in WWE were exhausting and super-awkward. I was mentally shot. I didn't feel like I had the energy to just jump right back into being on TV every week and dealing with all these people. What if this AEW just turned out to be another WWE? I just wanted space. I just needed to get my head right. A one-night stand sounded nice, but I wasn't looking for a long-term relationship. I didn't want to just jump right into a rebound fling and regret it as soon as I woke up naked in the bathtub at the Hard Rock with a contractual obligation to a company I knew nothing about.

But I liked everything I was hearing. I can play my music my own way, I am told. There are no scriptwriters.

What's more, though, was the timing. Such serendipity is hard to ignore. So much in this life is about timing. I didn't choose Double or Nothing. The way I saw it was, of all the people in this business, at what looked to be a seminal moment for the industry, the universe chose me. This was meant to be.

But my confidence was in the toilet. Before meeting Tony for the first time, I wondered what product I was even selling. It would have been the easiest thing in the world for me to make a truckload of cash just going around to every show in the country, hitting a Dirty Deeds and signing autographs. But that was the farthest thing from what I wanted. I certainly didn't want to get brought into a fledgling promotion with new television as a former WWE superstar. I didn't wanna be put on top anywhere because I had a name. I didn't wanna rely on any of that. I basically wanted to start over.

I also had no idea how the fans would react. I remembered back to when I first realized I wanted to leave WWE, and it occurred to me that if I did show up at a Ring

of Honor, for example, I might be violently rejected. Those fans are there because they are seeking an alternative to WWE. If the fucking guy from *Raw* with the ketchup and mustard shooters showed up, I thought they'd shit all over it. I wondered if I was now so synonymous with horseshit WWE creative that it would be impossible for me to ever be accepted anywhere.

Booked into oblivion in WWE and blackballed from the rest of the industry. Done. That was my fear.

I almost wanted to warn AEW: Thank you for your interest, but, trust me, you don't want to do this. I'm damaged goods, and if you bring me in I'll ruin your promotion before you even get it off the ground.

I finally met with Tony Khan. He, along with Cody and Brandi, came to my house in Vegas some weeks before Double or Nothing. The show was AEW's promotional debut, on PPV, from the MGM Grand, about 15 minutes from where we sat at my dining room table. I had never taken part in a clandestine business meeting before, so this was pretty cool. Funnily enough, the Uber driver who brought them to the house had driven Renée and me a few times. He was a fan and knew exactly what was going on: "So you're meeting with Dean?" he said.

Tony tipped him 200 dollars and he kept his mouth shut, but that must have been fun for him to know something no other wrestling fan in the world knew for a while.

We had a great little hangout. The first thing I noticed about Tony was he was, first and foremost, a wrestling fan. I was so jaded I had almost forgotten what it was like to be a pure, untainted fan of professional wrestling. Today, even though Tony is my boss, it just feels like he's my friend who's also a big wrestling fan. The phrase I hear most often from Tony when talking about wrestling-related matters is probably, "Dude, *sick.*" This guy is a factoid-remembering machine. He is familiar with any obscure reference you could dream up. That night we talked about ECW and old-school wrestling, he made a lot of points about current wrestling and what he planned to do differently, to which I replied every time, "Dude! I've been saying that for YEARS!"

He told me he used to do some shit in college that was like fantasy football for wrestling, and he had CZW-era Jon Moxley in his deal. This guy knew me to a degree. He wasn't just trying to buy up any available ex-WWE guys. After having some drinks and shooting the shit, we got down to brass tacks. I had some questions. ... I got them all answered. I laid out my thoughts, feelings, wants and needs. I wasn't looking to go to the highest bidder ... money never got brought up. I just wanted to be sure this was a fit. This was scary. I had just gone through a grueling divorce, and here we go again. This was a commitment.

All of our goals were in alignment.

There was no reason to say no other than fear of failure.

I made my position clear: If everything I've been told is true, if this is what we're doing, and this is how it's gonna be done. ... I'm in.

I'll ride with y'all.

MAY 25, 2019, LAS VEGAS

We watched *Batman* vs. *Teenage Mutant Ninja Turtles* and I took a nap. My mom was in town. We both agreed that movie was surprisingly good. I had let myself get a little too hyped up too early in the day. I had been waiting for this moment for a long time by this point. It's important to conserve your mental energy on the day of a TV or PPV. ... You don't wanna peak too early, so I took a siesta.

The rumor mill was running rampant. I tried to play coy with my mom about what my first move was gonna be. I can never bring myself to ruin a surprise for anybody. I often keep everyone in the dark, even my closest friends. My mom wasn't buying any of this bullshit, however. She was gonna be in Vegas one way or another. My mom is my biggest fan and good-luck charm. Everything seems to work out perfectly when she's in the audience.

I would need her tonight. If this crowd revolts at the sight of me, my career may be over. I would be the surprise at the end of the PPV and drop both Jericho and Kenny Omega, the *de facto* top heel and top babyface on the maiden voyage. If they didn't care about me or they hated me, it would be a disaster. I put all my chips on the table, and to AEW's credit, so did they, in a bet that I still had goodwill with the fans. It seemed like I was the only one with reservations. I had been thinking low-key, "off-Broadway." I kind of didn't want any attention. I just wanted to be free to exist again. This was the polar opposite. Jericho was certain it was gonna be the greatest thing. It was his idea: "And *boom*! ... You're the biggest star in the business," he told me over the phone.

Fuck.

I hope so.

No time to be a pussy about this, babe. Here we go.

I liked the ambiguity of taking out guys on both sides of the fence. If I was rejected, as I feared, I would be a heel. I was a heel in my mind going in. If they chant shit at me or make jokes, it doesn't matter. I'm gonna murder their hero in front of them. I would be a vicious, homicidal heel, and I would turn it into real visceral heat in no time at all. This was a defense mechanism. Thinking about it now ... nobody else saw it that way.

About 3:00 p.m., Cody sends me a video he took on his phone, walking the route from the ring over the rails through the crowd to stage. That's where I would throw Kenny off of some kind of set piece, what was a giant set of poker chips, a vision Kenny had that he brought to life. I familiarized myself with the terrain.

I choose to wear a pair of pants I got from a store in the mall called Robin's Jeans. I put them on, as well as a hoodie. I pack a small bag. I don't need much. Really, just the spray-painted MOX vest I made the other day. It didn't look too good, so Renée took some acrylic paint and doctored it up to make the orange really pop.

About 5:00 p.m., Atlas security arrives at my house to take my mother and me to the venue. I wear a full disguise: hood up, sunglasses, a bandana over my face. Arriving at MGM Grand as the pre-show is beginning. My mother is passed off to someone who will take her to her seat in the audience. Later, during the main event, she will be ushered to ringside. Ryan Loco, the best photographer in the game, who shot the cover of this very book, will be suspicious. He will ask her if she's here to see somebody, maybe a family member?

"I can't tell you," my mother will dutifully answer.

I am escorted to Cody's dressing room, where I will hide. An hour passes before I take my disguise off as people keep popping their heads in. Security finally locks the room down and I get comfortable. I shoot the shit with Cody and watch the show on the flat-screen TV mounted on the wall. Bret Hart presents the AEW World Championship belt. Dope. Jericho and Kenny come in, and we go over the deal. I haven't seen Chris in years. It's the first time I've met Kenny. I tell him my wife and I just watched his documentary and it was really good. I won't get a chance to take a look at or get a feel for this giant set of poker chips in person, but Kenny is confident he won't die. Referee Paul Turner comes in to confirm what I need from him. He will get a DDT, the first of his many. B.J. Whitmer pops in to say hi. It's good to see him. It's been forever. The show rolls on. Cody returns to the room, covered in Dustin's blood. He doesn't want to take a shower and close the book on the moment. I know the feeling.

No new visitors, I am left alone. The second-to-last match is going to the ring: the Young Bucks vs. the Lucha Bros. When I get home later, Renée and Amy Dumas, who happened to be over visiting, will note how much they enjoyed the Bucks' Elvis-inspired outfits.

I stretch out, stay loose, warm up and listen to music.

My confidence is growing. I feel good. I'm in the best shape I've been in some time. I got a fresh fade. More importantly, I had devised a plan months ago to drop a teaser trailer video promoting the return of MOX to professional wrestling at exactly midnight the day my contract expired. My goal was to paint a picture for the audience that would basically be like listening to the "Talk is Jericho" interview I eventually did that came out around this time. But now I wanted to tell the whole story without words in roughly 90 seconds. It was meant to set the stage for whatever was next. I think it ended up costing me eight grand. I spared no expense. I recruited Nick Mondo, deathmatch legend and filmmaker, to help me. He came up with a breaking-out-of-prison theme. We used a red camera — that's the real shit, like a *Lord of the Rings*-level camera, I learned. We filmed it in February. It was 48 hours of guerrilla filming in L.A. on my only 48 hours off of the road. We squeezed in one last shot at 4:00 a.m. on the second day and went to get a shot at the Viper Room. Just a nod to Dusty. It was only 10 minutes away, we had to. "I see you ... leather jacket, at the Viper Club."

I utilized Twitter for the first time since the Foley thing. Renée's people helped me sort it all out to change the name over from Dean Ambrose to Jon Moxley at exactly 12:00 a.m. and drop the video at the same time. As it turned out, 9:00 p.m. West Coast time, I happened to be on stage at the exact moment it happened, presenting the trainer's award to Cody Hawk at the Cauliflower Alley Club convention. I took a bunch of photos quick and rushed out of there with Ricker. He was there for Cody's night, too, and we shared a drink at the casino bar downstairs away from fans.

My phone was blowing up in my pocket as we caught up with each other. I didn't look at it. It just kept buzzing as I finished my drink and decided to order another. I got in a cab and by the time I got home, it had caught like wildfire. Mission accomplished. The stage was set.

An important facet of the teaser was it needed to look so good that fans would speculate it might be a WWE production. I hoped that no matter what theories or speculation was out there, that I was so ingrained in WWE that nobody would really believe it till they saw it.

The reaction to the video boosted my confidence. All of my fears and reservations were surface-level. When I think about it now, even though I wouldn't admit it to anybody, deep down in my heart I knew the crowd was gonna go nuts that night.

Main event's on. I will enter from the top of the arena. The atmosphere is now tense. I can feel it pouring in through cracks in the door. Security is getting antsy, they wanna go up. I've been doing this Shield shit long enough to gauge it. We can hold off. I close the door and continue to get into the proper headspace, doing hindu push-ups, bouncing around, music at full blast, the hidden track from Deftones' *Around the Fur* is playing somehow. It looks like they're going home. This is it. Time to go. When the nervous Atlas guy opens the door and looks at me again, this time I nod. I throw my hood on, shoulder through the door. We walk.

I've been caged. For how long I really don't even know anymore. Now I'm a weapon being deployed. I've been asleep. My eyes are blinking open and adjusting to the light. I don't know where I am. I may be volatile. Is this animal dangerous? We won't know what happens till I roll out of my sedentary position and stretch my muscles for the first time in eight years. What kind of sound will I make? As we walk up the stairs of the MGM, I imagine people with tranquilizer darts at the top waiting to put me down if I snap at anyone. I'm twitchy, and I feel unfamiliar energy sparking in my nerves, but it feels natural ... I like it. For all intents and purposes, I was literally in jail for eight years, and now I'm walking into a new world for the first time. That's the best way I can explain it. The cage door is about to open. Live TV, live crowd. Who really knows what the fuck is gonna happen.?

I hear Chris on the mic. I can't really make out what he's saying, but I know it's him. The pro of pros, he tees it up perfectly. I listen for my cue, he will demand a thank you. There will be no music, no pyro, no bells, no whistles. Just this motherfucker. I'm all I got. I think I heard it. Fuck it, I'm going. I walk down several flights of steps unnoticed; everyone's attention is on the ring. Halfway down I hear a shriek, a teenage-girl-getting-stabbed-in-a-horror-movie scream. The sound builds off of the scream as I continue down the stairs, taking my first shaky steps in what seems like forever, grimacing, sensitive to light and sound.

As I hit the floor and make a right turn, I get my feet underneath me and am bolstered by a monstrous roar from the collective crowd. Electricity jolts my heart alive as I jump the rail and slide into the ring — now a fully animated creature. So many colors, smells and sounds. I see Jericho. I identify him as a threat. He makes too sudden of a move and gets spiked with the hardest DDT I've ever DDT'd, while I'm still taking in my new environment. I pop up, nose in the air, sniffing, exploring, absorbing everything. The referee gets too close and is killed in an instant. Give wild animals their space. I feel the AEW ropes for the first time, leaning up on them, and I take the biggest goddamn breath of fresh air I've ever taken in my life.

This has been months of waiting, really longer than that. It has been at least a year since I even realized I was breathing artificial oxygen. The crowd chants "Moxley." That's my name. Moxley was not a famous name. I actually wasn't sure if that's what I was gonna go back to. I toyed with the idea of coming up with something completely new, but I had thought of The Misfits, who, in their original incarnation, were not a famous band. Years later, Metallica covered their music and Cliff Burton wore Misfits T-shirts on stage. Their records spread, and long after they broke up they were more famous than they'd ever been as a functioning band. I saw the original Misfits play in 2019, at the MGM Grand. Josh Barnett happened to be stageside doing security. Life is funny. Anyway, I thought of all the fans I've met over the years who didn't know who the hell I was until I started on TV with The Shield who told me how they went back and sought out all the old Moxley stuff. I banked on the fact that the Moxley name had some cachet.

I'm not ashamed to say that chant was music to my fuckin' ears. Jon Moxley was a barely functioning, socially dysfunctional, broke, drug abuser who disappeared off the face of the earth in May of 2011. It was May 2019, and now a sold-out arena was chanting his name. It was fuckin' wild.

I set my sights on a prone Kenny now. No person on planet Earth has considered this possibility. For a quick moment, there is silence as the audience registers what they are witnessing. Kenny is their guy. To me, he is a fresh kill I will claim for my own. I'm a predator, nondiscriminatory. I'm hungry. Kenny is defiant. We break out into a great brawl, walking the route laid out by Cody's cellphone video. The crowd now chants "A-E-DUB!" This makes me feel good. My thoughts now go from myself to the bigger picture. I helped! The people are happy! I am relieved.

One thing left to do. Just don't kill the top babyface on your first night in. I sail Kenny off the stack of poker chips to the floor below. I won't know for sure till I get to the back, but I sense he is OK.

I stand atop the mountain and own the world ... for one night at least. I am completely blown up. Coming down off the stage, I am a marauder. I make a full lap around the building, soaking in every single drop of this moment. I look like I wanna kill somebody, but I wanna be as close to these fans as possible, every single one of them, because I am grateful. I wanna give everybody in the building a close-up photo or video. I wanna drip sweat on all of them and make it a personal experience.

I eventually make my way to the back, where I have arranged a camera to be waiting. I walk into the room and see the red light blinking. I throw my vest down and deliver my first AEW promo, Jon Moxley's first words in eight years. One take. Easy money. The way it's supposed to be.

I remember Hunter talking to us in the early days of The Shield. We're all standing on the ramp at TV.

"Do you know what a paradigm shift is?" he asks us in a patronizing way, like he's talking to third graders. I found the way he said it insulting. I made some kind of small remark. I don't remember what. I was real testy back then. What? You don't think we know what words mean? "Yeah, we know what it means. ... Go on."

He looked at me quizzically. There was a pause and reset. "I want you guys to be a paradigm shift here," he continued. We did exactly that. We came in as new guys, middle fingers blazing, unapologetic. We pushed the pace and made everyone else keep up with us. We left backstage at WWE a lot better than we found it. That was 2012.

This was 2019. The industry has now changed with the advent of AEW. For the better. For a million reasons. To deny that would be ignorant. Bottom line is that AEW is great for the fans and the wrestlers. Many people, I'm sure, didn't want to believe that this was a real thing that would succeed, but it's working. Things are different now.

This is what was on my mind as I walked backstage, here at the first-ever AEW show. We're at the precipice of a new beginning. If you didn't feel it out there, I don't know what to tell you. It's in the people. ... Just look, just listen; there's an energy here that's undeniable. It's a new era in an industry gone lame as fuck and saccharine as shit.

This is what you call ... a paradigm shift.

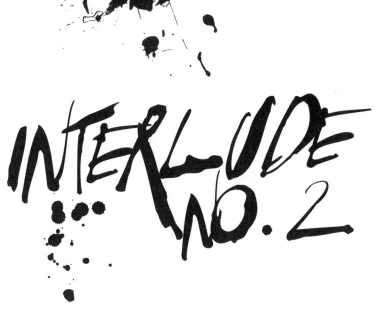

INTERLUDE NO. 2

I go through periods wear I swear off tanning. I always feel goofy going to the tanning bed. When the pandemic started and things were closed, I stopped going, eventually entering another one of my "Tanning is stupid, why do I need to have a tan to be in a fight?" phases. "How's a tan gonna help me win a match?" I will wonder aloud.

Then I'll see myself on the TV monitor one day, ghostly pale, and I'll be like, Dammit! How many times am I gonna have to learn this lesson? You just look so much better with a tan. In the summertime, it's easy to maintain a healthy brown because I'm usually shirtless 90 percent of the day, but in the winter, fans have probably tuned in and wondered when the F'n kid from *Powder* became a pro wrestler.

It's almost April. ... The weather in Vegas is getting good. Jacksonville is warming up too. A couple of months ago, I wrestled a 30-minute match, and it was so cold I literally wasn't sweating afterwards. At the PPV in August I was sweating so profusely before the bell even rang that it looked like I was pissing out of my eyebrows, which I prefer over the former ... but right now I think we're gonna be in a nice spring weather sweet spot. Since Daily's Place is outdoors, I should be able to spend plenty of time at TVs soaking up rays as I go about my business. Damn, now that I think about it — it's kinda crazy how we're still in Jacksonville. What is it, almost a year? At this point I think we've been at Daily's Place longer than we were doing *Dynamite* in a different city every week. Sometimes I see AEW commercials on TV with highlights from a packed arena, and that seems like a hundred years ago now.

I hope we get back on the road this year and bring AEW back live in-person with fans all over the country, and hopefully Europe. We were supposed to go to the UK this past summer before this all started. I miss going there. I miss those fans. I lived for European tours in WWE. Which reminds me: At shows over there, they always have sugar cubes at the coffee stand. Why don't we use sugar cubes more over here? It's easier than sugar packets and zero waste. Cubes are also more fun. ... Just dump a few of those bitches in there. I like those little tea biscuits and cookies they always have next to the coffee too. Hopefully we'll go sooner than later. I heard when we start traveling again, they want to do the Arena in Philly ... they call it the 2300 Arena now, like its 15th name. That would be dope. I hope we do that. I'd love to wrestle there again. Anyway, the point is, I hope to avoid having to go to a tanning bed till after summer is over. Also, I just decided I'm never gonna shave my chest again. Why do I need to shave my chest to be in a fight?

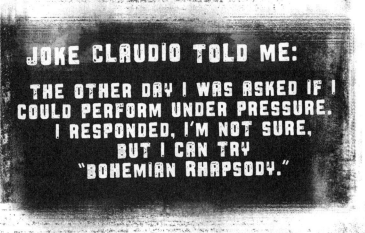

JOKE CLAUDIO TOLD ME:

THE OTHER DAY I WAS ASKED IF I COULD PERFORM UNDER PRESSURE. I RESPONDED, I'M NOT SURE, BUT I CAN TRY "BOHEMIAN RHAPSODY."

FLICK PICK: JURASSIC PARK, 1993

The other day I stumbled across a YouTube video discussing *Jurassic Park* fan theories. It was made by a guy who has an entire YouTube channel dedicated to such content. This man narrating the video was passionate. He spoke about events that have occurred in the *Jurassic Park* universe as if they happened in real life ... and he knew his stuff. He spoke with the confidence of an Ivy League professor when he talked about matters such as velociraptors, InGen, herbivores on Isla Sorna and the Lysine Contingency. He'd clearly spent hours upon hours of his life going over footage, scouring the internet for the secrets of *Jurassic Park*. He no doubt still spends many nights camped out on Reddit message boards, debating his colleagues with fervor about what we should expect from *Jurassic World: Dominion*, which has yet to come out as I write this. In fact, he released a 59-minute YouTube video titled "What We Can Expect From *Jurassic World: Dominion*," dated a year ago. This man is all in. I watched that first video and wondered what kind of adult man spends this much time on such matters. Does he have a job? Kids? A significant other? He can't, right? How could he dedicate so much of his energy toward a fictional world that doesn't exist in real life? ... Then I watched about 15 more of his videos and wondered how I, a man with a job and a wife, soon to have a kid, had enough time to absorb all the information in these videos. Then I was bummed out when I ran out of new videos to watch and finally I remembered that my entire life's work is based on a fictional world that doesn't exist in real life, and I wished I had this guy's phone number so I could call him and just talk *Jurassic Park* shop.

I'm pretty sure it was Omaha. Almost 48 hours have passed since I had that strange interaction with Road Dogg in the tunnel. We're at *SmackDown!* I am given a message delivered by Michael Hayes. I am told I am to go to the production truck to apologize to Kevin Dunn. Kevin Dunn, executive producer, is the guy responsible for all the nauseating camera cuts that might have given your children epileptic seizures while watching WWE programming.

I put two and two together and realized I must have sworn on camera at the PPV night before last. I had no problem apologizing to anybody if that's what happened, but I did find it odd that nobody said anything to me until two days later. I would have left the ring at the PPV and gone right to Vince or the truck, the head of USA network or the surgeon general and taken ownership of the mistake. This was what I signed up for, and I was willing to ply my trade within the parameters of the rules. Don't swear. ... That's fine, it's not hard. I don't need to swear to cut a promo.

However, in the ring it's possible that sometimes, shit just slips out. We communicate in the ring, with our partners, our opponents, the referees. This is largely imperceptible to the audience, but with the ring mic'd and all those HD cameras pointed at you, it's not out of the realm of possibility that an errant expletive word could come across on TV. What's more, a performer fully immersed in what they're doing might not have the network's standards and practices memo front and center on their mind while they are occupying the reality of their character. Sometimes you're just in the fucking zone.

I actually feel bad. Man, I fucked up. My bad. As I make my way to the production truck to talk to Kevin Dunn for probably the first time ever in my life, I begin to wonder if this isn't all a mistake. I couldn't have actually said "fuck." I've been with the company for two years, and feel I've done an exemplary job of ridding my vocabulary of all profanity while on camera. We'll know in a minute. I'm told I have to watch the tape in the truck. We'll get to the bottom of this.

I walk into the production truck and am met by Kevin Dunn, who is overly nice. He then pulls up the footage, and sure enough, there it is.

"Give me my fuckin' belt," I tell the referee shortly after the pinfall. Kevin plays it twice.

"Give me my fuckin' belt," I say. I'm in my own world, in the moment, sweat matting my hair, filled with the adrenaline of the pop of the crowd as the ref counted one, two, three, and I secured my first belt in WWE, a moment I've probably been picturing in one way or another since I was a little kid. I didn't scream it, but it was there, clear as day. I have no excuse.

I was 100 percent repentant. I took full responsibility. I sincerely apologized to Kevin, who had the responsibility of utilizing the seven- or eight-second delay to hit a button and bleep it out. It was my fault. I fucked up. I explained that I was in the moment, excited, and it was just a natural reaction, but I showed full contrition. Kevin went on and on about how he's had to have this talk with other guys and I was doing so well and he didn't want something like this to ruin things for me. I agreed. This was not the kind of stupid thing I wanted to fuck things up for me — or my partners, for that matter. I gotta be more careful, I thought.

Still, this whole thing felt a little overdramatic. Why didn't you just come and cuss me out right after it happened? I would have been cool with that. What's with this whole principal's-office thing? Just fine me a grand or fine me AND send someone to come kick me in the shin as hard as fuck. That's a good rule: Say "fuck" on TV, get kicked in the shin. This whole thing just feels a little weird, but I was the one in the wrong here and I am legitimately remorseful. I actually felt good leaving the truck. It was a good little reminder that one stupid little thing could fuck all this up, so keep your mouth in check. It almost seemed like Kevin was looking out for me. I appreciated his forthrightness in not letting it slide.

I thought it was a positive experience.

About an hour later, Michael comes up to me in the hallway again. He don't look happy. "*Weeell,*" he says, "I don't think ... that was the right kind of apology ... for the push we wanna give you."

I was flabbergasted. I have no clear memory of what I said to Michael then. I was in a little bit of shock. I did apologize. That's what I JUST DID. I thought this was over. I talked it out with Kevin and we shook hands. So ... it's not over? The only other thing I remember Michael saying is, "Look, I know you're a ... different type of cat."

The first time I'd heard that phrase. It wouldn't be the last. I didn't always necessarily take it as complimentary. In fact, many times I felt like I was being made fun of, but I wasn't in on the joke. I remember being by the ring and two top-producer types trying to get away with that sort of thing, subtly, but right to my face. I'm not fucking stupid. "Are we making fun of me right now?" I asked.

Their eyes went wide, and they changed the subject to laughing about something else seamlessly. Yeah, OK.

I can't say for sure whether this incident affected my career in any meaningful way or not. It doesn't matter now. ... It all worked out for me in the end. It's possible absolutely nothing would have been different.

But without a doubt, I could immediately feel a change in the air around me. I was treated differently. I was talked to differently. From that moment on, I think that's how I was viewed by WWE ... however I was described in the truck by Kevin Dunn that day.

Of course, this wasn't the first time I've felt myself viewed through a similar lens.

Elementary school, my desk placed out in the hallway. I have speech problems. They put words on a sheet of paper and I pronounce them correctly. I read sentences, and they don't like the way it sounds. I don't remember what the problem was, they just keep making me try over and over. I am not mentally present. I look at the drawings on the walls and escape into my mind.

"Look at me when I'm talking to you," the teacher says.

"I am," I say.

I stare into her pupils, locked on, and pronounce words. Then I'm looking at my shoes, counting the laces, and I hear, "Jonathan! Look at me!"

"I AM!"

I'm in seventh grade in the counselor's office. They want to put me on drugs. My mom is talking to people. Some lady who might be some kind of doctor is giving possible diagnoses. I just wanna get out of here. I refuse to take these drugs. I hate school. I don't need drugs. Why would I need drugs? All you people are the crazy ones, why don't YOU take some pills and just leave me alone, you psychos! God, I hate school.

A common experience I have is maybe after a show. Everyone is gathered around maybe the hotel bar or catering, relaxing and having a beer. Someone says to me something like, "I always thought you hated me," or "Y'know, I always thought you were a dick," then, "Turns out you're a pretty cool dude."

"Why would you think I hated you?" I will ask. This would have been a person I barely knew and had never had a conversation with. I have no reason to not like this person, and they certainly don't have any reason to believe I'm a dick. We will become friends.

What really shined a spotlight on this phenomenon was being with Renée. I have been deemed, fairly or not, unapproachable. She is disarming. That's why she's such a great interviewer. A great conversationalist and a ball of warm light, she has some God-given ability to make people want to pour their souls out to her. I remember when we first started dating, she said to me, "I can't believe how comfortable you are with making people uncomfortable."

"I don't know how you can just sit down at a table full of people and not say anything."

"What if I don't have anything to say?" I ask.

"If you don't make conversation, it makes people feel uncomfortable," she continued.

"Why would they feel uncomfortable? I'm comfortable." I say, perplexed.

Many people have described me as shy. I don't consider myself shy. I'm just not a chatty Kathy. That doesn't mean I'm necessarily shy. Also, you learn a lot more from listening than you do from talking. I can be antisocial at times, but overall I think I am a very friendly person. Being with Renée has made me more aware of all of this, and I have made some personal improvements in the area of social behavior. Well, maybe I haven't made a lot of improvements, but I'm definitely more aware of it.

Looking back on my life now, I've begun to see just how many things were likely affected by the way people perceived me. Even my family, I think, has probably had a hard time closing the distance with me. With the clarity I have now, I can see how at times they might just not have known what to make of me, but maybe at the time I didn't really know what to make of myself. This would have all been useful information to have when I was in seventh grade, but that's not how life works. The way I see it now, none of it matters. I am a pretty well-adjusted and successful adult, and I'm not gonna change for anybody now. If something about me bothers you, that's your problem.

Looking back on this incident years later, I began to wonder if maybe this was another case of my social awkwardness and obliviousness to those around me. Maybe when I went into the truck to give what, to me, was a sincere apology, I came off like a complete dick. It's not like that sort of thing hasn't happened before. It has been happening to me my whole life.

I told this story in an onstage sit-down interview with JR at a fan event in Baltimore in 2019. I hadn't thought about it in a really long time. It just kind of popped into my head. At this stage of my life, I was willing to accept that maybe I really did just plain come off bad. Thinking about it now, It's possible ... but ... Nah. Fuck that. I remember my compunction. I remember apologizing. I remember going above and beyond, saying that I was sorry for putting him in a bad spot, promising it would never happen again and thanking him for the talk. Kevin was *soooo* nice to me. We shared a hearty handshake on the way out, everything was good. IT WAS ALL GOOD. If I had gone in there and been an asshole, why didn't he just say, "Fuck you, then, you're being an asshole." No, he let me go through the whole song and dance, while being completely phony, pretending to accept my apology, pretending it was all good and we were friends. Then five minutes later this little cunt rat goes right to the rest of the office and says I didn't give a sufficient apology and whatever other bullshit he probably said about me, behind my back, no less. This dickless motherfucker ... and it was 48 hours later. Why didn't you just call me on the phone right when it happened and say, "Fuck you, we're all mad at you, and if you do it again, you're fired."? That would have been easy to understand. Instead, I got summoned to the secret castle to meet the Magical King Wizard who lives in the truck and controls the universe to beg for forgiveness? What are all these stupid little games?

The reality in a place like WWE is that one comment, one little seed planted by a guy in Kevin Dunn's position can be extremely detrimental to someone's future there. That's a lot of power, and that power breeds ego. Connecticut ... old, rich boys' club ego. I've heard all kinds of stories about that guy messing with people's careers, but this isn't that kind of book. Suffice to say that dude is a fuckbag. Maybe this is that kind of book. ... No! No! ... But for real, don't EVEN get me started on ... no ... this is *not* that kind of book. Fuck Kevin Dunn.

PUERTO RICO, 2006

I had a several-month stint in Puerto Rico. I turned 21 down there. This dude named Pipo, who seemed to own the whole island, took me and my roommate, a big, lovable southern fella named Mikal Judas, to every single bar in San Juan. I had sent a demo tape and got a call from "Bushwhacker" Luke Williams.

"I wanna put together a tag team, mate."

It was maybe the last place operating as an old territorial system. Four shows a week, 450 bucks a week. FOUR HUNDRED AND FIFTY BUCKS A WEEK? I was on a plane a few days later. Luke wanted a foreign heel tag team. I partnered with a guy named Hade from England. We were called the British Militia and waved the Union Jack. Since I couldn't pull off a decent English accent, I didn't speak in promos. We elicited mad heat from the passionate audiences. The red-hot energy of the fans in Puerto Rico created the most intense atmosphere I'd ever performed in up to that point, especially in the small towns.

We had a match in a gymnasium in Carolina, near where we stayed in crack central, against a couple babyfaces named El Chicano and Jumping Jeffrey. Luke described it as white heat. Damn, white heat must be hotter than red heat, I thought. A vision of a blacksmith pounding a molten-hot piece of wrought iron with a hammer came to mind.

Two conversations I had define this time period for me. Both very different. I was completely naive in all areas of life and wrestling. I'd barely ever been out of Ohio, and here I was on a Caribbean island with a wad of cash, living the dream. One of these conversations had a very positive impact on my future, the other not so much. Which to start with? Let's start with the bad and end with the good.

"*You wan cocay?*" I am asked by a wrestler on the card. That's a hell of a non sequitur. He sits down next to me in the locker room after the Sunday afternoon show, the last of the week.

"*Cocay.*" He makes a sniffing sound.

"Oh, nah, no I'm good," I say. I've never done cocaine. I really don't know anything about it. I communicate to him that I don't have enough money.

"You get paid tomorrow?" he asks. Yes, we get paid on my Mondays, I confirm.

"Only 80 dollar, you paid tomorrow. No problem." he says smoothly. Fair point. I did get paid tomorrow. My argument that I didn't have enough money quickly went out the window, and before I knew it I had bought my first bag of cocaine. I had no idea how much it weighed or if it was a good deal. We never got into the question of whether or not I actually wanted to buy it. What a salesman.

Our apartment was on the second floor. Luke lived across the hall. If you went out the kitchen door, you'd be above the office and you could walk across rooftops for a half mile or so. I was sitting out on the roof listening to music as the sun went down the next day considering my little stash. I smelled it, tasted it, rubbed a little on my gums and they went numb. I guess this stuff is OK. I dunno. I bit the end off of a McDonald's straw, poured a little out on my portable CD player, created a little baby line, and set about figuring out what this stuff was all about. I didn't really drink a lot back then. I was just really into uppers. That night however, with a giant white rocket up my ass, I would end up drinking like 20 Smirnoff Ices. The next morning, I woke up in the alley below our apartment feeling like a dried cactus and hoping nobody from the office saw me. The next Sunday, I was the one who approached the salesman. Thankfully, before long we were getting paid late, only paid half or not paid at all. If that territory had been on fire, I might not have survived.

Conversation Number Two started much the same way, in the dressing room, after a match. A veteran Puerto Rican wrestler comes in. He's got black hair and a goatee. A mean disposition. His face lights up when he sees me. He approaches and kneels down next to where I'm sitting on a bucket.

"Excuse me, sir," he says, his eyes become sweet. "You are great wrestler. One thing I want to tell you, please."

"Uh, yeah, please, for sure," I respond.

"If one thing ... how you say?" He struggles to find the perfect descriptor. ... "You be more ... bicious!" he growls emphatically.

"Bishes?"

"Bicious! Bicious!"

"Oh! Vicious!"

"Yes! Bicious!"

At the time, at 20 years old, I was experimenting with all kinds of shit in the ring, I didn't know exactly who I was as a wrestler yet. I was copying anything I saw that looked cool. I was playing around with all kinds of cute, technical wrestling and fancy little spots. I was quickly learning, however, that in Puerto Rico, you could come out and open with the fanciest, smoothest chain wrestling spot there is, and the people would still just sit on their hands.

But, if you just walked up and punched the good guy in the face, looked at the audience and said, "Fuck you," with a snarl on your face, they would go completely apeshit. Here, it was all about the local heroes selling their asses off and the role of the heel was simply to be ruthless and violent, getting heat, real heat. *Bicious*. Luke was coaching me on this. As the Sheepherders, he and his partner Butch had been exactly this kind of team. "Mate, I was hardcore before hardcore was hardcore," he was fond of saying, while describing all the barbwire, face-biting madness of the Sheepherders' glory days.

Luke was such an entertaining and funny character that sometimes the message would get lost in translation. I had to get my cool spots in. This gentleman in the locker room conveyed the message so simply and effectively that a lightbulb went off over my head. He mimicked gouging and tearing at the faces of opponents. I followed suit. Soon we were both mauling invisible babyfaces together on the dirt of the dressing room floor. He laughed and smiled. I thanked him for the advice. "God bless you, sir," he humbly told me as he shook my hand before disappearing.

The next time out I was mean as fuck. I made it my goal to get blown up while beating the shit out the good guys. Stomping, clubbing and biting until I was out of breath. It felt good, and I became a more rabid creature every time out. It felt energizing, liberating. This simple switch in focus from, What cool spot can I open with this week? to, Fuck it, let's just fuck somebody up, was a revelation. It was like putting on the most perfectly fitting pair of shoes or the most comfortable shirt you've ever owned. Yeah, this was me.

Over the years, as my style has evolved, *bicious* has remained a key component in the combustion. This was where the seeds were planted to spawn the creature that would stand toe to toe with the likes of Brain Damage or Minoru Suzuki. Even as a babyface, which I ended up being, somehow, some way, for so much of my career, this has served me well.

In the post-breakup of The Shield, my ability to change gears and tap into a vicious and hyper-aggressive nature is what brought the crowds to a frenzy as I ruthlessly and repeatedly attacked Seth every week like I was a dog chasing a mailman.

In all my research I have never been able to identify exactly who this man was who went out of his way to help me. Not with certainty. I can picture him clearly in my mind. He wasn't a regular, I don't think. I hardly ever saw him. Definitely never worked with him. But I'll tell you what, that guy knew his shit and I'll always be grateful for that little chat. God bless you, sir.

T-MOBILE ARENA, LAS VEGAS, JUNE 2016

The eye of the storm.

Chaos swirls around. HD cameras broadcasting live on PPV are pointed right at me. I've been dropped into a rabid pit of tens of thousands of iPhones ready to hit record. Somewhere some Gandalf-looking MFer is looking at the ring, an oversized feather pen in hand, ink dipped and ready to transcribe the forthcoming events onto the parchment and into the wrestling history books. I remain invisible.

I've been gifted a moment, a moment just for me. I'm at peace, in stillness and tranquility here. I'm underneath the ring at the T-Mobile arena in Las Vegas. The main event of WWE's Money in the Bank PPV is about to be sent to the ring, a match for the WWE World Heavyweight Championship. Roman Reigns defends against Seth Rollins. I've absconded by cover of a dozen emissaries wearing the same oversized WWE crew hooded sweatshirt as I am. We hurriedly rush from backstage, hoods up, crouched. The house lights are down, a video package plays on the screen as we circle the ring, seemingly performing routine maintenance. In less than 10 seconds I've slid under the apron to safety. I watch the soles of the men's boots in the inch between the floor and the bottom of the apron as they complete the circle around ring, retreating, the package delivered, their mission complete. I wish I could thank them.

I'm greeted by Nick Daw, who tosses me a bottle of water. An unsung WWE crew soldier, Nick is stationed underneath the ring at every televised WWE event, tightening cables and making necessary repairs on the spot. He organizes the weapons and props stored under the ring, making sure they're in the right positions, easily accessible. Nick is in charge of finding the desired structural integrity of those big, blocky WWE announce desks when there is a big table bump ... sometimes reinforcing them and sometimes sliding out from under the apron and strategically removing a piece or two from the framework, making the announce desk a live round, ready to blow. Tell Nick exactly what stunt you have in mind, and he'll tune her to the sweet spot.

In communication with Gorilla via headset, Nick lets them know I'm in position. I've spent a lot of time under the ring with Nick, lying on our stomachs, watching the tiny monitor like we're kids at a sleepover. Tonight is no different. I remember the first time The Shield was positioned under the ring for attack and we discovered the little clubhouse Nick had built for himself. We had plenty of time to kill down there, waiting for the lights to go out, our cue to spring into action and Triple Power Bomb the Rock through the announce desk in the dark. I thought, Wow, being underneath the ring is like being in the eye of the storm. No matter what's going on topside, it's eerily calm, the F'n Battle of the Bulge could be going on out in the arena, but under here all remains placid.

In a little over 30 minutes, I will be the WWE Champion.

I've never been more calm. I feel totally relaxed or, more accurately, I feel a sense of relief has washed over me as I take a comfortable position on a padded mat and indulge myself with a moment of reflection. ... I close my eyes and say a prayer, and images flash in my mind that I haven't seen in some time, memories of feelings I haven't felt in years. I remember starving. I could see my breath while sleeping in my truck in the winter. I remember putting one dollar and seven cents in my gas tank to make it to practice, mostly pennies and nickels. ... I remember the time it took us 22 hours to get to Philadelphia in a blizzard and sewing my own nipple back on outside Toronto. Images of sweltering gyms in the small towns of Puerto Rico come to mind, as well as the faces of the nurses in Germany, pulling shards of glass out of my body with tweezers. I feel the sensation of the Florida sun burning my eyes as I arrived in Tampa, at the base of this WWE mountain, what looked to be a possibly insurmountable climb above me. I will never kiss anybody's ass. I won't compromise my integrity, but I'll get to the top of this bitch by sheer force of will or die trying. I've been pouring my heart and soul out every night for WWE, on the road for years now. I've never taken a day off, never missed a show. I wrestled 199 matches in

2015. I'd wrestle 204 in 2016. Through injuries, illness, crippling back pain, walking pneumonia, knees and ankles swollen to cartoon proportions, coughing up so much blood in the shower in Las Cruces that I thought I was dying. ... All so I'd be ready to capitalize on an opportunity like this whenever and wherever it presented itself. Tonight, after having pushed the boulder all the way to the top of the hill time and time again, only to have it roll all the way back down, I will finally make good on my promises to those who have stuck by me through thick and thin. Tonight's as much for them as it is for me. I'd begun to worry I would never deliver the big win that they deserved after being punished for believing in me over and over. An albatross has been lifted off my shoulders. I am weightless.

Eyes on the small monitor now, Nick and I watch Roman walk the aisle with the WWE World Heavyweight Championship belt (as it was called then ... what a mouthful) in tow. I drove to Vegas from Los Angeles the previous night with Roman. We made it from the loading dock at the Staples Center to my front door in four hours flat. Somewhere around San Bernadino, I realized something was wrong. I could read it in Roman's face. He vaguely alluded to something, some shit was going down with Vince tomorrow, but I didn't have any clue and I didn't pry further.

He asked me who was winning the Money in the Bank match. All six participants had been at Staples all afternoon for "rehearsal," trying to come up with a plan. I told him I didn't know, even though I knew I was gonna win. Jericho, close enough to Vince, had asked him straight up. He said he wouldn't bother doing this rehearsal unless he knew the finish. Jericho wasn't supposed to tell me, so I didn't breathe a word. We played *Wolf of Wall Street* on a screen placed on the dashboard and flew through the desert. We got to my place, had a couple drinks on my back porch, talked movies and retired to bed.

The next day, I walked into the bowl at the brand-new T-Mobile arena. It was WWE's first show here. Jamie Noble, the producer for tonight's ladder match, rushed up to me and told me in a hushed yet aggressive tone, "Tonight's your night! It's about fuckin' time."

"Yep," I responded, unfazed.

"'Bout fuckin time, is all I'm saying," he said with his West Virginia twang as he gave me an emphatic fist bump. "Motherfuckers."

Jamie looked around and disappeared.

Roman, fresh from Vince's office, finds Seth and me in the locker room. Nobody else is around. He has news. We stand in a triangle. "You up tonight," he said to Seth, "Dean cashes in."

Roman went on to explain that he'd be serving a 30-day suspension for a discrepancy with the wellness policy. I don't remember saying anything. A little while later, Michael Hayes corrals the three of us into a room to give us the top-secret scoop, as he's done many times before. He doesn't tell us anything the three of us haven't already discussed. Nobody sells anything.

It's clear what needs to be done. It's a beautiful story, albeit not a planned one. Unfortunately, we can't give WWE credit for plotting a two-year story arc that tied up so beautifully. It happened by accident.

GRANT...

"Grant's gone," was the text I got from Dev. My blood ran cold. Like the feeling of ice literally pumping through the veins in my arms and wrists. I think Renée was preparing to make dinner. I wanted to say something, but words couldn't form in my larynx. I walked out to the garage and just stood there. After a few minutes, I began pacing small little circles, picking up things and putting them back down, searching for a suitable reaction. Twenty minutes had passed since I left Renée in mid-conversation. I had opened the garage door and was leaning on the back of my truck when she came out. Staring straight ahead, afraid to move. She said something, but I just couldn't fucking talk. I have no idea what words I used to convey what I had learned. I couldn't say it.

We started to walk. I just kept staring straight ahead. We ended up walking around the whole block. About halfway into the walk, I was able to talk about it a little, a few quick statements, just the necessary facts. I felt tears welling up behind my eyes like a drill was pushing out through my nose. I sucked it all in. I took a deep breath and bit my lip. I tried to just take it on the chin.

I remembered when my friend Casey died, back in Cincinnati. He was an MMA fighter and worked at the gym with me. We trained together a lot. We did a late-night conditioning session together one night at the gym after we got off work. He walked out the door about a minute before me into the night. It was 11:00 p.m. Ten hours later I got a call from a girl who worked the desk. Casey had shot himself. He was gone. Just like that. I carried guilt. At the wake, looking at the Ice Fights Middleweight Championship belt, the little local fight promotion, set amongst flowers and pictures of Casey with his loved ones, I just couldn't get it out of my head that I could have done something. I hadn't even known him all that long, but what if I'd have just been like, "Dude, you wanna come over and have a beer?"

"You wanna go throw rocks at fucking stop signs?"

Anything. How could I have known? Should I have known? What could I have done anyway? This haunted me for years.

Grant was so much worse. His wife, Brianne, had gone into a coma. Seemingly inexplicably. I've still never heard a good explanation as to why, if there is one. I prayed and prayed and fucking prayed that she would be OK. She passed away on April 4. Upon hearing the news of this worst possible outcome, while trying to process this horror, my thoughts immediately went to Grant's safety. I can't even fucking imagine the emptiness and the helplessness he must have felt. On top of that, we're right in the heat of a pandemic. That just added a sinister weirdness to the whole thing.

Grant was the kind of guy who could ingest an incredible amount of drugs on a good day. This was about as bad as a day can get, and I feared the ways in which he would try to escape or dull the pain. How do you say that to somebody delicately? Or should you just say it bluntly? Hey, I know you're going through unspeakable and unimaginable gut-wrenching hell right now but just a reminder: Don't do any drugs. Limit yourself to a couple of drinks, please. Good F'n luck. My core group that was tight with Grant stayed in regular communication with him and each other. We discussed Grant's wellbeing constantly. I'm sure other groups of friends close with him from different times and places were doing the same thing. That dude was loved. I'm sure we all feared the same thing.

Every time I talked to Grant and he seemed to be coping as well as anyone could, I felt a little bit of relief and said a prayer to keep us on track. I just wanted to go grab him, drag him to my house and lock him in a room where I could keep an eye on him. I was getting word through the grapevine from his wife's family, with whom he was close, that he was doing well. I started to really have hope he was gonna come out on the other side of this thing. I pictured us backstage at an indie show drinking beers one day again. I invited him out to Vegas all the time. I still had hope I'd get him to come do some hiking with me. I envisioned him designing all my T-shirts in perpetuity.

When I first left WWE and needed new artwork, I came to Grant immediately. He was a very talented artist and graphic designer. Always self-deprecating, of course he was all "AWW shucks, you don't wanna use any of my garbage. ... I'm no good." He created a MOX design with a grenade that I loved. When AEW asked if I had any ideas for a T-shirt, that was what I gave them. His last matches were in Japan for a GCW/Big Japan co-promotion. He had stepped away from the ring but decided to come back for this trip. Grant loved Japanese deathmatch wrestling. He had all the tapes. He could give you a whole dissertation of the history, narrating hours of footage. Eddie does the same thing with '90s All Japan. I heard about it and told him I was gonna check out his matches. He begged me not to. "Please don't. Just remember back to when you thought I was a somewhat serviceable wrestler." Very Grant. Of course, I went and watched him on that tour and thought he looked great, maybe better than ever. Danny Havoc the performer was absolutely fearless in the ring. He took some of the stupidest fucking bumps in the history of time, getting suplexed on his head with a ladder around his neck and shit like that. He had a connection with the audience that you can't buy, an unshakable bond built of respect, of his bodily sacrifice. He was so goddamn creative. I vividly remember him showing me the drawings in his notebook, his designs for the Cage of Death ... all kinds of crazy contraptions like a giant flyswatter made of chairs that would swing down from the top.

One of my favorite memories is sitting with Grant in the back of an SUV in Germany after a match in a big two-story nightclub. It was a main event for the title, and I made him do a regular match, I mean, mostly regular ... like PG-13. He just kept saying, "That's a bad idea. I suck. I can't wrestle."

"They love you. You're gonna do great," I insisted.

I don't know why we were in the back of this SUV, but I assume it had something to do with acquiring coke and/or ecstasy. I just remember we had a bottle of Jägermeister. The rumor was that Jäger had a certain opiate in it that really kicked you into fifth gear, but that it had been removed in any bottles sold in the U.S. In Germany, allegedly this was the real shit. I don't know if that's true, but we were floating six inches off the ground before too long. We sat there in a post-match afterglow, sweating on leather seats and starting to feel really good after a couple shots of this Jäger.

"Ya know, I was not the least bit confident I could put on a respectable performance tonight, but I must say, that was pretty fuckin' cool, and while I appreciate your confidence in me, don't ever ask me to do that again, it's way too stressful," he said.

The last time I saw Grant was when we had a WWE show in Philadelphia. I stayed around a couple days to hang out, see some friends, and show Renée around Philly. We met Grant at a wing spot in South Jersey we used to go to all the time ... it was close to his place. We took an Uber there from Downtown. Grant had just gotten off work. He ordered a Yuengling and a shot, and we began catching up. He was downing shots and beers at a clip, with that I-just-got-off-my-shitty-job-and-I-wanna-get-numb-real-quick urgency. We talked about the future. At closing time, he was hammered and attempted to drive home. Fuck no, I told him. We'll all go back in an Uber. It's this new brilliant thing, almost too good to be true. You don't even have to have your wallet or know where you live. They just come and pick you up anytime, anyplace, and take you home. It's great. He kept trying to get into his car. I practically had to wrestle him into this Uber and we took him home. He was pissed off that he would have to pick up his car the next day.

I'll pick it up, I told him. Things have evolved, there's no excuse to drive drunk these days. We're Uberin' your drunk ass. End of story. He was pissed.

The next day I awoke to a long Grant text. He wasn't much for long phone calls or constant no-effort emoji texts, but at times he would write long text message or eloquent email essays. Email was his preferred method of communication. I've started to get more into emails in the last year to try to take a page out of his book and keep this tradition alive. He apologized for being so faded in front of my wife. He hoped she didn't think he was some kinda shitbag and thanked me for forcing him into an Uber, as that was the right call. His wife had brought him to pick up his car in the morning and all was well. This was the last chance I'd ever have to look out for him.

He died of a broken heart. More than one person has tried to tell me about the coroner's statement or whatever, but I never wanna hear that. I don't care. I know what happened. He died of a broken heart.

I took it on the chin that first night. That was just my instinct. It is what it is, just eat it. The second night I felt a hole being drilled into my nasal cavity again and a little more came out. A few tears. I gritted my teeth and tried to take the blow. I was walking around like a cloud swelled up from the rain, dry thunder crackling in the distance. It was only a matter of time.

It came on the third day. We sat on the couch and the subject of Grant came up, a spark that lit the whole thing ablaze. I couldn't hold it in anymore. Tears shot out of my face like a broken faucet, surging convulsions in my guts. I stormed outside to our back porch in escape and sat on the steps. Renée followed behind and sat on the steps beside me as I wretched. It wouldn't stop, guttural screams coming from my bowels ... sounds I didn't think possible coming from my body. I totally lost control. It was like an exorcism. Snot, tears and spit spewing as I howled, a 230-pound limp sack of bones slumped over, my head resting on the stoop. I cried for two hours.

You happy now, motherfucker? Now I look like a pussy in my own book.

Walking off a plane in Dallas in tears after writing this, and people are staring at me and shit.

I will always miss you, Grant. I love you.

JOKE CLAUDIO TOLD ME:

I TOLD MY CHECK-IN LUGGAGE THAT WE WON'T BE TRAVELING MUCH DUE TO THE CORONAVIRUS. I SHOULDN'T HAVE DONE IT, BECAUSE NOW I'M DEALING WITH EMOTIONAL BAGGAGE.

JON MOXLEY'S GUIDE TO MARRIAGE

Blond, Canadian. There was a new broadcaster coming into WWE, I read, a chick from The Score in Toronto. There's a picture of her. Great smile, I thought.

RALEIGH, NORTH CAROLINA, 2013, SMACKDOWN!

It's that hectic time right before a Shield entrance: buckles snapping, zippers zipping, boots tightening. The burn of fresh Tiger Balm stings the inside of my nose and drips down the back of my throat. I smell of cocoa butter. I was really into cocoa butter back then. My biceps are the only exposed part of my body in this gear, might as well make 'em shine. There's good energy, last night on a five-day loop. I have a singles match with Bryan and we're up next. I'm doing some burpee/push-up combos when I hear, "We gotta go!"

I pop up off my belly and run down the hallway to catch up with the caravan of security.

"Let's do it, baby," I say.

The hallway is crowded and tight. I am slowed down by the traffic going both directions. I dart in and out of lanes, hopping and jogging past road cases and seamstress tables. Excuse me, excuse me, coming through. Rounding a corner now, open space in reach where I can kick it into a higher gear. I'm bobbing and weaving through, bouncing on my toes, when her face comes screaming into view.

That smile. It's that new chick.

She has a cup of tea in one hand. I see the little string hanging out ... she's a tea drinker. She has a stack of papers under her other arm, scripts and formats. That's right, she's a broadcaster.

"Hey!" she says, "Apparently everyone on Twitter thinks we're dating."

It's moments like this that separate the men from the boys.

I'm Wayne Gretzky on a breakaway, Rafiki back-fisting that hyena in *The Lion King*.

It's that scene from X-Men with the kid who runs so fast he sees everything in slow motion while Jim Croce's "Time in a Bottle" plays.

I slow my progress and turn my head and torso to the left. My arm swings back, not unlike the Sasquatch in the Patterson-Gimlin footage.

We are squared up with each other for just a second as I spin. I am now jogging backward down the hallway in the same direction. In less than a second, I will complete my rotation and disappear into the distance. But not before speaking the first words I ever will ... to my future wife.

"Well, hey. It looks good on ya."

Bullseye.

I don't care what Renée says. At this exact moment, it was all over.

Her goose was cooked.

It would take a while to reel her, in but she was firmly hooked.

If she had any doubt, if she thought for a moment the pang she felt in her gut was just indigestion, the nail would really get hammered home when we passed each other again about 30 minutes later. I made a quick glance in her direction as I passed, flanked by security moving through a loading dock area, tactical vest undone, my sweaty bang flopped over one side of my face, a fresh black eye on the other, blood dripping down my cheek. Just enough, a little drip. A perfect black eye. A gift from Bryan I don't think I ever thanked him for. Chicks dig stuff like that.

At this point in time, I was not looking for a relationship, much less a wife. I had long ago come to the conclusion that girlfriends were a waste of time and energy. What good could come of that? There's like a million girls out there. An official relationship just means somebody new to fight with. You ever get in a fight with

somebody you were dating casually? I didn't need anything in my life that could spark jealousy or negativity. I wasn't against the idea of monogamy, but it would have to be a situation where, I don't know ... like, the PERFECT girl came along. I didn't expect that to happen.

What rule out there says you have to have a significant other, a wife or a husband? I've seen so many people waste so much time in relationships that were doomed from the beginning. I think people get in a rush sometimes ... they just wanna have somebody, so they force it and start trying to push square pegs into round holes.

I still think my system is soundly designed. The proof is in the pudding, babe. It worked for me. It's really simple. ... Don't search. Just chill, relax, just wait, live your life, when the right one comes along, you'll know it. I was pretty certain I was destined to be a solo act and roam the earth alone forever, and I was good with that.

Then I met Renée.

About 47 seconds later it was just like, "Oh, OK, so we're just gonna be together forever, then? OK, cool."

It was that easy.

The first time we saw each other outside of work was in Vegas after a *SmackDown!* I had mentioned we should hang out after the show. I was careful not to ask her on an official date. Too risky. That would indicate I was chasing her. Girls don't like that. I just told her where I would be. The Crown and Anchor pub. The bait was set. Let's wait and see what she does.

I rode over with Seth and met my buddies Bonham and Farmer, and a few other people were there. Some steps led to a loft area overlooking the whole pub. We were shooting pool up there when she walked in, wearing a Dinosaur Jr. T-shirt. She showed up, all right. I watched her from the loft as she scanned the room. She wasn't just pretty ... she was cool. She was classy, but she didn't look out of place in such a disreputable establishment, my natural habitat.

I found out later she actually did think that she was going on an official one-on-one date that night, only to walk in and find a tray full of shots of Jack on a pool table, under a cloud of smoke surrounded by me and my scummy friends. The next move was clear.

The first time we really hung out just the two of us, a real "date," was in Orlando a short time later. I lived in Vegas, she lived in New York. This would be a summit on neutral ground. We had a PPV coming up in Miami, and I knew she was gonna be in Orlando for NXT, so I told her I was going straight to Florida to hang out for a couple days. I pretended like I was gonna be there anyway. I got a room at the Embassy Suites. We talked a lot on this walkie-talkie app called Voxer, and through these communications, I had mined a lot of useful information, such as her favorite drinks, snacks and candies. I stocked the room with Skinny Girl vodka, red wine and chips. I bought a big variety bag of fun-size Halloween candy. Game time looming close. I put on my battle attire, worn jeans and a fresh Hanes white T-shirt, straight out of the package.

Hours later, we sat on the couch still talking and laughing. I realized it was 4:00 a.m. I had been having such a good time, I almost forgot to have sex with her. Nobody is leaving here in the friend zone. Not on my watch. Time to hit the pay window.

We've basically been married ever since.

We actually got married for real on April 9, 2017, because I was in a bad mood.

We had gotten our marriage license a few months back. I had a house show in Reno and Renée came with me. Walking around downtown in the morning, we passed the courthouse and decided, Shit! We're in Nevada and we're already here, let's just get our marriage license so we have it loaded in the chamber whenever we decide to pull the trigger. One less thing. We were already planning to do a shotgun wedding of sorts in Vegas. A traditional wedding would be all of my nightmares rolled into one. Why don't I just stick my hand on this hot waffle iron and close the lid while I'm at it? Of course, if that's what she had wanted, I would have given it to her. Renée had no idea I had already acquired a pretty sick ring. I had used her friends to create a back channel for design intel, giving me insight into what kind of wedding ring she would want, without having to ask her directly and tip her off. It's rose gold, a hint bohemian. It's not all in your face. It doesn't try hard. ... It's just fuckin' cool. Very Renée.

I was in no rush. I figured when the day came, I would know it. There would be a sign. It would be a perfect sunset or a morning of sex and Bloody Marys. One day will be the perfect day to get married, and I'll know it when I see it.

That fuckin' marriage license started burning a hole in her pocket really quick. I started getting shit like, "Yeah, if you ever actually do it."

Goddamnit! I'm waiting for the magical fucking sign. Would you hold your horses! *Soooooorrry* for wanting to provide you with a perfect Disney-princess moment. Christ.

We started the day in Zion National Park in Utah, about five hours north. We had been planning this little trip for a while. There were no house shows, and I actually had a few days in a row off after Mania. I had hiked what's called Angels Landing that morning, getting up before dawn. It's a little gnarly. There's sheer cliffs, warning signs mounted that many people have fallen to their deaths. There are chains mounted into the rock face to grab onto as you traverse the path. I was pretty pumped afterwards. ... That had been on my to-do list for a while.

We sit down at a patio table at a little restaurant in town. I see Carrano's name pop up on my phone. MotherFUCK! This can't be good. I was getting drafted to *Raw* and had to fly to New York tomorrow morning. We have to drive home right now. We sat on the couch that night, and everyone was in a bad mood. Even the dog was side-eyeing me. I was angry and a little buzzed. I liked *SmackDown!* I didn't want to move, plus I was pissed that my trip got cut short. Renée went to bed. Bad vibes everywhere. She had been dropping more little "if we *eeeever* get married" hints out there. I started thinking about that.

It was like when you're mad about something else entirely, then notice an expired product in your fridge, then you check another and this shit's expired too! Before long, you're cleaning the whole thing out in a rage, hurling pickle jars and old Tupperware every which way.

I should just do this shit right now.

Yeah, I'm doing this shit RIGHT the fuck now.

I went to the garage and retrieved the ring. For a moment I felt the weight of the moment as I actually held it in my hand. This idea had popped into my head less than a minute ago. Am I sure? ... Nah, fuck all that. I'm doing this. I walked up the stairs. Surprisingly, I felt like I was on a roller coaster, chugging to the top of a hill. I got hit with nervous adrenaline I didn't expect. Renée was in bed with the dog. The TV was on. It's a bit of a blur. I just busted out the ring and said something in the vein of, "Well, you wanna do this or what?" Something close to that. She was in shock, but quickly her smile ... that smile ... spread across her face as big as I've ever seen it. Laughing, smiling, joy, excitement ... bullseye.

I look up the number for the Little Church of the West. It closes at 11:00 p.m. WTF!? Aren't Vegas chapels supposed to be open all night? Isn't that the whole point? We take to Yelp and find what turns out to be Pistol Pastor Pete's home number. An old lady answers. I explain our situation. She asks if we've been drinking.

"Well, yeah, but it's OK, I promise."

"OH, MY, you'll have to talk to the pastor," the lady tells me.

Pastor Pete says, "If you can drum up a witness, I can be there in thirty minutes. Two hundred fifty bucks. Cash only."

Done.

My good friend Sean Marshall answers his phone in the middle of the night ... he's in bed. Renée asks him to be the witness.

"I'm on my way," he responds without hesitation.

Sean and Pete arrive at the exact same time. We sign a few papers and open up a doggie ice cream for Blue. He shoves his face in it and we don't hear from him for another 20 minutes. By then it's over and we're officially betrothed. It goes down in the backyard under our big tree that's all lit up. Renée doesn't stop smiling that smile. I used a hair tie in place of a ring for purposes of the ceremony. I don't wear an actual wedding ring, because if I had one, I would lose it. I just got mine tattooed on a couple of days later. I couldn't lose that thing if I tried. We make the marriage official in the closet for some reason. It's a pretty big closet. I've never been so purely happy for one night as that night. Even a few hours later, when I had to leave, I was moving through the airport weightless, like I was on roller skates. Sometimes, if I'm on the road for a while, in Japan or stuck on a plane, I pull up the pictures of that night and relive it all over again in my mind.

The love of my life.

And ... I got that shit in writing.

Now that there's not a dry eye in the house and all the ladies in the audience are collecting themselves after being swept away in this tale of romance. ... Get ready to listen up and take notes, because it's time to get practical.

What have I learned after four years of husbandry?

...So, this is writers' block...

I had to have learned something. I guess I don't really know anything, and that's the first lesson. You don't know shit, so do a lot of listening. Remember at all times: Happy wife, happy life. Your main objective at all times is to keep your significant other happy. If you do that, everything else will fall into place, so stay focused on doing your job. Even if you're certain that you are right, you are wrong. Learn to live with being wrong. Sometimes it's good to be wrong. For example, if I had been left in charge of something like housewares, our cupboards would be full of paper plates and plastic sporks. I didn't think we needed a new fireplace. I still don't think we did. Was I right? Doesn't matter. She wanted a new fireplace, and the longer I pushed back against this idea the more it festered in her brain: Brain festering is to be avoided at all costs. Now, to my wife, the old fireplace began to look uglier and uglier as time went on. Then the furniture is ghetto, then the whole house is a mess, then there's dog hair everywhere, and now she's living in a double-wide, and Blue, Benny and I are dirty hooligans who have been banished to the yard.

The new fireplace brought balance to the universe. Happy wife, happy life. Do not engage in discussions about what color to paint the walls in any room of your house. This is not a hill to die on. Blue? Great. Eggshell or tan? Love 'em both. You have lost control of the colors of your walls — just accept it. When you're getting ready to go out, your wife may say she will be ready in 20 minutes. This is false. Plan accordingly. This is actually 45 minutes to an hour you have in which to run errands, get in a workout or anything else that needs to get done. Do not check on her progress ... they don't like to feel rushed. You will also notice up to three outfit changes. This is just their process. When asked your opinion on what she is wearing, do not engage in any discourse. Answer reflexively: Looks great. Love it. Otherwise, you'll never get to dinner and you will be starving.

Do not get piss on the floor. In fact, every once in a while, give the bathroom tiles a once-over with some Lysol just to be safe. If you get up in the middle of the night to pee, TURN THE LIGHT ON. That little toilet bowl light from *Shark Tank* is a useful tool as well, and if you're drunk, for the love of God, steady yourself on the wall. If you wake up before your partner, bring them coffee or tea in bed. Flowers. Flowers can't fix EVERYTHING. ... I mean when dumbass Gavin Rossdale went and banged the maid, a whole truckload of fuckin orchids couldn't have kept Gwen Stefani from kicking his ass to the curb, but flowers are very effective in almost any situation. So, flowers, flowers, flowers. Proactive flowers. ... Maybe you didn't do anything wrong and you see someone on the side of the road selling flowers on your way home. Better to have flowers than not, and who knows, maybe you did do something wrong. And if you didn't, it's always good to score points, run up the score. Tech-fall that F'n marriage.

Cards are good too, which reminds me ... unfortunately, Valentine's Day is a real thing, and, yes, they take it seriously. Be prepared ... have a battle plan. It's hard to remember all these holidays. I don't know what day it is half the time. I've actually forgotten my own birthday before. One time, I called my mother to remind me of her exact birthdate as I was booking her a flight. I pretended I didn't remember the year of her birth, but I did. What I was confused about was the day. It's February 6, but for years I would always get it confused with February 4 and 9. I think because if you write a 6 and flip it over that looks like a 9, and a 4 could look the same. When I called my mom to ask her this question it was February 6, her birthday. I had no fucking clue what day it was. You can see how I may have gotten myself in hot water regarding special days? You must go above and beyond on your significant other's birthday: Make a plan, have a surprise. Gotta crush the birthday.

Finally, and most importantly: Get it on. All the time. You can't have too much sex. In fact, if it feels like you've had too much sex, that's a good thing. Here's a pro tip, especially for those who spend time on the road. ... Don't watch porn. I know. Hear me out.

Instead, use your imagination. Fantasize about your significant other in all kinds of scenarios doing shit you could never get them to do in real life. Then when you get home, it's both your beautiful love who answers the door *and* the sultry chick from your dreams or whoever it so happens you concocted in your imagination.

The basic rule of thumb is: If you've run out of work to do at your job, grab a broom. There's always cleaning to be done. If you don't know what you should be doing right at this moment, have sex.

Here's one I can't take credit for; I learned this from my dad decades ago. Do not ever, under any circumstances, call a woman a bitch. Furthermore, even if she is acting like a total loon, do not call her crazy.

DEEP CUTS:
DOPE MATCHES YOU MAY NOT HAVE SEEN

Josh Barnett vs. Hideki Suzuki, Inoki Genome Federation, Fight for Japan, 12/31/2011
This match is on a card full of MMA fights and kickboxing matches, and is so realistic, it doesn't look out of place at all. This is Josh Barnett pro wrestling.

Tajiri vs. Psicosis, ECW Hardcore TV, 8/27/2000
Maybe the last great classic from the arena in the dying days of ECW. It's ON POINT!

Sami Callihan vs. Danny Havoc, CZW Cage of Death, 12/12/2009
Just fucking balls-out bonkers powerhouse of a match. IN THE CAGE OF DEATH! These guys kill each other. I watched this from the balcony. Sami has a gruesome scar on the back of his neck from this.

Yuko Miyamoto vs. Masashi Takeda, Big Japan Pro Wrestling, Scaffold/Construction Site Deathmatch, 7/12/2009
One of my all-time favorites. These are the kind of guys that can do a beautiful perfect bridging German suplex, high on their toes and their nose, but they choose to do it on a bundle of light tubes because they don't give a fuck what you think.

Nick Bockwinkel vs. Dory Funk Jr., WCW Slamboree '93: A Legends' Reunion, 5/23/199
An old-school battle of legends that garners a standing ovation. Cody Rhodes and I watched this before a house show, and it led to a competition in the locker room to see who could work the longest backslide every night. Claudio and I always won.

Norman Smiley vs. Minoru Suzuki, UWF, 7/20/1990
Norman is so underrated. This is an intensely competitive shoot-style match full of great shit.

Trent Acid vs. Homicide, ROH, WrestleRave 2003, 6/28/2003
Peak Trent Acid. RIP. Homicide is a national treasure.

Samoa Joe vs. Necro Butcher, IWA-Mid South, The Arena, 6/11/05
This is a classic. Brutal, completely brutal. I made Renée watch this on a plane.

INTERLUDE NO. 3

Vince doesn't own WWE. When Vince sells to Disney, they won't own WWE either. When Vince is gone, it won't matter how the shitshow that ensues between all those executives shakes out. They can sit in whatever chair they want, say whatever bullshit they want on investor calls, doesn't matter how much stock they own. WWE just did some astronomical deal with NBC to put their content on some shit called Peacock, but whatever that's about, library or not, NBC don't own shit and never will.

The fans own WWE. If you've ever been to a WrestleMania, for example, you will recall the passion of the fans, tidal waves of them in their T-shirts, wearing belts over their shoulders, holding up their homemade signs, smiles on their faces, their joy of being part of this experience. Maybe they've been fans since they were kids, and now they bring their kids to the matches at MSG. Maybe they're a couple from London on their honeymoon who enjoy PPVs together. Maybe they're from India or Australia, planning this trip for years. Maybe they're 13 and just started watching recently, bitten by the bug. They could have been first sucked in by Stone Cold, Bruno Sammartino, TLC matches, The Shield, perhaps Yokozuna captured their imaginations. Maybe they were big *Jersey Shore* fans and bought that one Mania just to see Snooki, and they got hooked. Whatever the case may be, they're all part of it … part of the magic. This is not something you can buy or sell. This is something that transcends material value that can be calculated on a spreadsheet by some bonehead in Stamford. It's an energy that cannot be contained, a life force that grows and grows, far beyond the parameters of control.

It got loose a long time ago, impossible to pinpoint exactly when. WWE took on a life of its own, an amalgamation of fans' passion, emotions and memories that will last a lifetime passed down through generations. That energy can't be put back in the box. Kinda like the dinosaurs in *Jurassic Park*. I'm one of these fans. Despite my obvious creative differences with the chairman and my general disdain for their product, I grew up with it. It's a big part of me.

It was pretty cool to really feel like part of the WWE family, flying on Vince's jet while eating sushi, working out at the office gym in Stamford, talking with Vince for like an hour in the hotel lobby at 2:00 a.m. I ran into him on his way to the gym. Renée and I had just had sex, and I was shirtless, going to the ice machine. It was the best conversation we ever had. I remember Stephanie and Hunter sent us a bottle of Jack Daniel's Sinatra Century, super-expensive, and flasks engraved with our initials when we got married.

I used to have a theory that Vince's plan was to scuttle the ship, intentionally crashing and burning WWE, like the Hindenburg, before he died so that nobody, not Hunter, Steph or Shane could ever take it over. I pictured him cackling maniacally while hundreds of drums of gasoline exploded atop Titan Towers, having the last laugh. Dude, remember that one promo where Vince brought back the NWO, and he's all like, "I'm gonna kill it! I'm gonna kill MY CREATION!" See what I'm saying? It makes perfect sense. What other explanation is there for this horseshit we're putting on TV? I wondered. I finally decided he'd just lost the plot and was so insulated in his own world, so disconnected from reality, he would never recover creatively. He's lost his magic, I decided, that Walt Disney magic that only Vince has, and when he dies it'll be gone forever. Hunter was smart enough to hire half the indies and take Instagram selfies with them, but he ain't got the magic. Shane would probably stick an M80 up his ass and light it if he thought that's what fans wanted to see, but he ain't got it either. Fortunately, though, when Vince is gone, that magic will live on in the hearts and minds of the fans forever.

Even if Vince did run the whole thing into the ground somehow, it still wouldn't take away my memories of watching Bret vs. Austin at Mania, my heart racing, nearly having an embolism when it briefly looked like Austin was gonna break the Sharpshooter. "NOBODY'S EVER BROKEN IT!" JR screamed. It wouldn't take away my memories of watching *Superstars* on Saturday mornings. It wouldn't take away my memories of the adrenaline I felt when *Raw Is War* first came out with that new badass intro with "Thorn in Your Eye" and all the exploding shit. Damn, WWE used to be cool. A moment like Daniel Bryan at WrestleMania 30 with that stadium full of fans chanting "YES!" ... You can't F'n tell me anybody owns that.

AEW is no different. When fans descend on an arena and sing "Judas" or go nuts when Orange Cassidy comes out, it's a moment when we've all been brought together in one place by our love of wrestling, something that's taken on a life of its own. It wasn't an investment from Tony Khan that created this promotion, it was the passion of the fans. It was already an idea, but they made it a reality. We know that, and as this thing grows and continues to succeed, I hope we never forget it.

MAY 14, 2021, CHICAGO ORD, ADMIRALS LOUNGE, 2:39 P.M.

I don't like to check bags. I like to stay fluid. They made me check my roller bag that I attach my little gym bag to, so now I gotta haul that around by the handles like a hitman. It makes my neck hurt worse. I had to check it cuz the storage was all full by the time I got to my gate. I was morning-drinking with Grizzly Kal at the Chili's in JAX until the last minute. Choices.

Yesterday was a long day. I wrestled two tag matches with Eddie, did a run-in at the end of *Dynamite*, and like a million promos and pretapes. Everything we did was fun and turned out great, but these Thursday AEW tapings, a necessary evil of the pandemic, have been long, laborious. I've gone full Lt. Murtaugh. Folks out here wrestling at 2:00 a.m. I can't wait to start touring again and just doing it all live.

Night before last, Wednesday live *Dynamite* was the shit. I've been working on facilitating a match with New Japan legend Yuji Nagata for well over a year, made difficult since I can't get into Japan right now. But as it turns out, I AM the fucking forbidden door. We were set to do it at an NJPW Strong taping in an empty arena with no fans, but Tony said, "Why don't you do it on *Dynamite*?" We're making shit happen, baby.

Renée is over 35 weeks pregnant. I told the baby to just stay in till I get through this match. She did not respond, but I'm sure she knew I meant business. Nagata is

53 years old and still fucking awesome. He's also a class act and a super-sweet man. I met with Nagata and Rocky, my boy and NJPW representative, at 4:30 p.m. It took us all of 15 minutes to discuss. I felt extra stress. I wanted Nagata to look great. This was my match that I called for, and Tony was gracious enough to put it on TNT, where Nagata last appeared on *Nitro* in '97. This legend has come all this way to be here.

Matches in New Japan match bring their own particular stress. There's often a language barrier, but wrestling is a universal language, and in Japan there are no time limits or commercial breaks so all you need is confidence in your skills. I know I can wrestle, sell, and perform my way out of any situation. Live, national television in the U.S. brings another type of stress that I'm well-accustomed to, and it doesn't even faze me by this point. Countless times as I'm about to go through the curtain I've got word that two segs, four and eight minutes, have now become three segs of three, three and six, or I think we've got two minutes left and the ref tells me we're going to commercial in 15 seconds. All different scenarios of that nature. You've gotta be able to improvise and think on your feet.

I told Tony, I don't wanna fuck with no commercial breaks. With our respective styles, I knew this would simply be a fight, hard strikes and submissions from the opening bell. A firefight till someone abruptly hit the pavement. I saw the match as one seg, foot to the gas pedal. We also need to see Nagata coming out of his locker room. It needs to feel like a Pride fight. I wanted the audience to immediately know they were seeing something different from the usual fare. Big fight feel. My boy TK set it up exactly as I asked and opened the show with us.

Still, what if some shit goes down with the times once we're live, you never know. It will all fall on my shoulders. I do NOT wanna have to tell Yuji F'n Nagata, Sorry, dude, we gotta go home. This was all the pressure of a big match in New Japan and all the stress of live TV all wrapped into one. For the first time in years, I found myself a little nervous. It didn't help that Eddie was more hyped than anyone in the building and kept trying to pump me up: "Lets fuckin' DO THIS, Mox! SHOW THESE MOTHERFUCKERS WATS UP!"

Dude. It's 5:00 p.m. I'm trying to stay all Zen. I don't wanna split my differential here. At 7:00 p.m., I get dressed and we film a quick hit warming up in the hallway. I jog around Daily's Place a little, pass Eddie smoking a Newport and use the code words "Dragon Breath." We converge in my trailer with the music loud. Eddie plays "WW III" by the Ruff Ryders. I'm getting warmed up, loosening my hips and moving around. One shot of Old No. 7 soccer-kicks me right in the face, mixing with the Tiger Balm in my sinuses and detonates a powerful explosion. It smells and tastes like victory.

There are butterflies in my stomach as we wait in the hall, "Nagata is walking. Thirty seconds." I hear from production. It's so much fun having Eddie here with me for this. I think he's more excited than I am, must be nice, that motherfucker doesn't have anything to remember or be prepared for in case of emergency. "Five, four, three, two ..."

I kick the fucking shit out of a glass door, and it bursts open. I hear the crowd roar, the energy supercharges my body, and I begin barking a litany of expletives before charging down the steps. Let's fucking go. In the ring, squared off with my opponent, I hear a flute. I think I'm hearing "Season of the Witch" by Donovan. I get briefly enraged as I wonder if they're playing house music and we've gone to commercial break but the song quickly fades, and the shit is on. After the match, holding the IWGP U.S. belt high, I realize I'm hearing "Wild Thing" by the Troggs. I assume that's my music now. That's pretty cool. I feel touched that Tony knows me well enough to know I would think it was cool. He was confident that he could surprise me with it and I wouldn't flip out. Nagata and I kicked and elbowed the piss out of each other in a glorious sprint that left my face busted open. Right under the eye, a blessing. Just a little drip. Renée, I'm sure, got turned on watching at home but that's not the sort of thing she would admit. I bowed to Nagata in sportsmanship and reverence; he bowed in return. My mother would text me later to tell me she cried, and I don't think she even knew who Nagata was. Trent cried too. This is everything great about professional wrestling. "Wild Thing" plays, and the crowd, still limited for safety, is going nuts; it feels like a full house. They are happy, I am happy, Blue Justice himself is happy. Eddie's probably crying worse than my mom cuz he gets emotional. Little bitch. Feels like every person in Jacksonville is smiling. For just a moment, everything was fucking good in the world. 2020 is in the rearview mirror. I'm as proud of that 10 minutes of television as anything I've ever done.

MONEY IN THE BANK 2014, TD GARDEN, BOSTON

Seth Rollins, who recently turned to the dark side, turning his back on his Shield brothers and breaking the hearts of fans worldwide, is a red-hot heel, aligned with HHH's Authority. He's only a few steps away from climbing the ladder and retrieving the MITB briefcase and a guaranteed shot at the championship any time, any place ... a virtual golden ticket to the top of the industry. I watch from Gorilla. I've been removed from the match by medical personnel, an innocuous moment meant to look like a legit shoulder injury. The crowd booed like an MFer as I furiously walked to the back, escorted by officials. A good sign, but that was the easy part — now would come the test. The next few moments would decide my fate, I knew that. Somehow I've become this ... good guy. Dean Ambrose, the unlikeliest of heroes, emerges from the curtain and races down the aisle to stop the villain from getting his hands on the prize. The crowd goes nuts. *THWACK!* I nail him in the back with a chair, and he falls off the ladder to the canvas. I proceed to beat the fuck out of him with a steel chair, which always sucks no matter how you slice it, exactly like he'd done to me on the night he went all evil.

The crowd roars with approval. They feel a certain catharsis. I look up to the sky: The MITB briefcase dangles above, tantalizing. The noise grows. I begin to climb the ladder, fighting through pain with every step. The volume around me is deafening as I near the top. As I touch the briefcase with my fingertips, I can't hear myself think, then *BOOM!* The pyro goes off ... the first notes of the classic music signaling the arrival of Kane, an agent of destruction retained by the Authority. The briefcase is swinging in circles now. I frantically try to get my hands on it, but I can feel Kane's presence closing the distance. The fix is in. The crowd in Boston ... IS ... PISSED.

Kane grabs my leg to yank me off the ladder, but I kick myself free, refusing to be denied. I dig deep, fighting off the movie monster with everything I have left. I make one last desperate scramble up. It's not over yet. ... I hear the high-pitched screams of girls in the crowd, pleading with me to climb. It's pandemonium. The monster finally overtakes me as he inevitably would, delivering a Chokeslam, and a Tombstone that puts me away, clearing the path for Seth to ascend the ladder and claim the prize.

The whole piece of business was incredibly exciting, and the heat is monstrous. The fans *reeaally* wanted me to grab that damn briefcase, and that's the important thing ... that's what I needed. What the fans screaming obscenities at the bad guys and the teenage girls fighting back tears might not have realized at the time was that, while I didn't grab the briefcase, I gained something so much more. I'm becoming fully entrenched as a scorned babyface with the fans firmly behind me as the story continues. I love storytelling. This night couldn't have worked out any better for Seth or me. The one thing I now knew without a doubt: When the time was right, I would get my revenge on the bad guys, acting as a proxy for those fans. We would get our revenge together, our big victory. The Death Star would blow up. One night soon would be our night.

Only problem is, that night never really came.

T-MOBILE ARENA, LAS VEGAS, JUNE 2016

Earlier tonight, I competed in another Money in the Bank ladder match. The last time, that night in Boston in 2014, I was prepared to jump out of the ceiling with my hair on fire into a pit of venomous scorpions if need be. Tonight my only goal was to not get hurt. Of all times, tonight was not the night for a catastrophic injury. As it was, I was basically limping into this PPV, beat to shit and half braindead, but I could have had a knife sticking out of my stomach and I still would have found a way to kayfabe it. Tonight, nothing was gonna stop me from grabbing that goddamn briefcase.

When it was over, I didn't even celebrate. This was just a means to an end. That wave of relief first hit me atop the ladder. We're almost there. I took my time. Those things seem to get higher and higher every year. The crowd was louder than I expected, slowly erupting as I finally unhooked the case. Many people couldn't have given a fuck less about me during the match. They were even booing me; they'd long given up hope. Joy, even shock and surprise overtook the arena when I secured the prize. I had called my shot on TV, a bold claim I might cash in on the same night when I won, but I'm sure few believed it. They'd been conditioned not to. Hell, even I didn't believe it ... but with the case and the contract in hand, it was now a real possibility. Maybe he will, a fan wonders briefly. Naaaaah, they sensibly decide, burned too many times.

Nick and I watch the little monitor without stress. It was nice to chill and watch my two friends, two great athletes, showcase their talents in the main event. Seth has just returned from a gruesome torn ACL. He has worked hard to return to get back to 100 percent, and he looks great out there. Seth had cashed in his briefcase at WrestleMania to become champion in a grand heist the previous year, before getting injured and having to relinquish the belt. Tonight, he has the chance to take back what he never lost. While Seth was champion, I made many attempts to wrest the belt from him, only to be derailed by the Authority's nefarious means time and again. Now, there's no Authority. Seth wants to prove he's the best by coming back from surgery and rehab, climbing the mountain and reclaiming his spot at the summit.

As the match wears on and nears the final stretch, I watch with one eye. I log-roll away from Nick to my own area and begin moving around as much as I can in my subterranean predicament, stretching, doing some push-ups, just getting some blood flow, focusing. There is but one thing left to do. *One, two, three!* The match concludes. Seth has pinned Roman clean in the middle ... maybe something of a shock to the audience, as a lack of Authority interference hasn't historically been Seth's MO.

Nonetheless, the audience is pleasantly surprised, Well, shit! Good for you, man! Congratulations! Well deserved! the crowd thinks as they applaud. Seth celebrates his enormous achievement. You can say whatever you want about how he acquired the MITB briefcase in the first place, or how he used it to hijack Roman's WrestleMania moment. Say whatever you want about the way Seth conducted business in the past. It doesn't matter because tonight he did it fair and fuckin' square, on his own talents, on his own merits that were always there. Not only that, tonight he overcame having his title stolen from him, and he overcame an injury that often ends careers. He came all the way back, reclaimed the top spot, and showed us all how great he is. And he did everything the right way! Now, FINALLY we can celebrate Seth Rollins.

I'm reminded of that scene at the end of *The Departed.* Matt Damon returns to his apartment, after all his lying and killing, but nobody is the wiser. He got off scot-free, a hero cop. He opens the door and sees Mark Wahlberg standing there with a gun, and he's dead before he can say anything. The loose end he forgot to tie up.

I hear Seth's music play, interrupted by mine. I've entered a mental space by this point where Nick no longer exists, though I hear him, as I always do, as I slide under the curtain "Watch your head!" *Thanks, Nick.* One thing left to do, put a slug in the back of this guy's skull.

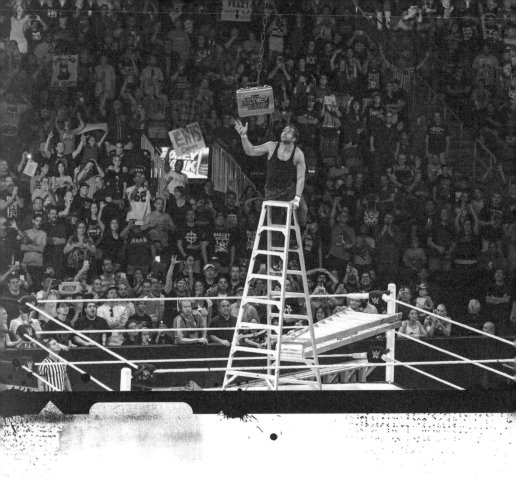

My music hits, the familiar *RRRRRRRRRRR*, that sound hasn't exuded real menace for some time, but right now, the crowd goes nuclear. Seth turns to the ramp, the poor sap, the oldest WWE trick in the book, the old music distraction. Nobody notices me rolling out from underneath the apron, but I appear, an apparition in the ring. I hear screams. I blast Seth in the skull with the steel briefcase, unapologetically. He won't recover. Anger, resentment, frustration, pain, agony begin to boil over as I move next to ringside. I look at senior referee Mike Chioda ... the crowd is F'n bonkers, but I can't acknowledge them. There's no time. ... This is an assassination, a hit.

"Kiki," I tell him. "I'm cashing this in. ... Right. Now."

The guttural roar in the arena as I hand Chioda the briefcase confirms, even to me, that this is real. I slide into the ring. Seth is searching with his hands, his vision blurred. ... His nightmares have come true; his past sins have come back to haunt him. I observe him without sympathy. I snatch him by the hair and pull him into a front facelock as the bell rings. I secure double underhooks and DDT him into oblivion.

CINCINNATI, PICCADLY, 1996

Donnie and Kevin got some of those foam belts once. Their grandma took them to a WWF show at Cincinnati Gardens when we were kids. I couldn't go because I didn't have any money. I was really bummed. I had been listening to the ads on WEBN for weeks. It was Bret and Taker in some kind of tag on top. Kev brought back a tag belt, and since he only had one, we paired it with a homemade companion. Donnie had the world belt. I really liked that thing. It was black and gold.

It's over, they know it. They know it's gonna be a three count, but they can't believe it. A certain magic lives between the moment you know it's over and the ref's hand slapping the mat for that final time. When you're not looking for a 2.95, a 1, 2, *nooooooo*!!! When you are not asking a question, "Could this be it?" When you're making a statement, "This is it." It's not like Tom Brady, up by six touchdowns in the fourth quarter, already posing for photographs, waiting for the last 11 minutes on the clock to run out, the game decided. It's an ultra-concentrated version of that. The audience has only seconds to fully grasp what's happening, process it, and decide how to respond. It's the subtleties leading up to that moment where the bad guy gets defeated that prepare them to believe this is it, it's over, we're ready to F'n blow. But nothing's really real until the ref hits three. When you nail it, that few seconds in between are pure distilled 100-proof joy and excitement, an entire arena orgasming at the exact same time. The best goddamn drug dealer in Amsterdam couldn't sell you that shit. If he could, I would have found him.

One, two ... *yep, fuck you*, three!!! The arena explodes. Nobody is sitting down, hands are in the air all the way to the ceiling, smiles. There's joy, catharsis, elation. This feeling is why they buy tickets, it's why they invest in performers. It's ... F'n ... loud. In the center of the ring, I feel like 747s are flying over my head. I finally release my grip on the fictional narrative and my character's plight after a few seconds. I try to hang on, but my hold immediately gives way to an outburst of emotion. A ball of rage inside me, I want to burst out something along the lines of, "Fuck all you fuckin' motherfuckers," but I instinctively hide it under my breath to an acceptable PG degree, as I've learned to do. Still, I let loose, finally celebrating.

I hold up the belt, standing on the turnbuckles, flexing a bicep pose. I look at the belt ... all that regular shit you do when you win a championship. I fall to my knees. All my rage has dissipated quickly. I'm exhausted, like I just got done running a bunch of 100-yard sprints. Even though my work in the main event consisted of doing exactly one move, I'm suddenly completely drained, a marathon of years and years, miles and miles, has come to an end. I celebrate with the audience for a long time. I shake every hand around ringside, take every picture, give every sweaty hug.

I'm the WWE champion, as I wrote down I would be on notebooks when I was 12, as I insisted to myself I could be internally through all the miles, the training, the studying, abject poverty, pain, frustration, doubt. I'm the WWE champ, and all the F'n pricks who said I wouldn't or couldn't make it at one point or another are all watching right now, and they can all suck my dick.

This isn't the end of the road, it's just a stop, the kind of really sweet truck stop where you load up on a bunch of shit you don't need. I hope the work is just beginning, I hope it only gets harder from here, because I'd relish the opportunity to show what I could really do with this thing. But the moment might be fleeting, so for right now, fuck tomorrow, cuz maybe all we have is tonight, and you better believe I'm gonna enjoy it.

I finally make it through the curtain. I'm startled by the round of applause and I feel awkward, my cheeks flushed. Gorilla is packed. Many friends are waiting to congratulate me: wrestlers, producers, writers, all kinds of people. I'm genuinely moved, but even though I would have had no problem swinging my dick around in a circle in front of the packed arena on the other side of the curtain five minutes ago, on this side of the curtain, in a more intimate setting, I feel embarrassed, self-conscious. I just want to not be the center of attention as quickly as possible. Renée is there. I didn't tell her what was gonna happen. I never do. It's a blur as I fist-bump and bro-hug through the crowd and make my way to Vince, looking all sentimental and shit, slapping me on the back hard.

Roman smiles as we embrace in a sweaty three-way Shield hug. At some point tonight, each one of the three of us held the title. Seth beams with pride. The story of our brotherhood seems to carry more emotional weight with fans than your typical storyline. We all know we're part of something special, and tonight wasn't just an unforgettable moment, but a beautiful ending to the story arc of the Shield, at least for now. There's always Monday.

Under normal circumstances, I'd drive to Phoenix tonight for *Raw*, but friends of mine — Farmer, Sean, Bonham — were all at the show and a bunch of people wanna come over to celebrate. So instead, I climb in the passenger seat of that goddamn

Mini Cooper Renée used to drive (I hated that thing, it was like driving a go-kart). I slide the seat back as far as it goes and recline. "Starman" by David Bowie plays on the stereo. I turn it up, roll down the windows and let the dry, desert night air rush over me. We don't speak, but I put "Starman" on repeat, and we listen to it three or four times in a row. Maybe 12 minutes later, we turn onto our street, passing the gas station on the corner about a half mile from the house. We pull into the driveway and turn off the car, Renée asks, "So what do you wanna do?"

"I wanna walk to the gas station, get a pack of cigarettes and a tallboy," I reply. That's exactly what we did.

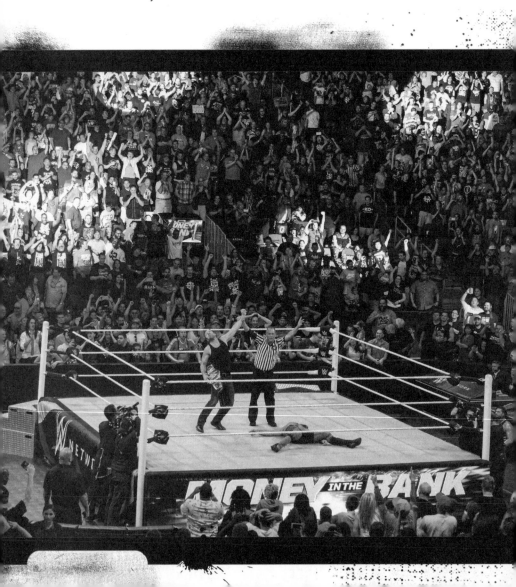

END OF THE BOOK

APRIL 9, TAMPA, FOUR POINTS SHERATON, 7:05 P.M.

I haven't showered today. There's still blood in my ears. I showered twice last night, but it's hard to get all that shit out. I wrestled Josh Barnett at Bloodsport last night at the Cuban Club in Ybor City, part of GCW's Collective. It's WrestleMania week. It's not as wild here as it would be traditionally. While things seem to be turning a corner as far as COVID is concerned, we're still a ways from back to normal. It wasn't even hard to book a hotel in Tampa; normally the whole city is sold out during Mania week. I'll probably never perform at WrestleMania itself again. There's really no need to ... the electricity I felt last night Bulldog Choking Josh and squeezing his head for every drop of juice I could after kneeing him in the face is just as supercharged and powerful as anything I could have gotten at the stadium on Sunday.

The last time I went toe to toe with a former UFC Heavyweight Champion during Mania week it was in front of 70,000 fans or some shit (Who knows, cuz they make all those numbers up). This time it was in front of a limited audience of 750, outdoors in a parking lot. There is a stark difference in the two experiences. In the first I felt dead, disconnected, like a dream I had once. In the second I felt alive, truly alive, testing my abilities as an athlete and using all my skills as a storyteller to create a piece of grotesque pro wrestling noir.

It's 7:28 now. I need to shower soon and get dressed. I went to bed around 7:00 a.m. after eating pizza on the street with Josh and Chris Dickinson and smoking Virginia Slims I got from a guy who, now that I think about it, for sure thought I was hitting on him. I woke up about noon, still on adrenaline with the worst headache I've had in years ... a combination of whiskey, said Virginia Slims and the fact that a 270-pound polar bear had opened my skull up with his elbow like he was trying to crack a giant walnut.

I gotta head back to the Cuban Club here soon, the show starts at eight, but I don't wanna get there before doors; I don't want fans to see me. I'm a surprise at the end of Joey Janela's Spring Break. I will confront Nick Gage, king of the deathmatches, folk hero and the guy who almost cut my tongue out with a pizza cutter 10 years ago. I'm not confronting him because I'm still mad about that or anything, but just cuz it's something we think people will want to see. I can't deny them that.

It's 7:39. A Korn concert, a performance from Woodstock '99 is playing on YouTube on the TV. Man, YouTube has come a long way. I sip a stiff cocktail. It burns. I'm coming to life now, visualizing this moment. I hope the people go nuts. I hope they're happy and excited. It's a good story: Two guys who nearly killed each other 10 years ago but haven't laid eyes on one another since. I told Nicky last night, the important thing was just don't move a muscle. I know you're gonna want to, but don't move an F'n muscle, I told him. Let 'em get their phones out and take their pictures. Let every image be imprinted on their brains like frames in a graphic novel. Let all the cameras do the work for us. Let the magic of pro wrestling happen. Ten years ago, Nicky went to prison for robbing a bank. In the interim, I went and did what I did ... sold a few T-shirts or whatever, but we find ourselves here again.

Today is my anniversary. I have a vagina on my head. My wife isn't mad at me yet. She might be later. I think I wanna DDT Nicky on a bundle of light tubes. ... It seems right to me: the button at the end of the night. Yeah, fuck it, it's gotta be light tubes. I haven't fucked with tubes in a decade. Once you add light tubes into the equation, everything changes. You're gonna get cut. I can wear a jacket, but the glass finds a way to crawl all over you, into any little crevice it can find. It's invasive, like fire ants ... but fuck ... it's gotta be tubes. I will stop and get a bunch of flowers before returning home tomorrow. I will ring the doorbell and play "Unchained Melody" on my phone, holding an ample amount of bouquets. Renée will open the door and smile. We will hug and kiss. She will be happy. We will have some sex. She didn't marry the guy who was too much of a pussy to stay an extra day in Tampa to DDT Nick FN Gage onto a pile of glass. She married the guy who did. 7:59. I called an Uber. he's eight minutes away. I'm gonna go shower.

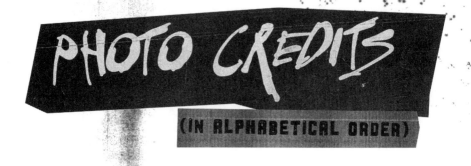

PHOTO CREDITS

(IN ALPHABETICAL ORDER)

ABOUT THE AUTHOR

Jon Moxley is one of the top professional wrestlers in the world. He is Pro Wrestling Illustrated's 2020 Wrestler of the Year and was Sports Illustrated's 2019 Wrestler of the Year. He was a WWE Grand Slam Champion, holding all WWE titles at least once, an IWGP Champion, and AEW World Champion. Known for his renegade style and hard-hitting interviews, he has seen it all and done it all in the wild business of pro wrestling—the sport he has loved since he was a child. He lives in Las Vegas with his wife Renee, their child, and two dogs.